T0275795

Cambridge Texts in Computer Science

Edited by D. J. Cooke, Loughborough University

Also in this series

1 An Introduction to Logical Design of Digital Circuits
C. M. Reeves 1972
2 Information Representation and Manipulation in a Computer
E. S. Page and L. B. Wilson, Second Edition 1978
3 Computer Simulation of Continuous Systems
R. J. Ord-Smith and J. Stephenson 1975
4 Macro Processors
A. J. Cole, Second Edition 1981
5 An Introduction to the Uses of Computers
Murray Laver 1976
6 Computing Systems Hardware
M. Wells 1976
7 An Introduction to the Study of Programming Languages
D. W. Barron 1977
8 ALGOL 68 – A first and second course
A. D. McGettrick 1978
9 An Introduction to Computational Combinatorics
E. S. Page and L. B. Wilson 1979
10 Computers and Social Change
Murray Laver 1980
11 The Definition of Programming Languages
A. D. McGettrick 1980
12 Programming via Pascal
J. S. Rohl and H. J. Barrett 1980
13 Program Verification using Ada
A. D. McGettrick 1982
14 Simulation Techniques for Discrete Event Systems
I. Mitrani 1982
15 Information Representations and Manipulation using Pascal
E. S. Page and L. B. Wilson 1983
16 Writing Pascal Programs
J. S. Rohl 1983
17 An Introduction to APL
S. Pommier 1983
18 Computer Mathematics
D. J. Cooke and H. E. Bez 1984
19 Recursion via Pascal
J. S. Rohl 1984
20 Text Processing
A. Colin Day 1984
21 Introdution to Computer Systems
Brian Molinari 1985
22 Program Construction
R. G. Stone and D. J. Cooke 1987
23 A Practical Introduction to Denotational Semantics
Lloyd Allison 1987
24 Modelling of Computer and Communication Systems
I. Mitrani 1987
25 The Principles of Computer Networking
D. Russel 1989
26 Concurrent Programming
C. R. Snow 1991
27 An Introduction to Functional Programming Systems Using Haskell
A. J. T. Davie 1992

28 Cambridge Computer Science Texts

Categories and Computer Science

R. F. C. Walters
Department of Computer Science, University of Sydney

CAMBRIDGE UNIVERSITY PRESS
Cambridge, New York, Melbourne, Madrid, Cape Town, Singapore, São Paulo

Cambridge University Press
The Edinburgh Building, Cambridge CB2 2RU, UK

Published in the United States of America by Cambridge University Press, New York

www.cambridge.org
Information on this title: www.cambridge.org/9780521419970

© Carslaw Publications 1991

First published by Carslaw Publications 1991
First Cambridge University Press edition 1992

A catalogue record for this publication is available from the British Library

ISBN-13 978-0-521-41997-0 hardback
ISBN-10 0-521-41997-2 hardback

ISBN-13 978-0-521-42226-0 paperback
ISBN-10 0-521-42226-4 paperback

Transferred to digital printing 2006

In memory of my father
Lynn David Walters

Preface

This book has its origins in an undergraduate course I have given on Categories and Computer Science over the past three years to a total of approximately 200 students at the University of Sydney. The course is a gentle introduction to category theory, with motivating examples taken from computer science, and was developed through interaction with the students.

Although this book is an undergraduate text, it contains quite a deal of original material, further details of which may be found in my reports and papers listed with the references. In particular, much of the discussion of distributive categories, data types, and imperative programs is new, and Chapter 7, §2 contains a description of a generalization of the Todd–Coxeter algorithm suitable for computing left Kan extensions developed with Sean Carmody; this section was written together with Sean.

The idea for the course came from discussions with Bill Lawvere while he was in Sydney in 1988. Since then we have held in Sydney, in addition to the Sydney Category Seminar (now 21 years old, chaired by Max Kelly), a further seminar — The Sydney Categories in Computer Science Seminar. I have learnt much from the members of this seminar, visitors to the seminar, and from my graduate students, fourth-year students, and vacation scholars. My thanks go to David Benson, Aurelio Carboni, Sean Carmody, Robin Cockett, Robbie Gates, Diana Gibson, Mike Johnson, Lesley Johnston, Giulio Katis, Wafaa Khalil, Stephen Lack, Mark Lauer, Phil Lavers, Mark Leeming, Stephen Ma, Gordon Monro, Wesley Phoa, Steve Schanuel, Usha Sridhar, Sun Shu-Hao, Andrew Solomon, Margaret Thiel, Phil Wadler, and Bill Unger. The research and visitors have been supported by an Australian Research Council Program Grant, and an Australian Research Council Small Grant.

The main assistance in actually producing the book has come from Sean Carmody, Wafaa Khalil, and Karl Wehrhahn. Their help has been invaluable. Additional assistance has been received from Mike Johnson, Stephen Lack, and Wesley Phoa. A further important debt is to my friend and collaborator in Milan, Stefano Kasangian, who first introduced me to the community of computer scientists interested in category theory.

R. F. C. Walters walters_b@maths.su.oz.au
31 May 1991.

Contents

Introduction

It is always exciting and fruitful when two disparate scientific fields are found to have much in common. Each field is enriched by the different perspective and insights of the other. This has happened recently with category theory and theoretical computer science.

The relations between category theory and computer science constitute an extremely active area of research at the moment. Some evidence of this is given in the short list of references at the end of the book. Among the many places where research is being done are: Aarhus, Carnegie-Mellon, Cambridge, Edinburgh, Glasgow, London, Milan, Oxford, Paris, Pennsylvania, Pisa, Stanford, and Sydney. Topics of current interest include the connections between category theory and functional programming, polymorphism, concurrency, abstract data structures, object-oriented programming, and hardware design.

This book is an introduction to category theory in which several of the connections with computer science are discussed in sufficient detail to give the reader some technical expertise and a feeling for the rich possibilities arising from the happy connection between these two subjects.

What is category theory?

The notion of function is one of the most fundamental in mathematics and science. Functions are used to model variation — for example, the motion of a particle in space; the variation of a quantity like temperature over a space; the symmetries of a geometric object, or of physical laws; the variation of the state of a system over time.

Category theory is the algebra of functions; the principal operation on functions is taken to be composition.

A category is an abstract structure: a collection of objects, together with a collection of arrows between them. For example, the objects could be geometric figures and the arrows could be ways of transforming one into another; or the objects might be data types and the arrows programs.

Category theory was invented by S. Eilenberg and S. Mac Lane in 1945 and arose out of their work in algebraic topology. Since then it has influenced many areas of mathematics; for example, algebraic geometry, through the work of A. Grothendieck, and logic, through the work of F. W. Lawvere. It is a revolutionary and infectiously attractive way of comprehending mathematics.

How is category theory related to computer science?

Briefly

* ⋆ An important aspect of computer science is the construction of functions out of a given set of simple functions, using various operations on functions like composition, and repeated composition. Category theory is exactly the appropriate algebra for such constructions.
* ⋆ Computing is concerned with machines — that is, dynamical systems, which have sets of states which vary over time. They are built up out of functions or elementary machines by an essentially algebraic process. Again underlying this is the theory of functions and composition.
* ⋆ Since category theory is an algebra of functions we can consider categories which are purely formal, and which don't really consist of functions. This is the syntactical side of computer science. Programs and languages are formal things which are intended to describe or specify actual functions. Category theory is well adapted to deal with the relation between syntax and semantics.

Some computer science topics we will deal with in this book are: grammars and languages; data types; boolean algebra; circuit theory; flow charts; imperative programming; specification; and lambda-calculus.

For the mathematical reader

Although this book is primarily about applications of category theory to computer science, category theory arose in algebraic topology and has proved useful to many areas of mathematics. We have included a small number of examples from other areas of mathematics so that the book may be useful for readers intent on pursuing further mathematics.

The computer science topics will be described in detail so that no particular background in computer science is necessary to read this book.

Chapter 1

The Algebra of Functions

A category is an algebra of functions with composition being the main operation. Whenever you calculate by composing functions (for example, in iterating a function) there is a category behind your calculations.

In dealing with functions you have to consider two sorts of things — the functions themselves and the sets they go between. So a category has two sorts of things — *objects* (= sets) and *morphisms* (= functions). This complicates the definition of category, but also leads to the amazing expressiveness of the notion of category.

The aim of this chapter is first to make a formal definition of category and then to develop some experience with the concept by examining examples.

§1. Categories

We begin by giving the formal definition. Immediately following that we will describe categories a little more intuitively.

Definition. A category $\mathbf{A}$ consists of a set of *objects* (called obj $\mathbf{A}$) and a set of *morphisms* or *arrows* (called arr $\mathbf{A}$). The objects are denoted

$$A,\ B,\ C,\ \ldots,\ X,\ Y, \ldots,$$

and the morphisms are denoted

$$f,\ g,\ h,\ \ldots,\ \alpha,\ \beta,\ \gamma,\ \ldots.$$

Further:

(i) Each morphism has a designated *domain* and *codomain* in obj $\mathbf{A}$. When the domain of f is A and the codomain of f is B we write $f : A \to B$.

(ii) Given morphisms $f : A \to B$, $g : B \to C$, there is a designated *composite* morphism

$$g \circ f : A \to C.$$

(iii) Given any object A there is a designated *identity* morphism $1_A : A \to A$.

(iv) The data above is required to satisfy the following:

- *Identity laws.* If $f : A \to B$ then

$$1_B \circ f = f \qquad \text{and} \qquad f \circ 1_A = f.$$

- *Associative law.* If $f : A \to B,\ g : B \to C$ and $h : C \to D$ then

$$h \circ (g \circ f) = (h \circ g) \circ f : A \to D.$$

Note. Although I speak of a category as an algebra of functions it is important to realize that the notion of category is axiomatically defined and formal — the objects of a category need not be actual sets, and the arrows need not be actual functions. As is usual with axiomatic definitions this allows great flexibility in the construction of categories. This flexibility is crucial in the application of categories to computer science.

Remark. Informally, a category is an algebra of functions between sets, and hence looks something like this:

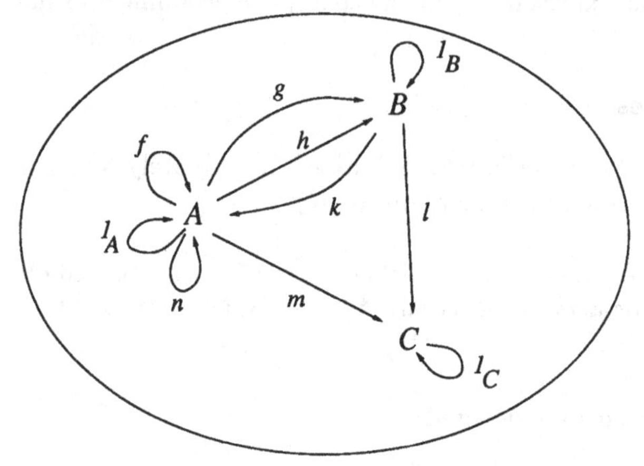

The principal operation in a category is composition. Hence for example, given $g : A \to B$ and $l : B \to C$ we can form $l \circ g : A \to C$; in the example above $l \circ g$ must be m since m is the only arrow from A to C.

The principal axiom on a category is the associativity of composition. This axiom means we can leave out brackets in a composition of arrows; for example, we can write $l \circ g \circ k \circ h \circ f \circ f$ (or even $lgkhf^2$) instead of $(l \circ ((g \circ k) \circ (h \circ (f \circ f))))$.

Remark. It may seem surprising that we take composition as the main operation on functions. In high school the usual operations on functions are addition and multiplication. We will see later that these operations can be expressed using composition.

Remark. Notice that a category is a mixture of graphical information and algebraic operations. Computer science is similarly a mixture of graphs and algebra.

Let's now look at some examples of categories.

Example 1. If we take all sets A, B, C, ... to be objects and all functions $f : A \to B$, $g : B \to C$, ... to be morphisms we get a category called **Sets**. Composition is composition of functions; that is, $g \circ f(a) = g(f(a))$. (A function $f : A \to B$ is defined on all elements of A, but is not necessarily surjective.)

The associative law holds since

$$(h \circ (g \circ f))(a) = h((g \circ f)(a)) = h(g(f(a))) = (h \circ g)(f(a)) = ((h \circ g) \circ f)(a).$$

That's a large example. Let's look at some small ones.

Example 2. One object A; one arrow, which must therefore be the identity arrow.

$$1_A : A \to A; \qquad 1_A \circ 1_A = 1_A.$$

Example 3. No objects; no arrows.

Example 4. One object A; two arrows $1_A : A \to A$, $\alpha : A \to A$. To specify a category we have to give all composites $1_A 1_A$, $1_A \alpha$, $\alpha 1_A$, $\alpha\alpha$ and to check the identity and associative laws.

Let's write the compositions down as a table — in the f, g position of the table we put $g \circ f$.

The only question is what to take for $\alpha \circ \alpha$.

There are two possible choices, either $\alpha\alpha = 1_A$ or $\alpha\alpha = \alpha$. Let's look at both possibilities.

Case (i). Suppose $\alpha\alpha = 1_A$. That is, the composition table is:

	1_A	α
1_A	1_A	α
α	α	1_A

(1)

In fact, this does give a category. All that needs to be checked is the associative law. Notice that composition is a fully defined operation.

You may recognise the composition table as

- addition modulo 2, or
- the cyclic group of order 2,

and these are well known to be associative.

Case (ii). Suppose that $\alpha^2 = \alpha$.

This also yields a category, with composition table:

	1_A	α
1_A	1_A	α
α	α	α

(2)

Again we need to check the associative law, but can we instead recognise this category? For example, can we represent the one object as a set and the arrows as functions closed under composition? In that case the associative law will be automatic (see the note below).

We can: take A to be the set $\{0, 1\}$. Let 1_A be the identity function $A \to A$. Let α be the function given by

$$\begin{aligned} \alpha \quad : \quad & 0 \longmapsto 0, \\ & 1 \longmapsto 0. \end{aligned}$$

Clearly,

$$\begin{aligned} \alpha^2 \quad : \quad & 0 \longmapsto 0 \longmapsto 0, \\ & 1 \longmapsto 0 \longmapsto 0. \end{aligned}$$

Hence $\alpha^2 = \alpha$ as required.

Here is another way of representing this example in terms of sets and functions. Let A be the plane, and 1_A the identity function. Now take α to be the projection onto the x-axis. That is,

$$\alpha : (x, y) \mapsto (x, 0).$$

Then clearly $\alpha^2(x, y) = \alpha(x, 0) = (x, 0) = \alpha(x, y)$, and so $\alpha^2 = \alpha$ as required.

Note. Any collection of sets and functions containing the identity for each of the sets and closed under composition is a category (a *sub*category of **Sets**). The associative law holds by the argument given in Example 1.

Definition. An arrow $\alpha : A \to A$ in a category satisfying $\alpha^2 = \alpha$ is called an *idempotent*.

Idempotents are an abstraction of the notion of projection.

Example 5. Two objects A, B; three arrows $1_A : A \to A$, $1_B : B \to B$, and $\alpha : A \to B$. The compositions we have to give are $1_A 1_A = 1_A$, $1_B 1_B = 1_B$, $\alpha 1_A = \alpha$, and $1_B \alpha = \alpha$. These are all forced by the identity laws, and are easily checked to satisfy the associative law. Hence we have a category. Its composition table (only partially defined as is usual with categories) is

	1_A	1_B	α
1_A	1_A		α
1_B		1_B	
α		α	

It can easily be represented as sets and functions — just take A and B to be two sets, and α to be any function from A to B.

Example 6. One object A; four arrows

$$1_A,\ e_1,\ e_2,\ e_1 e_2$$

from A to A, such that $e_1 e_2 = e_2 e_1$, $e_1^2 = e_1$, and $e_2^2 = e_2$. We can fill out the composition table (fully defined, since there is only one object):

	1	e_1	e_2	$e_1 e_2$
1	1	e_1	e_2	$e_1 e_2$
e_1	e_1	e_1	$e_1 e_2$	$e_1 e_2$
e_2	e_2	$e_1 e_2$	e_2	$e_1 e_2$
$e_1 e_2$	$e_1 e_2$	$e_1 e_2$	$e_1 e_2$	$e_1 e_2$

Is this a category? We must check the associative law.

Again the easiest way is to find a representation in terms of sets and functions. One way to do that is as follows: Let A be the plane; and define e_1, e_2 by

$$e_1(x, y) = (x, 0),$$
$$e_2(x, y) = (0, y).$$

Then $e_1 e_2(x, y) = (0, 0) = e_2 e_1(x, y)$.

The four functions 1, e_1, e_2, and $e_1 e_2$ are closed under composition and hence we have a category.

Example 7. Let X be a set. We are going to form a category, denoted by $\mathcal{P}X$, whose objects are the subsets of X. The arrows in $\mathcal{P}X$ are inclusion functions between these subsets.

As an example, let $X = \{0, 1, 2\}$. Consider all subsets and inclusions between them:

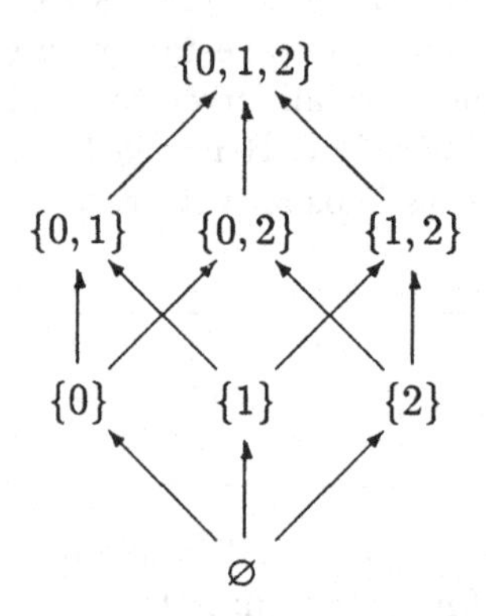

Inclusion functions are closed under composition. Identities are inclusions. Notice that to simplify the picture we have not drawn all the arrows. Identities have been omitted as well as composite arrows like $\varnothing \to \{0, 1\}$.

Now let's generalise a bit the examples we've seen so far.

§2. General Examples

Example 8. (Only identity arrows.) Given any set of objects there is a category with only identity arrows:

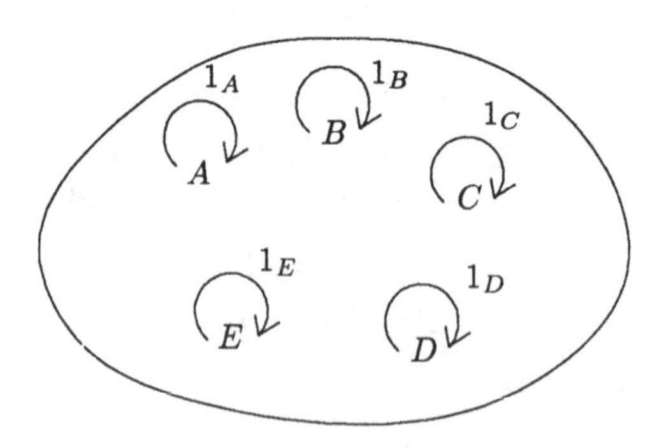

(This category may be thought of as just the set $\{A, B, C, ...\}$.)

Example 9. (Exactly one object.) Suppose the one object is A, and the set of arrows is $\{1, f, g, h, \ldots\}$. Then composition is fully defined; the category is determined by the composition table.

The only requirement is the associative law.

Example 10. Given any group $G = \{1, f, g, ...\}$ we get a category with one object A. Composition is the product of elements in the group which is, of course, associative.

Definition. A category with one object is called a *monoid*.

The special feature of groups, among monoids, is that to each arrow $\alpha : A \to A$ there is an arrow $\alpha^{-1} : A \to A$ such that $\alpha\alpha^{-1} = 1_A$, $\alpha^{-1}\alpha = 1_A$. Arrows with this property are important in any category.

Definition. An arrow $\alpha : A \to B$ in a category for which there exists another arrow $\alpha^{-1} : B \to A$ such that

$$\alpha\alpha^{-1} = 1_B, \qquad \alpha^{-1}\alpha = 1_A$$

is called an *isomorphism* (we then say A and B are isomorphic objects, and write $A \cong B$).

Let's see two special examples of monoid.

Example 11. One object A; arrows 1_A, e, e^2, e^3, $e^4, \ldots$. Composition is given by

$$e^m e^n = e^{m+n}.$$

This monoid can be thought of as the natural numbers under addition. One role it plays in computer science is that of discrete time.

Example 12. One object A; arrows

$$\ldots, e^{-2}, e^{-1}, 1_A, e^1, e^2, \ldots.$$

Composition is again given by the formula $e^m e^n = e^{m+n}$. This monoid may be thought of as the integers under addition.

Example 13. (At most one arrow from any one object to any other object.) Consider a category with:

- many objects A, B, $C, \ldots$;
- at most one arrow from one object to another.

Notation. If there is an arrow from A to B denote it by $A \leq B$.

Now the existence of identities says exactly that $A \leq A$ for all objects A. The existence of composition says exactly that $A \leq B$ and $B \leq C$ implies $A \leq C$.

The identity laws and the associative law are automatically satisfied since they are the requirements that two given arrows with the same domain and codomain are equal, something that is always true when there is at most one arrow from one object to another.

Definition. A category with the property that if A and B are objects then there is at most one arrow from A to B, is called a *preordered set*.

Note. In a preordered set we can have $A \leq B$ and $B \leq A$ without necessarily $A = B$. In fact, if $A \leq B$ and $B \leq A$ then A is isomorphic to B.

Example 14. Given a set X the category $\mathcal{P}X$ of all subsets of X is a preordered set.

§3. Free Categories; Generators and Relations

A common way of describing an algebraic structure is to specify:

- some of the elements (which are called *generators*); and
- some equations between values of the operations (called the *relations*).

The remaining elements of the structure, and the remaining values of the operations, can be deduced from the given ones.

This method of description is called *presenting the algebra by generators and relations*.

Categories can be presented in this way. We specify:

- all of the objects and some of the arrows (these are called generators of the category); and
- some equations between composites of given arrows (these are the relations of the category).

Example 15. Consider the category presented by one object A, one arrow $e : A \to A$, and one relation $e^4 = 1_A$.

In this category there is just one object A. We must consider as possible arrows in the category

$$1_A,\ e,\ e^2,\ e^3,\ e^4,\ e^5,\ldots.$$

The relation implies that

$$e^4 = 1_A,\ e^5 = e,\ e^6 = e^2,\ e^7 = e^3,\ e^8 = 1_A, \ldots,$$

and hence the only arrows we need are 1_A, e, e^2, e^3. Further the whole composition can be deduced from the one relation:

	1_A	e	e^2	e^3
1_A	1_A	e	e^2	e^3
e	e	e^2	e^3	1_A
e^2	e^2	e^3	1_A	e
e^3	e^3	1_A	e	e^2

In fact, this is a category (either check the associative law, or observe that it is modulo 4 addition). It follows that it is the category presented by the generators and relations above.

Notice that we need to be sure that we have made all possible deductions from the given relations — for example we need to be sure that it is not possible to deduce that $e^3 = e$, say. But the composition table above shows that there is a category in which the relation $e^4 = 1$ is true, but in which $e^3 \neq e$ and hence $e^3 = e$ is not deducible from the relation.

Example 16. Take the generators to be one object $*$, and a set of arrows $\Sigma = \{a, b, c, \ldots, z, A, B, C, \ldots, Z\}$ from $*$ to $*$. Take *no* relations.

Think of Σ as being an alphabet.

This category has one object $*$. The arrows are all 'words in letters of alphabet Σ', including the *empty* word which consists of no letters.

For example, the word 'Mathematics' is the composite of the arrows

$$\mathrm{s} : * \to *,\ \mathrm{c} : * \to *,\ \mathrm{i} : * \to *,\ \mathrm{t} : * \to *,\ \ldots,\ \mathrm{h} : * \to *,\ \mathrm{t} : * \to *,\ \mathrm{a} : * \to *,\ \mathrm{M} : * \to *$$

in that order:

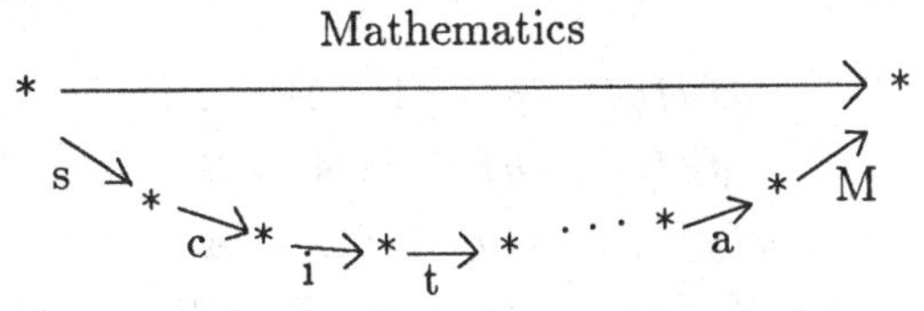

$$\begin{array}{c} * \xrightarrow{\text{Mathematics}} * \\ * \xrightarrow{\mathrm{s}} * \xrightarrow{\mathrm{c}} * \xrightarrow{\mathrm{i}} * \xrightarrow{\mathrm{t}} * \cdots * \xrightarrow{\mathrm{a}} * \xrightarrow{\mathrm{M}} * \end{array}$$

It is clear that all these words must be arrows — we must be able to form all composites — and that no further arrows are necessary.

The composition of two words u, v,

$$* \xrightarrow{u} * \xrightarrow{v} *,$$

is the concatenation vu of u and v (notice the order).

The identity $1_* : * \to *$ is the empty word.

It is easy to see that this gives a category.

Remark. This category is called the *free monoid* on the alphabet Σ. It is obviously fundamental in the study of language. Languages are subsets of a free monoid — sets of well-formed words or sentences.

So far I have given examples of generators and relations for monoids. The remaining examples involve several objects.

Example 17. Take as generators

- two objects A, B, and
- two arrows $f : A \to B$, $g : B \to A$.

Take one relation $gf = 1_A$.

The possible arrows in the category presented by these generators and relations are:

- $gfgf \cdots gfgf : A \to A$,
- $fgfgf \cdots gfgf : A \to B$,
- $gfgf \cdots gfg : B \to A$,
- $fgfgf \cdots gfg : B \to B$.

But we are given that $gf = 1_A$ and so:

$$\begin{aligned} gfgfgf \cdots gf &= 1_A : A \to A, \\ fgfgf \cdots gf &= f : A \to B, \\ gfgfgf \cdots gfg &= g : B \to A, \\ fgfgfgf \cdots gfg &= fg : B \to B. \end{aligned}$$

So there are five possible arrows

$$1_A, \qquad 1_B, \qquad f : A \to B, \qquad g : B \to A, \qquad fg : B \to B.$$

The composition table is:

	1_A	1_B	f	g	fg
1_A	1_A		f		
1_B		1_B		g	fg
f		f		1_A	f
g	g		fg		
fg		fg		g	fg

The free category on a graph

Definition. A (directed) *graph* is a set of objects and a set of arrows, each with a prescribed domain object and codomain object.

Note. There is no composition! That is the difference between graphs and categories.

Given a graph **G**, and no given relations, we can form a category generated by **G** called the *free category* on **G**.

The objects of the free category are the same as those of **G**. Arrows from object A to object B are paths of arrows from A to B with domains and codomains matching up, i.e.

$$\left(A \xrightarrow{f_n f_{n-1} \cdots f_1} B\right) = \left(A \xrightarrow{f_1} A_1 \xrightarrow{f_2} \cdots \xrightarrow{f_{n-1}} A_n \xrightarrow{f_n} B\right).$$

Composition is concatenation of paths; the identities are the empty paths.

Example 18. Consider the graph:

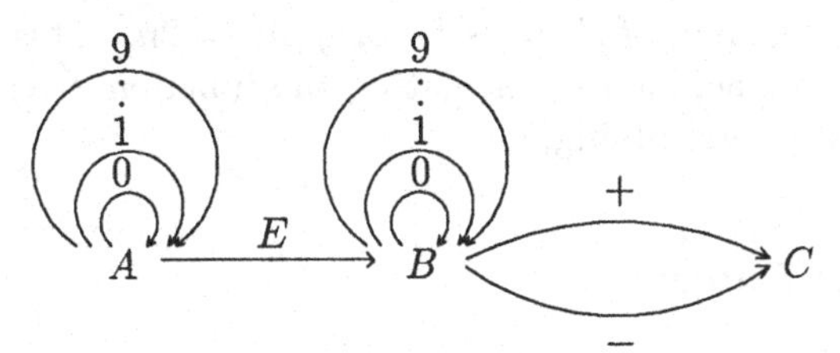

There are 10 loops about both A and B, in both cases labelled 0, 1, 2, 3, ..., 9.

What are the arrows from A to C in the free category on this graph? A typical example is

$$-102E274 = A \xrightarrow{4} A \xrightarrow{7} A \xrightarrow{2} A \xrightarrow{E} B \xrightarrow{2} B \xrightarrow{0} B \xrightarrow{1} B \xrightarrow{-} C.$$

In general, the arrows from A to C may be identified with signed numbers with a non-negative exponent.

Remark. We will see in Chapter 5 that graphs may be used as grammars to describe subsets of free monoids, and so free categories are fundamental to the theory of languages

A last example of generators and relations.

Example 19. Consider the graph with objects I, N and arrows

$$o : I \to N, \qquad s : N \to N, \qquad f : N \to N.$$

Take the relations to be

$$fo = o, \qquad fs = ssf.$$

Among the arrows from I to N are the arrows of the form $ssss \cdots ssso : I \to N$; these may be thought of as natural numbers; for example, $s^5 o$ may be thought of as 5.

What is $fsssssso = fs^5 o$? Using the relations we see that

$$\begin{aligned} fsssssso &= ssfsssso \\ &= ssssfssso = ssssssfsso \\ &= ssssssssfso = ssssssssssfo \\ &= s^{10} o. \end{aligned}$$

This calculation may be thought of as saying that $f(5) = 10$.

It is clear that in general $fs^n o = s^{2n} o$ or $f(n) = 2n$. This presentation of a category is a little machine for calculating the function $f(n) = 2n$, a key idea behind functional programming.

§4. Some Large Categories

So far we've looked at one large category **Sets**, the category of sets and functions, and many small categories. If this were a book about categories applied to mathematics, rather than to computer science, we would study other large categories like:

Vect:	objects	–	finite-dimensional vector spaces
	arrows	–	linear maps
Grps:	objects	–	groups
	arrows	–	group homomorphisms
MetrSp:	objects	–	metric spaces
	arrows	–	continuous maps
Rel:	objects	–	sets
	arrows	–	binary relations
	composition	–	composition of relations
Par:	objects	–	sets
	arrows	–	partial functions

and so on.

In fact every area of mathematics gives rise to one or more categories which are the main topic of interest of that subject.

In this book we may occasionally look at **Vect**, but not **Grps** or **MetrSp**.

A category you know well which is related to **Vect** is **Matr**, the category of matrices (with entries in $\mathbb{R}$, say).

The category **Matr** has objects: natural numbers $0, 1, 2, \ldots$; and the arrows from n to m are $m \times n$ matrices. The composition of arrows is matrix multiplication which is associative when defined.

For example,

$$2 \xrightarrow{\begin{pmatrix}1 & 1\\ 1 & 0\end{pmatrix}} 2 \xrightarrow{\begin{pmatrix}1 & 2\\ 0 & 1\\ 1 & 0\end{pmatrix}} 3 = \begin{pmatrix}1 & 2\\ 0 & 1\\ 1 & 0\end{pmatrix}\begin{pmatrix}1 & 1\\ 1 & 0\end{pmatrix} = \begin{pmatrix}3 & 1\\ 1 & 0\\ 1 & 1\end{pmatrix}.$$

Note. Writing $A : n \to m$ is just another way of saying A is $m \times n$.

Note. It is important to include the unique $0 \times n$ matrix, and the unique $n \times 0$ matrix to handle the 0-dimensional vector space.

In this book we do want to look at a variety of large categories relevant to computer science. I will introduce them later.

§5. The Dual of a Category

Given a category $\mathbf{A}$, an easy way to construct a new category is to reverse all the arrows of $\mathbf{A}$. The new category so obtained is called the *dual* or *opposite* of $\mathbf{A}$ and is denoted by $\mathbf{A}^{\mathrm{op}}$.

To be precise:

- The objects of $\mathbf{A}^{\mathrm{op}}$ are the same as the objects of $\mathbf{A}$. For convenience, to make it easier to distinguish between $\mathbf{A}$ and $\mathbf{A}^{\mathrm{op}}$, we make a notational difference between the objects of $\mathbf{A}$ and those of $\mathbf{A}^{\mathrm{op}}$: if A is an object of $\mathbf{A}$ we denote the corresponding object of $\mathbf{A}^{\mathrm{op}}$ by $\overline{A}$.
- If $f : A \to B$ is an arrow of $\mathbf{A}$ then $\overline{f} : \overline{B} \to \overline{A}$ is an arrow of $\mathbf{A}^{\mathrm{op}}$. The arrows of $\mathbf{A}^{\mathrm{op}}$ are precisely those obtained in this way.
- If 1_A is the identity of A in $\mathbf{A}$ then $\overline{1_A}$ is the identity of $\overline{A}$ in $\mathbf{A}^{\mathrm{op}}$.
- If $g \circ f$ is the composite of $A \xrightarrow{f} B \xrightarrow{g} C$ in $\mathbf{A}$ then $\overline{g \circ f}$ is the composite of $\overline{C} \xrightarrow{\overline{g}} \overline{B} \xrightarrow{\overline{f}} \overline{A}$ in $\mathbf{A}^{\mathrm{op}}$; that is,

$$\overline{f} \circ \overline{g} = \overline{g \circ f}.$$

The associative law is easy:

$$\begin{aligned} \overline{h} \circ (\overline{g} \circ \overline{f}) &= \overline{h} \circ (\overline{f \circ g}) \\ &= \overline{(f \circ g) \circ h} \\ &= \overline{f \circ (g \circ h)} \qquad \text{(associative law in } \mathbf{A}) \\ &= (\overline{g \circ h}) \circ \overline{f} \\ &= (\overline{h} \circ \overline{g}) \circ \overline{f}. \end{aligned}$$

Example 20. The dual of

$$A \xrightarrow{f} B \xleftarrow{g} C$$

is

$$\overline{A} \xleftarrow{\overline{f}} \overline{B} \xrightarrow{\overline{g}} \overline{C}.$$

Example 21. The dual of the category with one object A and three arrows 1_A, e_1, e_2 satisfying

$$e_i e_j = e_i \qquad (i, j = 1, 2)$$

is the category with one object $\overline{A}$ and three arrows $\overline{1_A}$, $\overline{e_1}$, $\overline{e_2}$ satisfying

$$\overline{e_j}\,\overline{e_i} = \overline{e_i} \qquad (i, j = 1, 2).$$

Compare the composition tables of these two categories:

	1_A	e_1	e_2
1_A	1_A	e_1	e_2
e_1	e_1	e_1	e_2
e_2	e_2	e_1	e_2

	$\overline{1_A}$	$\overline{e_1}$	$\overline{e_2}$
$\overline{1_A}$	$\overline{1_A}$	$\overline{e_1}$	$\overline{e_2}$
$\overline{e_1}$	$\overline{e_1}$	$\overline{e_1}$	$\overline{e_1}$
$\overline{e_2}$	$\overline{e_2}$	$\overline{e_2}$	$\overline{e_2}$

Now it is an amazing but not obvious fact that the duals of many well-known categories are also well-known categories.

Example 22. The dual of **Vect** is **Vect**.

Example 23. The dual of $\mathbf{Sets}_{finite}$ (finite sets and functions) is $\mathbf{BoolAlg}_{finite}$ (finite boolean algebras and boolean algebra maps).

Many famous theorems of mathematics assert that the dual of one category is another — Stone Duality, Gelfand Duality, Pontryagin Duality. I won't give any details of these examples; but let's look at a simple example.

Example 24. The dual of $\mathcal{P}X$ is $\mathcal{P}X$. To make this example clear it has become urgent to define what it means for categories to be isomorphic (we've taken it for granted so far).

Definition. Let **A** and **B** be categories. An isomorphism from **A** to **B** is a bijection Φ from the objects and arrows of **A** to the objects and arrows of **B**, respectively, such that:

(i) if $f : A_1 \to A_2$ in **A** then

$$\Phi(f) : \Phi(A_1) \to \Phi(A_2) \text{ in } \mathbf{B}$$

(Φ preserves domains and codomains);

(ii) if $f : A_1 \to A_2$ and $g : A_2 \to A_3$ in **A** then

$$\Phi(gf) = \Phi(g)\Phi(f)$$

(Φ preserves composition);

(iii) if 1_A is an identity in **A** then

$$\Phi(1_A) = 1_{\Phi(A)}$$

(Φ preserves identities).

If there is an isomorphism Φ from **A** to **B** we say that **A** and **B** are *isomorphic* categories, and we write $\mathbf{A} \cong \mathbf{B}$. We can think of an isomorphism as renaming the objects and arrows — isomorphic categories differ only in the names of the objects and arrows.

Example 25. Category **A**, with one object A and arrows 1_A, α such that $\alpha^2 = \alpha$, is isomorphic to the category **B** with one object $*$ and arrows 1_*, e such that $e^2 = e$.

The isomorphism $\Phi : \mathbf{A} \longrightarrow \mathbf{B}$ is given by

$$\Phi(A) = *, \qquad \Phi(1_A) = 1_*, \qquad \Phi(\alpha) = e. \tag{3}$$

One of the things an isomorphism must satisfy is $\Phi(\alpha\alpha) = \Phi(\alpha)\Phi(\alpha)$. But

$$\Phi(\alpha\alpha) = \Phi(\alpha) = e = ee = \Phi(\alpha)\Phi(\alpha). \tag{4}$$

Example 26. The two categories of Example 4 are not isomorphic. For suppose the first category is **A** with one object A and arrows 1_A, α such that $\alpha^2 = \alpha$, and the second is **B** with one object $*$ and arrows 1_*, e such that $e^2 = 1_*$.

The only possible candidate for an isomorphism is (3), but then

$$\Phi(\alpha\alpha) \neq \Phi(\alpha)\Phi(\alpha),$$

as we see in (4). So $\mathbf{A} \not\cong \mathbf{B}$.

Note. If **A**, **B** are preorders then conditions (ii) and (iii) for an isomorphism $\Phi : \mathbf{A} \to \mathbf{B}$ are automatically true, since they are equations between parallel arrows and in a preorder any two parallel arrows must be equal.

An isomorphism of preorders amounts to a bijection from the objects of **A** to objects of **B** such that for each pair of objects A_1, A_2 of **A**,

$$A_1 \leq A_2 \qquad \text{if and only if} \qquad \Phi(A_1) \leq \Phi(A_2). \tag{5}$$

Condition (5) just means that Φ takes arrows $A_1 \to A_2$ to arrows $\Phi(A_1) \to \Phi(A_2)$ and is a bijection on arrows.

Example 27. We are now in a position to see that $(\mathcal{P}X)^{\text{op}}$ is isomorphic to $\mathcal{P}X$. Let's sketch the two categories when $X = \{0, 1, 2\}$. Remember that the arrows in $\mathcal{P}X$ are inclusions, while those in $(\mathcal{P}X)^{\text{op}}$ are the reverse of inclusions.

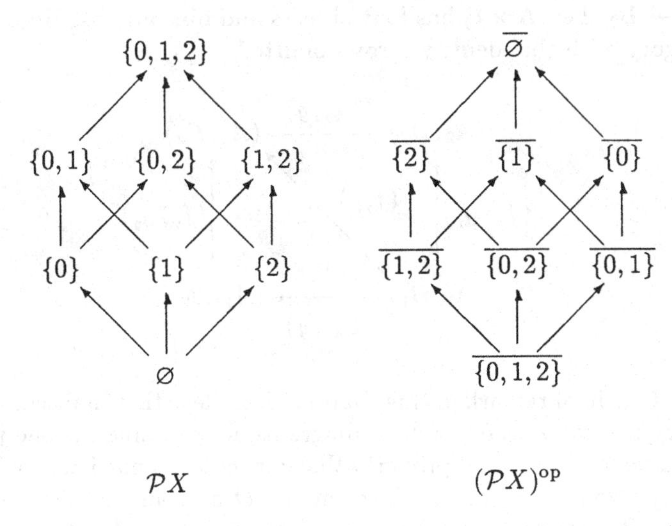

As drawn, the two categories look the same. What is the bijection which makes them look the same?

Answer. If U is a subset of $X = \{0,1,2\}$ then

$$\Phi(\overline{U}) = \neg U \qquad \text{(the complement of } U \text{ in } X\text{).}$$

This is clearly a bijection between objects of $(\mathcal{P}X)^{\mathrm{op}}$ and those of $\mathcal{P}X$ since $\neg\neg(U) = U$. Further, there is an arrow from $\overline{U}$ to $\overline{V}$ in $(\mathcal{P}X)^{\mathrm{op}}$ if and only if $V \subset U$, if and only if $\neg U \subset \neg V$, if and only if there is an arrow from ΦU to ΦV in $\mathcal{P}X$. Hence Φ is an isomorphism.

Here is one more way of making new categories out of old.

Definition. If $\mathbf{A}$, $\mathbf{B}$ are categories then $\mathbf{A} \times \mathbf{B}$, the *product* of $\mathbf{A}$ and $\mathbf{B}$, is defined by the following:

- the objects of $\mathbf{A} \times \mathbf{B}$ are pairs (A, B) of objects, A from $\mathbf{A}$ and B from $\mathbf{B}$;
- the arrows from (A_1, B_1) to (A_2, B_2) are pairs (f_1, g_1) of arrows

$$(f_1 : A_1 \to A_2, g_1 : B_1 \to B_2).$$

Composition is performed component by component.

Example 28. Suppose that $\mathbf{A}$ has two objects A_1, A_2 and three arrows 1_{A_1}, 1_{A_2} and $f : A_1 \to A_2$ and $\mathbf{B}$ has two objects B_1, B_2 and three arrows 1_{B_1}, 1_{B_2}

and $g : B_1 \to B_2$ then $\mathbf{A} \times \mathbf{B}$ has four objects and nine arrows. Here is a sketch of the category with the identity arrows omitted:

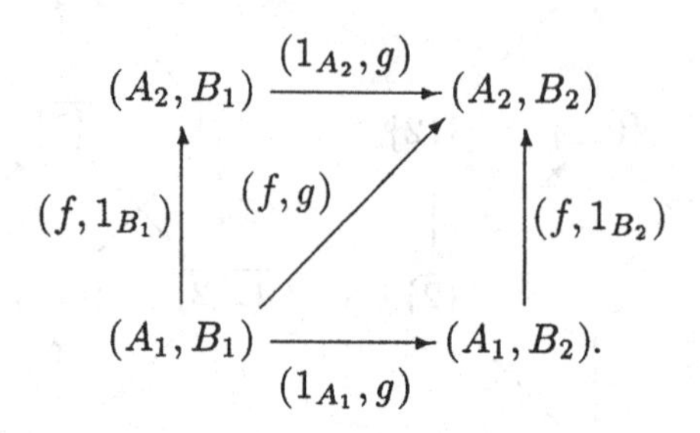

Remark. One final remark in this chapter. It is clear that in discussing arrows in a category it is very useful to draw diagrams, for example the one just above. Some diagrams have a special property that makes them particularly interesting — given any two objects in the diagram, P, Q say, any composite of arrows beginning at P and ending at Q yields the same result. We then say that the diagram *commutes*.

The diagram we drew in the last example commutes, since

$$(f, 1_{B_2})(1_{A_1}, g) = (f, g) = (1_{A_2}, g)(f, 1_{B_1}).$$

Problems 1

1. Give an example of two functions $f, g : \mathbb{R} \to \mathbb{R}$ such that $g \circ f \neq f \circ g$.

2. Decompose the following functions $f : \mathbb{R} \to \mathbb{R}$ into composites of simple functions:

(i) $f(x) = 1 + e^{2\sin^2 x + 1}$;

(ii) $f(x) = xe^{(\sin x + x)}$.

3. Write down the composition table for each of the following subcategories of **Sets**:

(i) the set $\{0, 1\}$; all functions from the set to itself;

(ii) the sets $\{0, 1\}$ and $\{2\}$; all functions between them.

4. Sketch the category of all subsets of $\{0, 1, 2, 3\}$ with the morphisms being inclusion functions.

5. Show that the number of categories with exactly n arrows is less than or equal to $(n + 1)^{n^2}$.

6. Represent each of the following categories as a category of sets and functions:

(i) Two objects X, Y; arrows $s : X \to Y$, $p : Y \to X$ with $ps = 1_X$;

(ii) One object X; arrows 1_X, α, α^2 such that $\alpha^3 = 1_X$;

(iii) One object X; arrows 1_X, α, α^2 such that $\alpha^3 = \alpha^2$;

(iv) One object X; arrows 1_X, α, α^2 such that $\alpha^3 = \alpha$;

(v) One object X; arrows 1_X, α_1, α_2 such that $\alpha_i\alpha_j = \alpha_i$ $(i, j = 1, 2)$;

(vi) One object X; arrows 1_X, α_1, α_2 such that $\alpha_i\alpha_j = \alpha_j$ $(i, j = 1, 2)$.

7. Show there are exactly 11 different categories with three arrows.

8. Represent each of the following monoids in terms of sets and functions:

(i) arrows 1, e, e^2, e^3, e^4 satisfying $e^5 = e$;

(ii) arrows 1, e, α such that $e^2 = e$, $e\alpha = \alpha e = \alpha^2 = \alpha$.

9. (i) Here is a picture of an endomorphism α of $\{0, 1, 2, 3, 4, 5\}$:

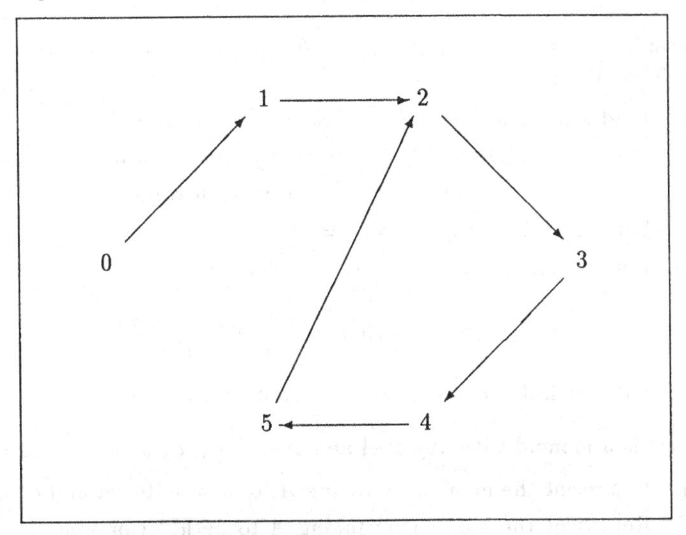

(each arrow indicates where an element goes under α). Calculate the composition table for the monoid generated by α;

(ii) Show that if α is an endomorphism of a finite set X then there are natural numbers k, l $(k < l)$ such that $\alpha^k = \alpha^l$.

10. Consider the monoid generated by arrows x_1, x_2, $\ldots$, x_n and satisfying $x_i^2 = x_i$, $x_ix_jx_i = x_ix_j$ $(i, j = 1, 2, \ldots, n)$. Show that the monoid is finite.

11. Represent each of the following categories, given in terms of generators and relations, as a category of sets and functions:

(i) one object X; arrows 1_X, α, such that $\alpha^4 = \alpha^2$;

(ii) one object X; arrows 1_X, α, β, such that $\alpha^2 = \alpha$, $\beta^2 = 1_X$, $\alpha\beta = \alpha$;
(iii) one object X; arrows 1_X, α, β such that $\alpha^2 = \alpha$, $\beta^3 = 1_X$, and $\alpha\beta = \beta\alpha$.

12. Show that the category given by generators

$$\alpha : X \to Y, \qquad \beta : Y \to X$$

satisfying the relation $\alpha\beta\alpha = \alpha$ is finite.

13. Determine all the arrows in the category with generators three objects A, B, C and three arrows $f : A \to B$, $g : B \to C$, $h : C \to A$ satisfying the relations

$$hgf = 1_A, \qquad fhg = 1_B, \qquad gfh = 1_C.$$

Find a representation of the category in terms of sets and functions.

14. Consider the category given by generators $o : I \to N$, $s, f : N \to N$, and relations $fo = o$, $fs = ssf$. Find a representation of this category in terms of sets and functions.

15. Consider the graph with objects I, N and arrows $o : I \to N$, $s : N \to N$ and $f : N \to N$.

(i) Find a finite number of relations which imply that

$$fs^n o = \begin{cases} so & \text{if } n \text{ is even,} \\ o & \text{if } n \text{ is odd,} \end{cases}$$

but which do not imply $s^m o = s^n o$ unless $m = n$.

(ii) Find a finite number of relations which imply that

$$fs^n o = \begin{cases} s^{n-1} o & \text{if } n > 0, \\ o & \text{if } n = 0, \end{cases}$$

but which do not imply $s^m o = s^n o$ unless $m = n$.

16. There is a monoid with object A and arrows 1_A, α, α^2, α^3, α^4 satisfying $\alpha^5 = \alpha^2$.

(i) Represent the monoid by taking A to be a finite set and α to be a function.
(ii) Represent the monoid by taking A to be $\mathbb{R}^n$ (for some n), and α to be a linear transformation.

17. Show that $\mathcal{P}\{0,1,2,3\}$ is isomorphic to $\mathcal{P}\{0,1\} \times \mathcal{P}\{2,3\}$.

18. Show that if $\alpha : A \to B$ and $\beta : B \to C$ are isomorphisms in a category $\mathbf{A}$ then so is $\beta\alpha : A \to C$.

19. Suppose that $\alpha : A \to B$ is an arrow with two inverses $\beta_1 : B \to A$ and $\beta_2 : B \to A$. Show that $\beta_1 = \beta_2$.

20. Show that if $\mathbf{G}$ is a group (regarded as a one-object category) then $\mathbf{G}^{\mathrm{op}}$ is isomorphic to $\mathbf{G}$.

21. Show that if $\alpha : A \to B$ and $\beta : B \to A$ are arrows in $\mathbf{A}$ such that $\beta\alpha = 1_A$ then $\alpha\beta$ is an idempotent.

22. Consider a category $\mathbf{A}$ with the following properties:

(i) every arrow in $\mathbf{A}$ has an inverse;

(ii) for each pair of objects A, B there is an arrow from A to B;

(iii) for each object A there are exactly n arrows with domain A.

Show that the total number of endomorphisms (loops) in $\mathbf{A}$ is n.

23. How many objects and how many arrows are there in the category $\mathcal{P}\{1, 2, 3, \ldots, n\}$?

24. Consider the category **Lin** whose objects are

$$\mathbb{R}^0, \qquad \mathbb{R}^1, \qquad \mathbb{R}^2, \quad \ldots$$

and whose arrows are all *linear* transformations.

Show that **Lin** is isomorphic to **Matr**.

25. (i) Show that the category given by generators

$$\alpha : X \to Y, \qquad \beta : Y \to X$$

satisfying the relation $\beta\alpha\beta\alpha = 1_X$ is finite;

(ii) Consider the category generated by the two arrows $a : X \to Y$, $b : Y \to X$ and satisfying the relations

$$abab = ab, \qquad baba = 1_X.$$

Show that the category has at most five arrows, and find a representation of the category in terms of sets and functions.

26. Verify that the following describes a category, denoted **Rel**:

objects	–	sets $X, Y, Z, \ldots$;
arrows	–	$\rho : X \longrightarrow Y$ are binary relations, i.e. subsets of $X \times Y$;
composition	–	if $\rho : X \longrightarrow Y$ and $\tau : Y \longrightarrow Z$ then $(x, z) \in \tau\rho$ if there exists a y such that $(x, y) \in \rho$ and $(y, z) \in \tau$.

Prove that $\mathbf{Rel}^{\mathrm{op}} \cong \mathbf{Rel}$.

Chapter 2

Products and Sums

So far we have discussed functions of one variable, but any algebra of functions must be able to deal with the fact that there are functions of two variables; for example, functions $f : \mathbb{R} \times \mathbb{R} \to \mathbb{R}$.

Example 1.

$$\begin{aligned} \textit{add} \quad : \quad & \mathbb{R} \times \mathbb{R} \longrightarrow \mathbb{R} \\ & (x, y) \longmapsto x + y, \end{aligned}$$

$$\begin{aligned} \textit{multiply} \quad : \quad & \mathbb{R} \times \mathbb{R} \longrightarrow \mathbb{R} \\ & (x, y) \longmapsto x \cdot y. \end{aligned}$$

To express the notion of function of several variables we need to be able to talk about ***products of objects***. Then a general function of two variables will be an arrow of the form

$$f : X \times Y \to Z.$$

We have already described arrows with special properties in a category — 'idempotents' and 'isomorphisms'. In this chapter we will define objects with special properties — ***products*** and ***sums***.

To lead up to these definitions we will first describe something simpler.

§1. Initial and Terminal Objects

In **Sets** the empty set $\varnothing$ and the one point set $\{*\}$ both have properties which characterise them, and which can be formulated purely in terms of functions.

1. **A characteristic property of the one point set $\{*\}$.** Given any set X there is exactly one function from X to $\{*\}$.

The function takes any $x \in X$ to $*$. Clearly this *is* a function and is the only possible function from X to $\{*\}$. We will denote this function by $! : X \to \{*\}$.

2. **A characteristic property of the empty set $\varnothing$.** Given any set X there is exactly one function from $\varnothing$ to X.

To see this you need to think carefully about what a function is. A function from Y to X is a subset U of $Y \times X$ satisfying the property that to each $y \in Y$ there is exactly one pair in U with first coordinate y. Hence a function from $\varnothing$ to X is a subset of $\varnothing \times X = \varnothing$ — and there is only one such subset, namely $\varnothing$, and it satisfies the property vacuously. We will also denote this function by $! : \varnothing \to X$.

1.1 Proposition. Property 2 characterizes the empty set.

Proof. Suppose Z is another set with the property that, for any set X, there is exactly one function $Z \to X$. Then this property of Z implies that there is exactly one function $\alpha : Z \to \varnothing$, and one function $Z \to Z$, which must be the identity function 1_Z.

The same property of $\varnothing$ says there is exactly one function $\beta : \varnothing \to Z$ and one function $\varnothing \to \varnothing$ (which must be $1_\varnothing$).

But $\alpha\beta : \varnothing \to \varnothing$ and hence must be $1_\varnothing$. Similarly, $\beta\alpha : Z \to Z$ and hence must be 1_Z. Thus Z and $\varnothing$ are isomorphic sets. ∎

A similar argument shows that Property 1 characterises the one point set, again *up to isomorphism* — that is to say, any two sets satisfying Property 1 are isomorphic. Notice that while there is only one empty set there are in fact many one-point sets, but they are all isomorphic.

Definition. In a category **A** an object O is called *initial* if for any object X in **A** there is a unique arrow $O \to X$. An object I is called *terminal* if for any object X there is a unique arrow $X \to I$.

Note. The reason for my choice of symbols to denote the initial and terminal objects is that O looks like 0 — the number of elements in the empty set ; and I looks like 1 — the number of elements in the one-point set. (Unfortunately I is also the first letter of initial, but don't let this confuse you.)

The terminal object I is characterised by arrows into I (that is, with codomain I). What are the arrows out of I?

Example 2. **(Sets.)** What is a function $\{*\} \to X$?

Such a function is completely determined by where the single point $*$ goes to. In other words, there are just as many functions from $\{*\}$ to X as elements of X. This enables us to define what is an *element* of an object in a general category.

Definition. If I is terminal in **A** we call arrows $I \to A$ *elements* of A (or *points* or *constants* of A).

Example 3. **($\mathcal{P}X$.)** The subset X itself is terminal in $\mathcal{P}X$ since every object U has an arrow to X; that is each subset U is contained in X.

The empty subset $\varnothing$ is initial in $\mathcal{P}X$ since there is an arrow from $\varnothing$ to U for each object U; that is, $\varnothing$ is contained in every subset U.

It is clear that in a preorder the uniqueness part of the definition of initial and terminal is superfluous, and in fact a terminal object is a maximum element of the preorder, and an initial object is a minimum element of the preorder.

Remark. Not every category $\mathbf{A}$ has initial and terminal objects.

Example 4. The only monoid to have a terminal object is the monoid with exactly one arrow — a monoid has only one object and if that is terminal there is only one arrow from the object to itself.

Note. In general, 'large' categories tend to have initial and terminal objects; 'small' categories don't.

Remark. There is an obvious similarity between the definitions of initial and terminal objects. They are *dual* definitions. What this means technically is that if $\overline{A}$ is a terminal object in $\mathbf{A}^{\mathrm{op}}$ then A is an initial object in $\mathbf{A}$ — and conversely.

Proof. $\overline{A}$ is terminal in $\mathbf{A}^{\mathrm{op}}$ means that there is exactly one arrow $\overline{f} : \overline{X} \to \overline{A}$ for each $\overline{X}$ in $\mathbf{A}^{\mathrm{op}}$, which means that there is exactly one arrow $f : A \to X$ in $\mathbf{A}$; that is, A is initial in $\mathbf{A}$. ∎

Example 5. Recall that $\overline{\varnothing}$ is the top element and $\overline{X}$ is the bottom element in $(\mathcal{P}X)^{\mathrm{op}}$.

§2. Products

The cartesian product of two sets X and Y is the set denoted by $X \times Y$ whose elements are the pairs (x, y) with x in X and y in Y. Our purpose in this section is to characterise $X \times Y$ using only functions and composition of functions. If we can do that, then we can define the product of objects in any category — even formal categories whose objects are not sets.

We cannot so characterise $X \times Y$ in **Sets** on its own; we need its relation with X and Y.

The obvious relation is that there are two projection maps:

$$X \xleftarrow{p_1} X \times Y \xrightarrow{p_2} Y$$

$$x \longleftarrow\!\shortmid (x, y) \longmapsto y.$$

If we have a terminal object I and an 'element' $\alpha : I \to X \times Y$ of $X \times Y$, then composing α with p_1, p_2 gives us 'elements' x, y of X and Y.

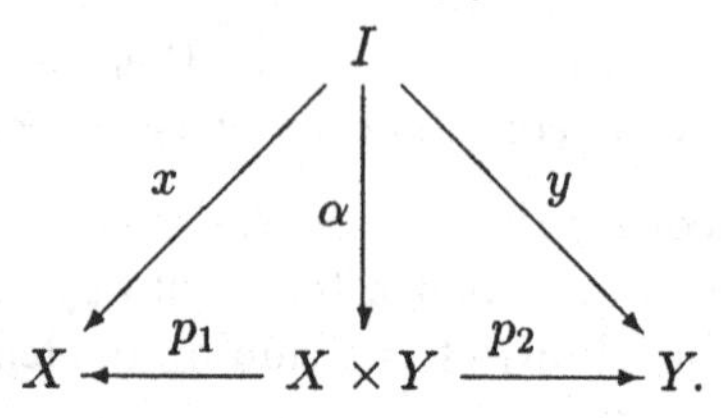

One property of $X \times Y$ is that there is a bijection between 'elements' of $X \times Y$ and pairs of 'elements', one of X and one of Y.

This does translate the usual definition into one in terms of functions and composition. However there is a stronger property of $X \times Y$ and its projections, namely that, given *any* set Z there is a bijection between functions $Z \to X \times Y$ and pairs of functions $Z \to X$, $Z \to Y$. This property does not rely on the existence of a terminal object.

Let's check this property. Consider a function

$$\alpha : Z \longrightarrow X \times Y$$
$$z \longmapsto \alpha(z).$$

Notice that $\alpha(z)$, being an element of the cartesian product, has two components $\alpha_1(z) \in X$ and $\alpha_2(z) \in Y$. Hence we get two functions

$$Z \xrightarrow{\alpha_1} X, \qquad Z \xrightarrow{\alpha_2} Y.$$

Conversely, we can put together two functions $Z \to X$, $Z \to Y$ to get one function $Z \to X \times Y$.

We now define products of objects in any category.

Definition. In a category **A**, an object $X \times Y$ with two arrows

$$X \xleftarrow{p_1} X \times Y \xrightarrow{p_2} Y$$

is called a *product* of X and Y if, given any object Z and arrows $x : Z \to X$, $y : Z \to Y$,

($\star$) there is a unique arrow $\alpha : Z \to X \times Y$ such that

$$p_1 \cdot \alpha = x, \qquad p_2 \cdot \alpha = y.$$

Note. The defining property of products is sometimes called *the universal property of products*. It is often useful to break condition ($\star$) of the definition into two parts, namely:

(i) (Existence.) Given arrows $x : Z \to X$, $y : Z \to Y$ there *exists* an arrow $\alpha : Z \to X \times Y$ such that

$$p_1 \cdot \alpha = x, \qquad p_2 \cdot \alpha = y;$$

(ii) (Uniqueness.) Given 2 arrows $\alpha, \beta : Z \to X \times Y$ such that

$$p_1 \cdot \alpha = p_1 \cdot \beta, \qquad p_2 \cdot \alpha = p_2 \cdot \beta$$

then $\alpha = \beta$.

Note. A useful name for the arrow $\alpha : Z \to X \times Y$, induced by the pair $f : Z \to X$, $g : Z \to Y$, is

$$(f, g) : Z \to X \times Y.$$

2.1 Proposition. The product of two objects in a category is unique up to isomorphism.

Proof. Suppose

$$X \xleftarrow{\;q_1\;} Q \xrightarrow{\;q_2\;} Y$$

is also a product of X, Y (with projections q_1, q_2). We want to show that Q is isomorphic to $X \times Y$.

The defining property of $X \times Y$ means that there is an arrow $\alpha : Q \to X \times Y$ such that $p_1\alpha = q_1$, $p_2\alpha = q_2$:

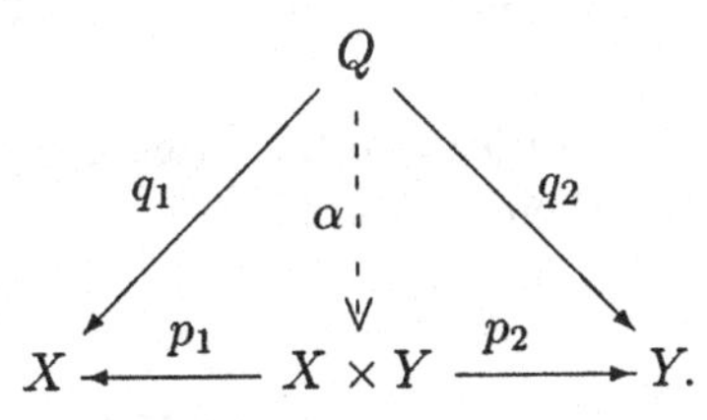

The defining property of Q means that there is an arrow $\beta : X \times Y \to Q$, such that $q_1\beta = p_1$, $q_2\beta = p_2$:

$$\begin{array}{ccccc} X & \xleftarrow{\;p_1\;} & X \times Y & \xrightarrow{\;p_2\;} & Y. \\ & {\scriptstyle q_1}\nwarrow & \downarrow{\scriptstyle \beta} & \nearrow{\scriptstyle q_2} & \\ & & Q & & \end{array}$$

Hence:

$$q_1\beta\alpha = p_1\alpha = q_1 = q_1 1_Q,$$
$$q_2\beta\alpha = p_2\alpha = q_2 = q_2 1_Q.$$

That is, the following diagram, with either one of the arrows 1_Q, $\beta\alpha$ across the diagonal, commutes:

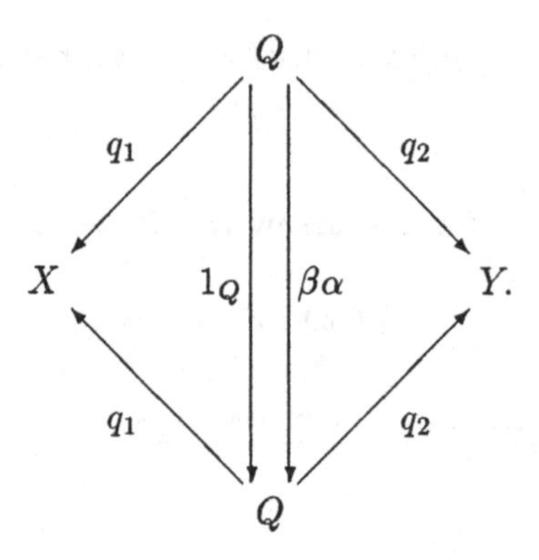

The uniqueness property of products implies that $\beta\alpha = 1_Q$.

By symmetry, we also have that $\alpha\beta = 1_{X\times Y}$, and hence that Q is isomorphic to $X \times Y$ — by a unique isomorphism which, composed with the projections of $X \times Y$, produces the projections of Q.

Remark. Not all categories have products of objects. Large categories usually do; small categories usually don't, though the next example is an exception.

Example 6. Each pair of objects in the category $\mathcal{P}X$ has a product. Consider subsets U, V of X. Then their product is

$$U \longleftarrow U \cap V \longrightarrow V.$$

Certainly $U \cap V$ is contained in both U and V. Further suppose

$$U \longleftarrow W \longrightarrow V.$$

That is, W is contained in both U and V. Then W is contained in $U \cap V$. The rest of the definition of product just says that certain (composites of) arrows are equal. But this is automatic since $\mathcal{P}X$ is a preorder — between any pair of objects there is at most one arrow.

To summarize, in any preorder the product of two objects, if it exists, is their intersection — the greatest lower bound of the two objects.

Example 7. The monoid with object A and two arrows 1 and α, satisfying $\alpha^2 = \alpha$, does not have products.

The product of A and A would have to be A — there is no other object. From the definition of product there is a bijection between pairs of arrows

$$A \to A, \qquad A \to A$$

and single arrows

$$A \to A \times A = A.$$

No bijection is possible since there are four pairs of arrows $(A \to A, A \to A)$, but only two arrows $A \to A$.

It turns out that the definition of product given above allows a great variety of constructions used in mathematics connected with functions of several variables.

Example 8. Given a set X there is a function,

$$\begin{aligned} \Delta : X &\longrightarrow X \times X \\ x &\longmapsto (x, x), \end{aligned}$$

called the *diagonal function*. It is sometimes called the *copy* function since it produces two copies of x.

In an arbitrary category with products the diagonal arrow is defined as the arrow with components 1_X, 1_X. That is, Δ_X is the unique arrow making the following diagram commute:

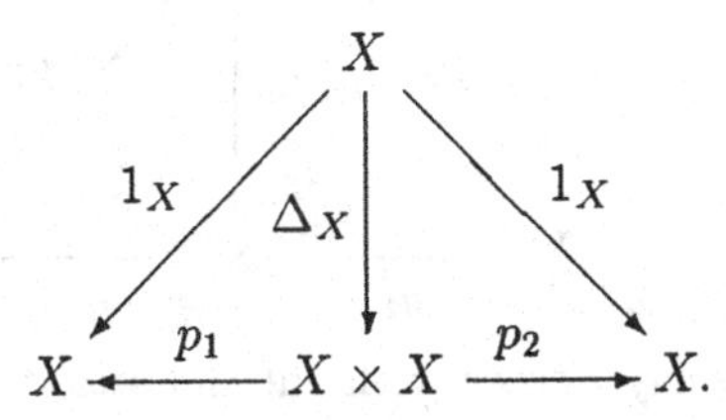

Example 9. In **Sets**, given two functions $f : X_1 \to Y_1$, $g : X_2 \to Y_2$ there is a function denoted by:

$$\begin{aligned} \mathrm{f} \times \mathrm{g} : X_1 \times X_2 &\longrightarrow Y_1 \times Y_2 \\ (x_1, x_2) &\longmapsto (f(x_1), g(x_2)). \end{aligned}$$

This function $f \times g$ may be thought of as the two functions f and g in *parallel*.

How can we define this operation in an arbitrary category with products?

Given arrows $f : X_1 \to Y_1$, $g : X_2 \to Y_2$ in a category with products, the arrow $f \times g$ is defined to be the unique arrow from $X_1 \times X_2$ to $Y_1 \times Y_2$ such that

$$p_{Y_1}(f \times g) = f p_{X_1},$$
$$p_{Y_2}(f \times g) = g p_{X_2},$$

where the p's are projections. That is, $f \times g$ is the unique arrow making the following diagram commute:

$$\begin{array}{ccccc} X_1 & \xleftarrow{p_{X_1}} & X_1 \times X_2 & \xrightarrow{p_{X_2}} & X_2 \\ \downarrow{\scriptstyle f} & & \downarrow{\scriptstyle f \times g} & & \downarrow{\scriptstyle g} \\ Y_1 & \xleftarrow[p_{Y_1}]{} & Y_1 \times Y_2 & \xrightarrow[p_{Y_2}]{} & Y_2. \end{array}$$

Example 10. In **Sets**, given two sets X, Y there is a function

$$twist_{X,Y} : X \times Y \longrightarrow Y \times X$$
$$(x, y) \longmapsto (y, x).$$

In an arbitrary category with products, $twist_{X,Y} : X \times Y \to Y \times X$ is defined as follows. Let p_1, p_2 be the projections of $X \times Y$ and q_1, q_2 the projections of $Y \times X$. Then $twist_{X,Y}$ is the unique arrow such that the following diagram commutes:

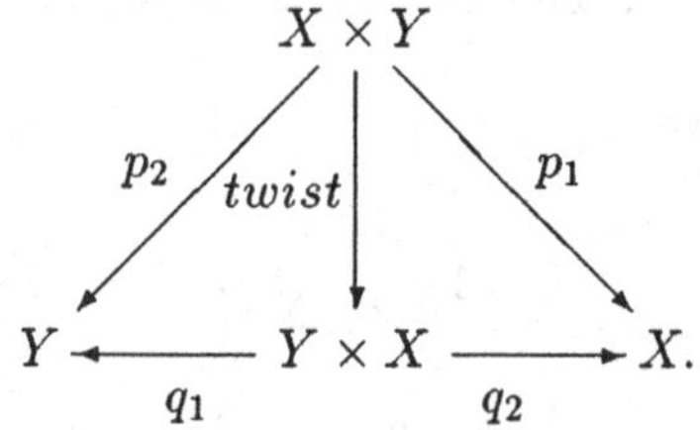

A definition which clearly agrees with the definition in **Sets**.

Note. The product $X \times Y$ is defined in terms of arrows *into* $X \times Y$. What are arrows *out of* $X \times Y$? These are 'functions of 2-variables'.

§3. Categories with Products – Circuits

Example 11. Let $\mathbf{B} = \{0, 1\}$. The following is a category, which we shall call **Circ**:

- Objects: $\mathbf{B}^0$, $\mathbf{B}^1$, $\mathbf{B}^2$, $\mathbf{B}^3$, ... where $\mathbf{B}^0 = \{*\}$, $\mathbf{B}^1 = \mathbf{B}$, and $\mathbf{B}^m = \{(x_1, x_2, \ldots, x_m); x_i \in \mathbf{B}\}$ for $m > 1$.
- Arrows: all functions between these sets.

There are 2 functions from $\mathbf{B}^0$ to $\mathbf{B}^1$, namely

$$\begin{aligned} \mathit{true} \ : \ \mathbf{B}^0 &\longrightarrow \mathbf{B}^1 \\ * &\longmapsto 1, \end{aligned}$$

and

$$\begin{aligned} \mathit{false} \ : \ \mathbf{B}^0 &\longrightarrow \mathbf{B}^1 \\ * &\longmapsto 0. \end{aligned}$$

Some further interesting functions in this category:

$$\begin{aligned} \neg \ : \mathbf{B}^1 &\longrightarrow \mathbf{B}^1 \\ 0 &\longmapsto 1 \\ 1 &\longmapsto 0, \end{aligned} \qquad \text{(sometimes called } \mathit{not}\text{)}$$

$$\begin{aligned} \& \ : \ \mathbf{B}^2 &\longrightarrow \mathbf{B}^1 \\ (0,0) &\longmapsto 0 \\ (0,1) &\longmapsto 0 \\ (1,0) &\longmapsto 0 \\ (1,1) &\longmapsto 1, \end{aligned} \qquad \begin{aligned} \mathit{or} \ : \ \mathbf{B}^2 &\longrightarrow \mathbf{B}^1 \\ (0,0) &\longmapsto 0 \\ (0,1) &\longmapsto 1 \\ (1,0) &\longmapsto 1 \\ (1,1) &\longmapsto 1. \end{aligned}$$

Claim. The category **Circ** has products. In fact, the product of $\mathbf{B}^m$ and $\mathbf{B}^n$ is $\mathbf{B}^{m+n}$ with the following projections:

$$\begin{array}{ccccc} \mathbf{B}^m & \xleftarrow{\ p_1\ } & \mathbf{B}^{m+n} & \xrightarrow{\ p_2\ } & \mathbf{B}^n \\ (x_1, \ldots, x_m) & \longleftarrow\!\shortmid & (x_1, x_2, \ldots, x_m, \ldots, x_{m+n}) & \longmapsto & (x_{m+1}, \ldots, x_{m+n}). \end{array}$$

Let's check the property of products. Consider the following diagram:

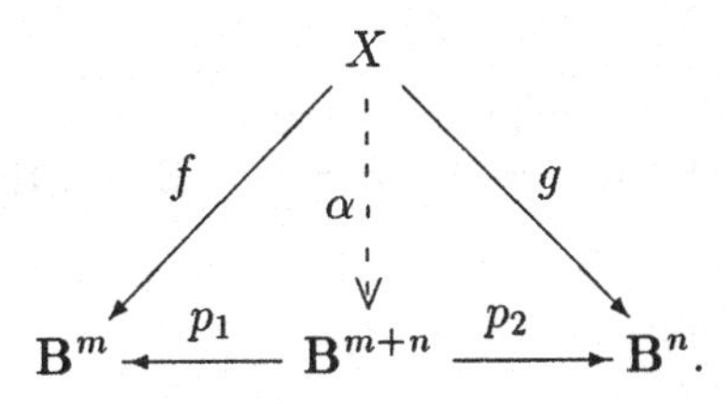

Suppose

$$f(x) = (f_1(x), f_2(x), f_3(x), \ldots, f_m(x))$$

and $$g(x) = (g_1(x), g_2(x), g_3(x), \ldots, g_n(x)).$$

Then $$\alpha(x) = (f_1(x), f_2(x), \ldots, f_m(x), g_1(x), g_2(x), \cdots, g_n(x)),$$

and clearly $p_1\alpha = f$, $p_2\alpha = g$. Further, α is the only function with this property.

Now to show what kind of functions can be constructed using products let us consider the following question.

Question. What arrows can be constructed in **Circ**, starting with *true*, *false*, $\neg$, &, *or*, identity maps, and projections using only composition and the property of products?

Answer. All arrows can be so generated.

We will not give a formal proof of this result, but instead we will give an example which makes the general case clear.

Consider the following function:

$$\begin{aligned} f :\quad \mathbf{B}^3 &\longrightarrow \mathbf{B} \\ (0,0,0) &\longmapsto 1 \\ (0,0,1) &\longmapsto 0 \\ (0,1,0) &\longmapsto 0 \\ (0,1,1) &\longmapsto 0 \\ (1,0,0) &\longmapsto 0 \\ (1,0,1) &\longmapsto 1 \\ (1,1,0) &\longmapsto 0 \\ (1,1,1) &\longmapsto 0. \end{aligned}$$

I claim that

$$f(x, y, z) = (\neg x \& \neg y \& \neg z) \ or \ (x \& \neg y \& z).$$

To see this, notice that $f(x, y, z)$ is 1 if either of the two parts $(\neg x \& \neg y \& \neg z)$ or $(x \& \neg y \& z)$ is 1.

The first part is 1 precisely when $x = 0$ and $y = 0$ and $z = 0$; the second part is 1 precisely when $x = 1$ and $y = 0$ and $z = 1$. Hence the result.

Using this expression for f we can decompose f into $\neg$, &, *or*, using products and composition as follows.

$$\mathbf{B}^3 \xrightarrow{\Delta_{\mathbf{B}^3}} \mathbf{B}^3 \times \mathbf{B}^3 = \mathbf{B}^6$$
$$(x, y, z) \longmapsto (x, y, z, x, y, z)$$

$$\mathbf{B}^6 \xrightarrow{\neg \times \neg \times \neg \times 1_{\mathbf{B}} \times \neg \times 1_{\mathbf{B}}} \mathbf{B}^6$$
$$(x, y, z, x, y, z) \longmapsto (\neg x, \neg y, \neg z, x, \neg y, z)$$

$$\mathbf{B}^6 \xrightarrow{\& \times 1_{\mathbf{B}} \times \& \times 1_{\mathbf{B}}} \mathbf{B}^4$$
$$(\neg x, \neg y, \neg z, x, \neg y, z) \longmapsto (\neg x \& \neg y, \neg z, x \& \neg y, z)$$

$$\mathbf{B}^4 \xrightarrow{\& \times \&} \mathbf{B}^2$$
$$(\neg x \& \neg y, \neg z, x \& \neg y, z) \longmapsto (\neg x \& \neg y \& \neg z, x \& \neg y \& z)$$

$$\mathbf{B}^2 \xrightarrow{or} \mathbf{B}$$
$$(\neg x \& \neg y \& \neg z, x \& \neg y \& z) \longmapsto f(x, y, z).$$

Note. We have used the following easily checked facts about this category:

$$(\mathbf{B}^m \times \mathbf{B}^n) \times \mathbf{B}^p = \mathbf{B}^{m+n+p} = \mathbf{B}^m \times (\mathbf{B}^n \times \mathbf{B}^p),$$

and the same is true for arrows, namely,

$$(f \times g) \times h = f \times (g \times h).$$

It is because of these facts that we have omitted brackets above.

This decomposition corresponds to the way such a function might be implemented using boolean gates; that is, using a circuit (without feedback) consisting of wires and components:

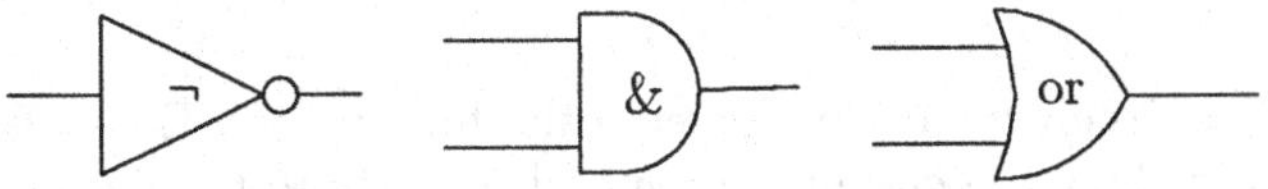

The set **B** is the set of possible states (the state space) of each wire — each wire can be at zero volts or one volt, say.

The function $\neg : \mathbf{B} \to \mathbf{B}$ is implemented by the component

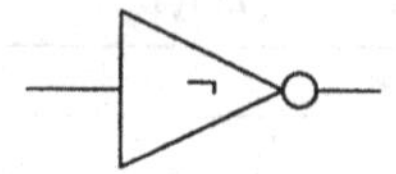

The function $\& : \mathbf{B}^2 \to \mathbf{B}$ is implemented by the component

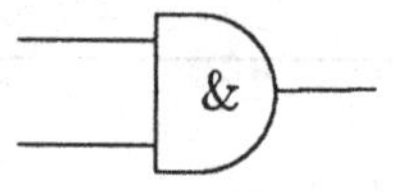

The function $or : \mathbf{B}^2 \to \mathbf{B}$ is implemented by the component

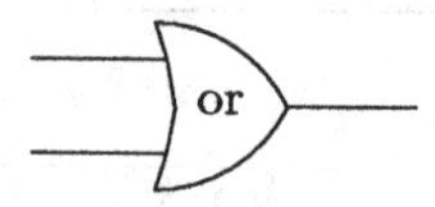

What can we do with wires and components?

- We can split up wires. This corresponds to the diagonal function,

$$\Delta_{\mathbf{B}} : \mathbf{B} \to \mathbf{B}^2.$$

- We can put 2 components side by side. This corresponds to the function,

$$f \times g : \mathbf{B} \times \mathbf{B} \to \mathbf{B} \times \mathbf{B}.$$

- We can put two components in series. This corresponds to composition,

$$g \circ f : \mathbf{B} \to \mathbf{B}.$$

- We can twist two of the wires. This corresponds to the function,

$$twist : \mathbf{B} \times \mathbf{B} \to \mathbf{B} \times \mathbf{B}.$$

Let us draw a circuit which implements the function $f : \mathbf{B}^3 \to \mathbf{B}$ in the above example; notice how the circuit corresponds exactly to the decomposition given above.

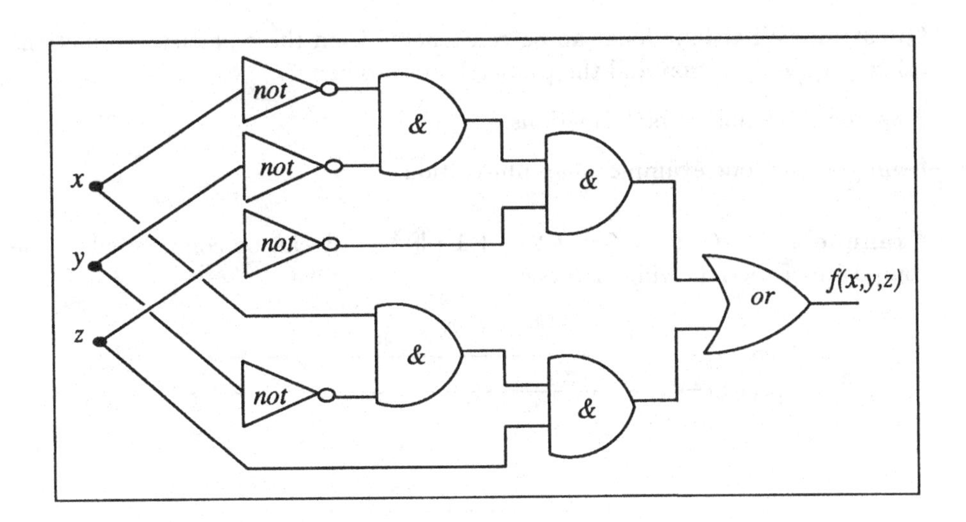

Going from left to right in this circuit corresponds exactly to the successive functions in the composite:

$$\mathbf{B}^3 \xrightarrow{\Delta} \mathbf{B}^6 \xrightarrow{\neg\times\neg\times\neg\times 1\times\neg\times 1} \mathbf{B}^6 \xrightarrow{\&\times 1\times\&\times 1} \mathbf{B}^4 \xrightarrow{\&\times\&} \mathbf{B}^2 \xrightarrow{\text{or}} \mathbf{B}$$

Summarising:

(i) Using wires, we can implement products.

(ii) Every function $\mathbf{B}^m \to \mathbf{B}^n$ can be implemented using $\neg$, &, *or, true, false*, using products and composition.

(iii) A decomposition of function f into &, *or*, *not*, using products and composition, corresponds to an implementation of f by a circuit.

Example 12. A second example of a category with products.

- Objects: $\mathbb{R}^0, \mathbb{R}^1, \mathbb{R}^2, \ldots$.
- Arrows: all functions between these sets.

Here are some particular functions in this category:

(i) To each real number r there is the function $\lceil r \rceil : \mathbb{R}^0 \to \mathbb{R}$ (called the *name* of r) which takes the single point of $\mathbb{R}^0$ to $r \in \mathbb{R}$;

(ii) $add : \mathbb{R}^2 \to \mathbb{R}$ which takes (x, y) to $x + y$;

(iii) $multiply : \mathbb{R}^2 \to \mathbb{R}$ which takes (x, y) to xy.

Question. What functions can be constructed from these particular functions using only composition and the properties of products?

Answer. The polynomial functions.

I will give just one example as an illustration.

Example 13. $f(x,y) = 3x^2 + 2xy + 1 : \mathbb{R}^2 \to \mathbb{R}$ can be constructed as the composite of the following arrows:

$$\begin{array}{ccc} \mathbb{R}^2 & \xrightarrow{\Delta \times 1_{\mathbb{R}}} & \mathbb{R}^3 \\ (x,y) & \longmapsto & (x,x,y), \end{array}$$

$$\begin{array}{ccc} \mathbb{R}^3 & \xrightarrow{\Delta \times 1_{\mathbb{R}^2}} & \mathbb{R}^4 \\ (x,x,y) & \longmapsto & (x,x,x,y), \end{array}$$

$$\begin{array}{ccc} \mathbb{R}^0 \times \mathbb{R}^2 \times \mathbb{R}^0 \times \mathbb{R}^2 \times \mathbb{R}^0 & \xrightarrow{\ulcorner 3 \urcorner \times 1_{\mathbb{R}^2} \times \ulcorner 2 \urcorner \times 1_{\mathbb{R}^2} \times \ulcorner 1 \urcorner} & \mathbb{R}^7 \\ (x,x,x,y) & \longmapsto & (3,x,x,2,x,y,1), \end{array}$$

$$\begin{array}{ccc} \mathbb{R}^7 & \xrightarrow{mult \times 1_{\mathbb{R}} \times mult \times 1_{\mathbb{R}^2}} & \mathbb{R}^5 \\ (3,x,x,2,x,y,1) & \longmapsto & (3x,x,2x,y,1), \end{array}$$

$$\begin{array}{ccc} \mathbb{R}^5 & \xrightarrow{mult \times mult \times 1_{\mathbb{R}}} & \mathbb{R}^3 \\ (3x,x,2x,y,1) & \longmapsto & (3x^2,2xy,1), \end{array}$$

$$\begin{array}{ccc} \mathbb{R}^3 & \xrightarrow{add \times 1_{\mathbb{R}}} & \mathbb{R}^2 \\ (3x^2,2xy,1) & \longmapsto & (3x^2+2xy,1), \end{array}$$

$$\begin{array}{ccc} \mathbb{R}^2 & \xrightarrow{add} & \mathbb{R} \\ (3x^2+2xy,1) & \longmapsto & (3x^2+2xy+1). \end{array}$$

Note. We have used the following easily checked facts about this category:

(i) $(\mathbb{R}^m \times \mathbb{R}^n) \times \mathbb{R}^p = \mathbb{R}^{m+n+p} = \mathbb{R}^m \times (\mathbb{R}^n \times \mathbb{R}^p)$; and the same is true for arrows, namely $(f \times g) \times h = f \times (g \times h)$. It is because of these facts that we have omitted brackets above.

(ii) $\lceil r \rceil \times f : \mathbb{R}^0 \times \mathbb{R}^1 \to \mathbb{R}^1 \times \mathbb{R}^1$ takes x to $(r, f(x))$.

§4. Products of Families

We have spoken so far of products of pairs of objects. We can similarly define products of finite (or infinite) families of objects.

Definition. If $(X_k)_{k \in K}$ is a finite family of objects of **A** then the product of the family is an object $\prod_{k \in K} X_k$ together with a family of projections

$$p_l : \prod_{k \in K} X_k \to X_l \qquad (l \in K),$$

which has the following property.

Given any object Z and a family of arrows

$$f_l : Z \to X_l \qquad (l \in K),$$

there is a unique arrow $\alpha : Z \to \prod_{k \in K} X_k$ such that $p_l \alpha = f_l \quad (l \in K)$.

Diagrammatically,

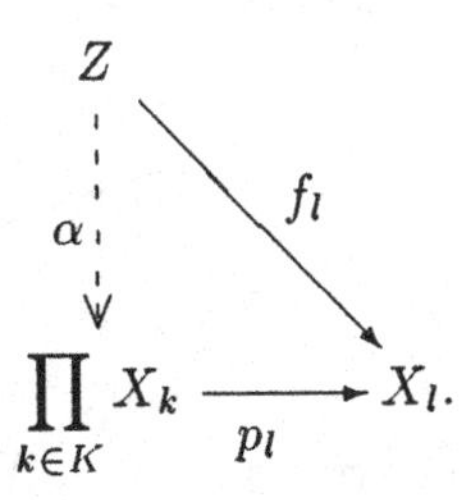

Note. A product of the empty family is a terminal object; the family is empty so that the only requirement of the product is that, given Z, there is a unique arrow from Z to the product.

4.1 Proposition. The product $\prod_{k \in K} X_k$, if it exists, is determined up to isomorphism.

Proof. Same as for a pair of objects. ∎

4.2 Proposition. If products of all pairs of objects exist in **A** and a terminal object exists then products of finite families exist.

Proof. I will prove that triple products — products of three objects — exist by showing that $(X_1 \times X_2) \times X_3$, with suitable projections, is the product of the family $(X_k)_{k \in \{1,2,3\}}$.

The projections of the triple product are the following composites of projections:

$$p_1 = p_{X_1} \cdot p_{X_1 X_2}, \qquad p_2 = p_{X_2} \cdot p_{X_1 X_2}, \qquad p_3 = p_{X_3},$$

illustrated in the diagram:

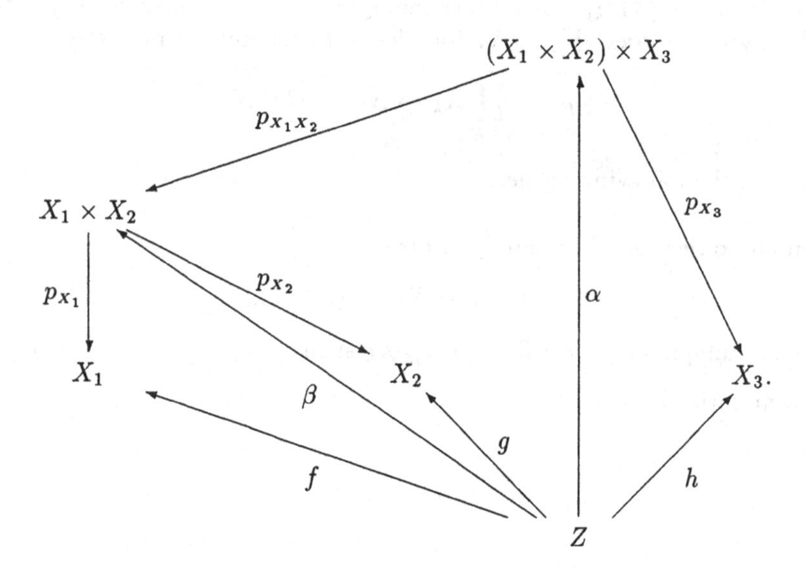

Consider an object Z and three arrows $f : Z \to X_1$, $g : Z \to X_2$, and $h : Z \to X_3$.

To verify the property of the triple product we need to construct an arrow $\alpha : Z \to (X_1 \times X_2) \times X_3$.

Certainly, since $X_1 \times X_2$ is a product, there is an arrow $\beta : Z \to X_1 \times X_2$ such that $p_{X_1}\beta = f$, $p_{X_2}\beta = g$.

Now consider $\beta : Z \to X_1 \times X_2$ and $h : Z \to X_3$. Since $(X_1 \times X_2) \times X_3$ is a product there is an arrow $\alpha : Z \to (X_1 \times X_2) \times X_3$ such that $p_{X_1 X_2} \cdot \alpha = \beta$, $p_{X_3} \cdot \alpha = h$.

Hence,

$$(1) \qquad p_1\alpha = p_{X_1} \cdot p_{X_1X_2} \cdot \alpha = p_{X_1} \cdot \beta = f,$$
$$(2) \qquad p_2\alpha = p_{X_2} \cdot p_{X_1X_2} \cdot \alpha = p_{X_2} \cdot \beta = g,$$
$$(3) \qquad p_3\alpha = p_{X_3} \cdot \alpha = h,$$

as required.

Suppose $\gamma : Z \to (X_1 \times X_2) \times X_3$ is another arrow satisfying (1), (2) and (3).

Then $p_{X_1X_2} \cdot \alpha$ and $p_{X_1X_2} \cdot \gamma$ have the same composites with projections onto X_1, X_2 (by (1) and (2)). Hence $p_{X_1X_2} \cdot \alpha = p_{X_1X_2} \cdot \gamma$ by the uniqueness property of the product $X_1 \times X_2$. Hence α and γ have the same composites with the projection onto $X_1 \times X_2$. But (3) implies that α, γ have the same composite with the projection onto X_3. Hence, by the uniqueness property of the product $(X_1 \times X_2) \times X_3$ we have that $\alpha = \gamma$.

We have now verified the required existence and uniqueness properties for the triple product. ■

4.3 Corollary. $X_1 \times (X_2 \times X_3) \cong (X_1 \times X_2) \times X_3$.

Proof. Both are triple products, hence isomorphic to $X_1 \times X_2 \times X_3$, and hence isomorphic to each other. ■

Note. Let the three projections of $X_1 \times (X_2 \times X_3)$ be denoted by q_{X_1}, $q_{X_2}q_{X_2X_3}$, and $q_{X_3}q_{X_2X_3}$. Then the isomorphism of the corollary,

$$a : X_1 \times (X_2 \times X_3) \to (X_1 \times X_2) \times X_3,$$

is characterised by the fact that

$$p_{X_1}p_{X_1X_2}a = q_{X_1}, \; p_{X_2}p_{X_1X_2}a = q_{X_2}q_{X_2X_3}, \; p_{X_3}a = q_{X_3}q_{X_2X_3}.$$

Example 14. In the category **Circ** of Example 11, with the product chosen as we did in the previous section, the isomorphism of the corollary is the identity function. We then say that the product is *strictly associative*.

Example 15. In **Sets** the usual cartesian product of sets is not strictly associative. The isomorphism a is given by

$$(X_1 \times X_2) \times X_3 \xrightarrow{a} X_1 \times (X_2 \times X_3)$$
$$((x_1, x_2), x_3) \longmapsto (x_1, (x_2, x_3)).$$

Notice, however, that there is an appropriate triple product (or, more generally, an n-ary product)

$$X_1 \times X_2 \times X_3 = \{(x_1, x_2, x_3); x_1 \in X_1, x_2 \in X_2, x_3 \in X_3\}.$$

To avoid a proliferation of brackets we shall usually use the n-ary product rather than repeated binary products.

§5. Sums

The notion dual to product is *sum* or *coproduct*.

Definition. The sum of two objects X_1, X_2 in a category is an object X_1+X_2 with two *injections*

$$X_1 \xrightarrow{i_1} X_1 + X_2 \xleftarrow{i_2} X_2,$$

such that, given any object Z and two arrows $f : X_1 \to Z$, $g : X_2 \to Z$, there is a unique arrow $\alpha : X_1 + X_2 \to Z$ such that

$$\alpha i_1 = f, \qquad \alpha i_2 = g.$$

Diagrammatically,

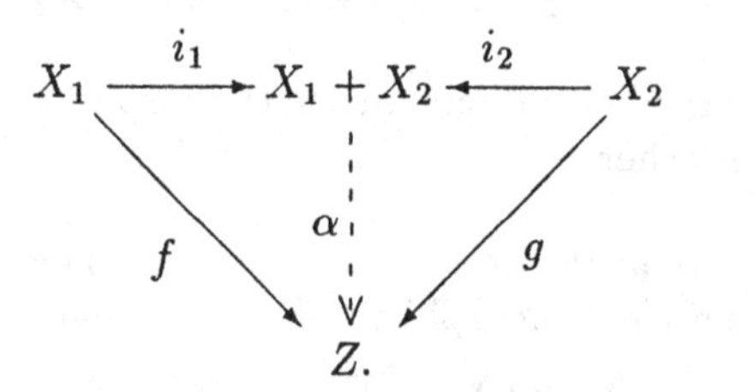

Example 16. **(Sets.)** If X_1, X_2 are sets then the sum of X_1, X_2 is the disjoint union,

$$X_1 + X_2 = \{(x_1, 0) : x_1 \in X_1\} \cup \{(x_2, 1) : x_2 \in X_2\},$$

together with injections

$$X_1 \xrightarrow{i_1} X_1 + X_2 \xleftarrow{i_2} X_2$$

$$x_1 \longmapsto (x_1, 0)$$

$$(x_2, 1) \longleftarrow x_2.$$

Given $f : X_1 \to Z$, $g : X_2 \to Z$ the required function $\alpha : X_1 + X_2 \to Z$ is given by

$$\alpha : X_1 + X_2 \longrightarrow Z$$

$$(x_1, 0) \longmapsto f(x_1)$$

$$(x_2, 1) \longmapsto g(x_2).$$

This function certainly has the property that

$$\alpha i_1(x_1) = \alpha(x_1, 0) = f(x_1),$$
$$\alpha i_2(x_2) = \alpha(x_2, 1) = g(x_2).$$

Clearly α is the only function with this property.

Note. The function $\alpha : X_1 + X_2 \to Z$ corresponding to the pair of arrows $f : X_1 \to Z$, $g : X_2 \to Z$, is often denoted by

$$\begin{pmatrix} f \\ g \end{pmatrix} : X_1 + X_2 \to Z.$$

Note. We usually think of $(x_1, 0)$ as a 'copy of' x_1 (and $(x_2, 1)$ as a copy of x_2), and the functions i_1, i_2 as inclusion functions.

Note. A function out of a sum of sets is defined by cases.

Remark. Since the definition is dual to that of product (obtained by reversing arrows) all the constructions for products can be imitated.

Example 17. There is an arrow $\nabla : X + X \to X$ called the *codiagonal* defined to be the unique arrow making the following diagram commute:

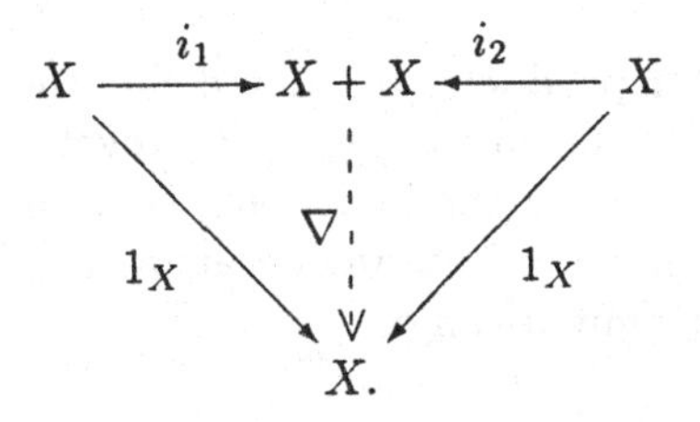

In **Sets** the codiagonal is:

$$\nabla : X + X \longrightarrow X$$
$$(x, 0) \longmapsto x$$
$$(x, 1) \longmapsto x.$$

It is the function 'forget cases'.

Example 18. Given $f : X_1 \to Y_1$, $g : X_2 \to Y_2$, there is an arrow $f + g : X_1 + X_2 \to Y_1 + Y_2$, defined to be the unique arrow making the following diagram commute:

$$\begin{array}{ccccc}
X_1 & \xrightarrow{i_1} & X_1 + X_2 & \xleftarrow{i_2} & X_2 \\
\Big\downarrow f & & \Big\downarrow f+g & & \Big\downarrow g \\
Y_1 & \xrightarrow[j_1]{} & Y_1 + Y_2 & \xleftarrow[j_2]{} & Y_2.
\end{array}$$

You may think of $f + g$ as the function 'in the first case do f, in the second case do g'.

Example 19. Given two objects X, Y there is an arrow $twist_{X,Y} : X + Y \to Y + X$ (which in **Sets** takes $(x, 0)$ to $(x, 1)$ and $(y, 1)$ to $(y, 0)$) defined as follows. Suppose i_1, i_2 are the injections of $X + Y$ and j_1, j_2 the injections of $Y + X$. Then $twist$ is the unique arrow making the following diagram commute:

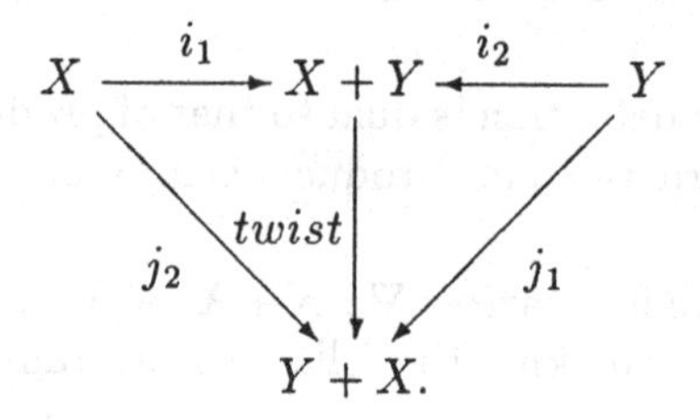

Remark. Just as for products, we may define the sum of a family $(X_k)_{k \in K}$ of objects. The sum is an object $\sum_{k \in K} X_k$ together with a family $i_l : X_l \to \sum_{k \in K} X_k$ $(l \in K)$ of arrows (the injections) such that given a family of arrows $f_l : X_l \to Z$ $(l \in K)$, there is a unique arrow $\alpha : \sum_{k \in K} X_k \to Z$ such that $\alpha i_l = f_l$, $l \in K$. Diagrammatically:

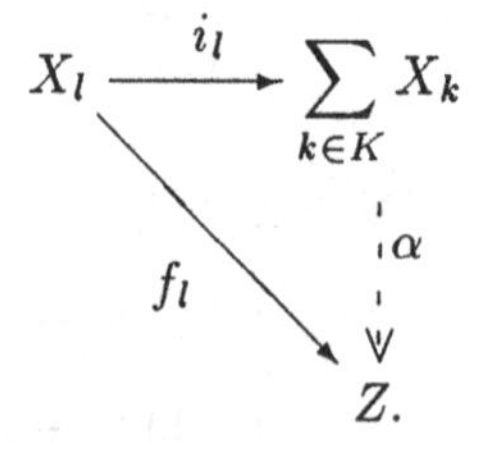

Remark. A sum of the empty family is an initial object. Furthermore, all finite sums can be constructed using binary sums and an initial object.

Note. In **Sets** the usual choice of sum of sets is not strictly associative;

however, there is an appropriate choice of n-ary sum, namely,

$$X_0 + X_1 + \cdots + X_{n-1} = \bigcup_{k=0}^{n-1} \{(x_k, k); x_k \in X_k\},$$

which we will use in preference to repeated binary sums.

Let us now look at some examples of categories with sums.

§6. Categories with Sums – Flow Charts

Example 20. **($\mathcal{P}X$.)** The sum of two objects U, V is their union. The property of sums is: $U + V$ is an upper bound for U and V (since $U \to U + V$ and $V \to U + V$). Further, given any other upper bound W of U and V (that is, given arrows $U \to W$, $V \to W$) then $U + V$ is contained in W (that is, there is an arrow $U + V \to W$).

In general in a preorder:

- the product of a family of objects is the greatest lower bound, or infimum, of the objects;
- the sum of a family of objects is the least upper bound, or supremum of the objects.

Example 21. Consider the preorder whose objects are real numbers, and with an arrow from r to s if $r \le s$ as real numbers. Then

$$\prod_{k \in K} r_k = \inf_{k \in K} r_k,$$

$$\sum_{k \in K} r_k = \sup_{k \in K} r_k.$$

A larger example:

Example 22. Consider the category, which we shall call **Flow**, with

- objects: $0{\bullet}\mathbb{R} = \varnothing$, $1{\bullet}\mathbb{R} = \mathbb{R}$, $2{\bullet}\mathbb{R}$, $3{\bullet}\mathbb{R}$, $\ldots$, where

  $m{\bullet}\mathbb{R} = \{(x,0) : x \in \mathbb{R}\} \cup \{(x,1) : x \in \mathbb{R}\} \cup \cdots \cup \{(x, m-1) : x \in \mathbb{R}\}$ $(m > 1)$;

- arrows: all functions between these sets.

The category **Flow** has sums which are strictly associative. In fact,

$$m{\bullet}\mathbb{R} + n{\bullet}\mathbb{R} = (m+n){\bullet}\mathbb{R}.$$

The injections are:

$$m{\bullet}\mathbb{R} \xrightarrow{i_1} (m+n){\bullet}\mathbb{R} \xleftarrow{i_2} n{\bullet}\mathbb{R}$$

$$(x,k) \longmapsto (x,k)$$

$$(x, l+m) \longleftarrow\!\shortmid (x,l).$$

It is easy to see that the property of a sum holds. Given $f : m{\bullet}\mathbb{R} \to Z$ and $g : n{\bullet}\mathbb{R} \to Z$ then

$$\begin{pmatrix} f \\ g \end{pmatrix}(x,i) = \begin{cases} f(x,i) & \text{if } 0 \le i \le m-1; \\ g(x, i-m) & \text{if } m \le i \le m+n-1. \end{cases}$$

As before, we'll take a special class of functions and see what functions can be generated out of them using sums and composition.

We take as the special functions:

- all continuous functions from $\mathbb{R}$ to $\mathbb{R}$, and
- the function which tests whether x is positive or not:

$$test_{x>0} : \mathbb{R} \longrightarrow 2{\bullet}\mathbb{R} = \mathbb{R} + \mathbb{R}$$

$$x \longmapsto (x,0) \text{ (if } x \le 0)$$

$$x \longmapsto (x,1) \text{ (if } x > 0).$$

Question. What functions can be generated out of these special functions using composition and the property of sums?

Let's look at some examples.

Example 23. The discontinuous function,

$$f : \mathbb{R} \longrightarrow \mathbb{R}$$

$$x \longmapsto \begin{cases} \sin x & \text{if } x \le 0 \\ e^x & \text{if } x > 0, \end{cases}$$

can be constructed as the composite of the following arrows:

$$\mathbb{R} \xrightarrow{test_{x>0}} \mathbb{R}+\mathbb{R}$$
$$x \longmapsto \begin{cases}(x,0) & \text{if } x \leq 0\\ (x,1) & \text{if } x > 0,\end{cases}$$

$$\mathbb{R}+\mathbb{R} \xrightarrow{\lceil \sin x\rceil + \lceil e^x \rceil} \mathbb{R}+\mathbb{R}$$
$$(x,0) \text{ if } x \leq 0 \longmapsto (\sin x, 0) \text{ if } x \leq 0$$
$$(x,1) \text{ if } x > 0 \longmapsto (e^x, 1) \text{ if } x > 0,$$

$$\mathbb{R}+\mathbb{R} \xrightarrow{\nabla} \mathbb{R}$$
$$(\sin x, 0) \text{ if } x \leq 0 \longmapsto \sin x \text{ if } x \leq 0$$
$$(e^x, 1) \text{ if } x > 0 \longmapsto e^x \text{ if } x > 0.$$

Example 24. The test function,

$$test_{x\geq 1} \; : \; \mathbb{R} \longrightarrow \mathbb{R}+\mathbb{R}$$
$$x \longmapsto \begin{cases}(x,0) & \text{if } x < 1\\ (x,1) & \text{if } x \geq 1,\end{cases}$$

can be constructed as the composite of the following arrows:

$$\mathbb{R} \xrightarrow{\lceil 1-x \rceil} \mathbb{R}$$
$$x \longmapsto (1-x),$$

$$\mathbb{R} \xrightarrow{test_{x>0}} \mathbb{R}+\mathbb{R}$$
$$(1-x) \longmapsto \begin{cases}(1-x,0) & \text{if } 1-x \leq 0\\ (1-x,1) & \text{if } 1-x > 0,\end{cases}$$

$$\begin{array}{ccc} \mathbb{R}+\mathbb{R} & \xrightarrow{twist} & \mathbb{R}+\mathbb{R} \\ (1-x,0) \text{ if } x \geq 1 & \longmapsto & (1-x,1) \text{ if } x \geq 1 \\ (1-x,1) \text{ if } x < 1 & \longmapsto & (1-x,0) \text{ if } x < 1, \end{array}$$

$$\begin{array}{ccc} \mathbb{R}+\mathbb{R} & \xrightarrow{\lceil 1-x \rceil + \lceil 1-x \rceil} & \mathbb{R}+\mathbb{R} \\ (1-x,0) \text{ if } x < 1 & \longmapsto & (x,0) \text{ if } x < 1 \\ (1-x,1) \text{ if } x \geq 1 & \longmapsto & (x,1) \text{ if } x \geq 1. \end{array}$$

Example 25. The piecewise-continuous function,

$$f : \mathbb{R} \longrightarrow \mathbb{R}$$

$$x \longmapsto \begin{cases} \sin x & \text{if } x \leq 0 \\ e^x & \text{if } 0 < x < 1 \\ \cos x & \text{if } 1 \leq x, \end{cases}$$

can be constructed as the following composite:

$$\begin{array}{ccc} \mathbb{R} & \xrightarrow{test_{x>0}} & \mathbb{R}+\mathbb{R} \\ x & \longmapsto & \begin{cases} (x,0) & \text{if } x \leq 0 \\ (x,1) & \text{if } x > 0, \end{cases} \end{array}$$

$$\begin{array}{ccc} \mathbb{R}+\mathbb{R} & \xrightarrow{1_{\mathbb{R}} + test_{x \geq 1}} & \mathbb{R}+\mathbb{R}+\mathbb{R} \\ (x,0) \text{ if } x \leq 0 & \longmapsto & (x,0) \text{ if } x \leq 0 \\ (x,1) \text{ if } x > 0 & \longmapsto & \begin{cases} (x,1) & \text{if } 0 < x < 1 \\ (x,2) & \text{if } 1 \leq x, \end{cases} \end{array}$$

$$\begin{array}{ccc} \mathbb{R}+\mathbb{R}+\mathbb{R} & \xrightarrow{\lceil \sin x \rceil + \lceil e^x \rceil + \lceil \cos x \rceil} & \mathbb{R}+\mathbb{R}+\mathbb{R} \\ (x,0) \text{ if } x \leq 0 & \longmapsto & (\sin x, 0) \text{ if } x \leq 0 \\ (x,1) \text{ if } 0 < x < 1 & \longmapsto & (e^x, 1) \text{ if } 0 < x < 1 \\ (x,2) \text{ if } 1 \leq x & \longmapsto & (\cos x, 2) \text{ if } 1 \leq x, \end{array}$$

$$\begin{array}{ccc} \mathbb{R}+\mathbb{R}+\mathbb{R} & \xrightarrow{1_{\mathbb{R}} + \nabla} & \mathbb{R}+\mathbb{R} \\ (\sin x,0) \text{ if } x \leq 0 & \longmapsto & (\sin x, 0) \text{ if } x \leq 0 \\ (e^x,1) \text{ if } 0 < x < 1 & \longmapsto & (e^x, 1) \text{ if } 0 < x < 1 \\ (\cos x,2) \text{ if } 1 \leq x & \longmapsto & (\cos x, 1) \text{ if } 1 \leq x, \end{array}$$

$$\begin{array}{ccc} \mathbb{R}+\mathbb{R} & \xrightarrow{\nabla} & \mathbb{R} \\ (\sin x,0) \text{ if } x \leq 0 & \longmapsto & f(x) \text{ if } x \leq 0 \\ (e^x,1) \text{ if } 0 < x < 1 & \longmapsto & f(x) \text{ if } 0 < x < 1 \\ (\cos x,1) \text{ if } 1 \leq x & \longmapsto & f(x) \text{ if } 1 \leq x. \end{array}$$

It is more or less clear that any piecewise continuous function with a finite number of discontinuities can be constructed in this way. Some functions with an infinite number of discontinuities — like

$$\begin{array}{ccc} \mathbb{R} & \longrightarrow & \mathbb{R} \\ x & \longmapsto & \begin{cases} 0 & \text{if } \cos^2 x < 0.5 \\ 1 & \text{if } \cos^2 x \geq 0.5, \end{cases} \end{array}$$

— can also be constructed.

Notice that corresponding to such decompositions there is a flow chart (without feedback) which implements the function. A flow chart may be built up out of components like functions and tests:

test(x)false x

x f f(x) x test

test(x)true x

The way a flow chart can be built up is analogous, but dual, to the way circuits are built up. Components may be joined in series (which corresponds to composition) or side by side (which corresponds to the sum of functions). Two edges may be joined, which corresponds to the codiagonal function. Each edge of the flow chart has state space IR; that is, when following through a flow chart you carry with you one real number. Below we give the flow charts corresponding to the last three examples. A study of these flow charts will show that a flow chart is just a graphical representation of the decomposition of a function using sums.

Example 23′.

$$f : \mathsf{IR} \longrightarrow \mathsf{IR}$$
$$x \longmapsto \begin{cases} \sin x & \text{if } x \leq 0 \\ e^x & \text{if } x > 0. \end{cases}$$

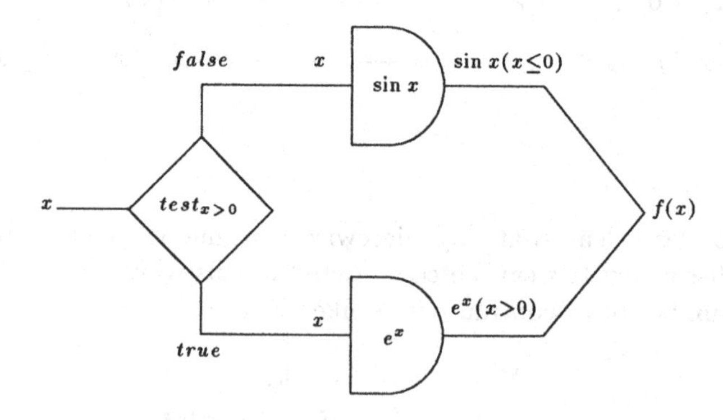

Going from left to right in this flow chart corresponds exactly to the successive functions in the composite:

$$\mathsf{IR} \xrightarrow{test_{x>0}} \mathsf{IR} + \mathsf{IR} \xrightarrow{\lceil \sin x \rceil + \lceil e^x \rceil} \mathsf{IR} + \mathsf{IR} \xrightarrow{\nabla} \mathsf{IR}.$$

Example 24′.

$$test_{x\geq 1} \;:\; \mathbb{R} \longrightarrow \mathbb{R}+\mathbb{R}$$

$$x \longmapsto \begin{cases}(x,0) & \text{if } x<1\\ (x,1) & \text{if } x\geq 1.\end{cases}$$

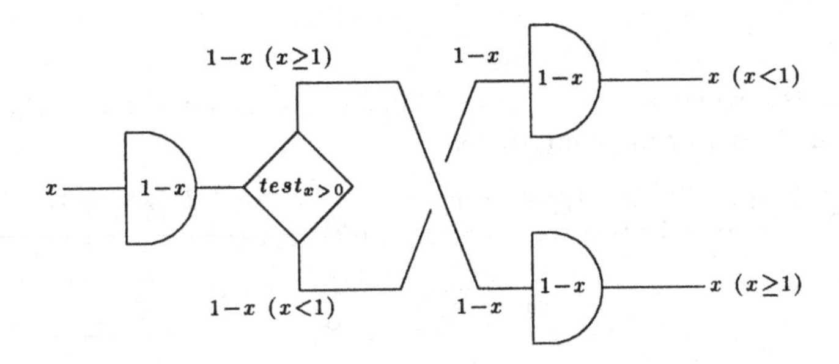

Going from left to right in this flow chart corresponds exactly to the successive functions in the composite:

$$\mathbb{R} \xrightarrow{\lceil 1-x\rceil} \mathbb{R} \xrightarrow{test_{x>0}} \mathbb{R}+\mathbb{R} \xrightarrow{twist} \mathbb{R}+\mathbb{R} \xrightarrow{\lceil 1-x\rceil+\lceil 1-x\rceil} \mathbb{R}+\mathbb{R}.$$

Example 25′.

$$f:\mathbb{R} \longrightarrow \mathbb{R}$$

$$x \longmapsto \begin{cases}\sin x & \text{if } x\leq 0\\ e^x & \text{if } 0<x<1\\ \cos x & \text{if } 1\leq x.\end{cases}$$

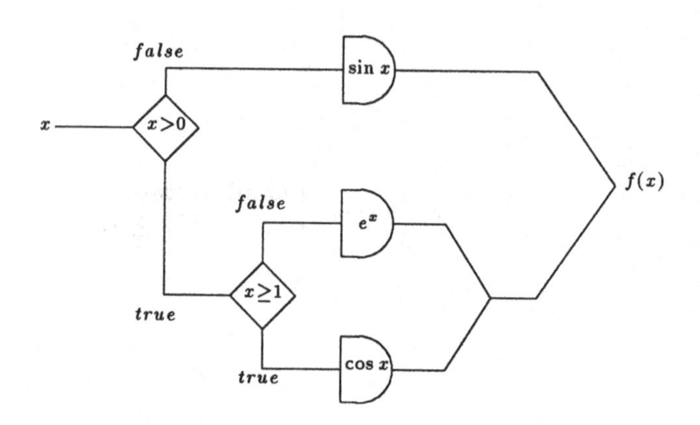

Going from left to right in this flow chart corresponds exactly to the successive functions in the following composite:

$$\mathrm{IR} \xrightarrow{test_{x>0}} 2{\bullet}\mathrm{IR} \xrightarrow{1_{\mathrm{IR}} + test_{x\geq 1}} 3{\bullet}\mathrm{IR} \xrightarrow{\lceil \sin x \rceil + \lceil e^x \rceil + \lceil \cos x \rceil} 3{\bullet}\mathrm{IR}$$

$$\xrightarrow{1_{\mathrm{IR}} + \nabla} 2{\bullet}\mathrm{IR} \xrightarrow{\nabla} \mathrm{IR}.$$

Problems 2

1. Suppose that I is a terminal object in a category $\mathbf{A}$.
   (i) Show that if A is also terminal in $\mathbf{A}$ then A is isomorphic to I.
   (ii) Show that if A is isomorphic to I then A is terminal.

2. Consider a product $A \times B$ of A and B with projections $p_1 : A \times B \to A$, $p_2 : A \times B \to B$. Show that if P is isomorphic to $A \times B$ then P with suitable projections is also a product of A and B.

3. Show that if I is a terminal object in a category $\mathbf{A}$ and X is any object of $\mathbf{A}$ then the product $X \times I$ exists, and in fact X is the product of X and I.

4. Consider the two functions
$$f,\ g : \mathrm{IR} \to \mathrm{IR}$$
defined by $f(t) = \cos t$, $g(t) = \sin t$.
   (i) Describe the function $\alpha : \mathrm{IR} \to \mathrm{IR} \times \mathrm{IR}$ arising from f, g using the defining property of products.
   (ii) The function α defines a curve in $\mathrm{IR} \times \mathrm{IR}$. Sketch the curve.

5. Consider $\mathbf{B} = \{0,1\}$. Express each of the functions $f : \mathbf{B}^3 \to \mathbf{B}$ in terms of *true*, *false*, $\neg$, &, and *or* using composition and products:

   (i) $f(0,0,0) = 1$, $f(1,1,1) = 1$; $f(x,y,z) = 0$ otherwise.

   (ii) $f(0,0,1) = 1$, $f(0,1,1) = 1$, $f(1,0,1) = 1$; $f(x,y,z) = 0$ otherwise.

   In each case sketch a circuit implementing the function.

6. Consider sets X, Y and the function $twist_{X,Y} : X \times Y \to Y \times X$.

   Show how to deduce from the properties of products that

$$X \xrightarrow{\Delta} X \times X \xrightarrow{twist_{X,X}} X \times X \quad = \quad X \xrightarrow{\Delta} X \times X.$$

7. Express the function $f : \mathbb{R}^2 \to \mathbb{R}$ given by

$$f(x,y) = xy^2 + x^2y$$

   in terms of $add : \mathbb{R}^2 \to \mathbb{R}$ and $multiply : \mathbb{R}^2 \to \mathbb{R}$, using composition and products.

8. If object $\overline{P}$ in the category $\mathbf{A}^{op}$, together with projections $\overline{p_1} : \overline{P} \to \overline{A}$, $\overline{p_2} : \overline{P} \to \overline{B}$, satisfies the property of a product in $\mathbf{A}^{op}$, write down what property P, together with p_1, p_2, satisfies in $\mathbf{A}$; that is the *dual property*.

9. Show that if the sum $X + Y$ of two objects X, Y is initial ($X + Y \cong O$), then X and Y are both initial ($X \cong O \cong Y$).

10. Consider the category with objects $0{\bullet}\mathbb{R}, 1{\bullet}\mathbb{R}, 2{\bullet}\mathbb{R}, \ldots$, and arrows all functions. Show how to construct out of the continuous functions from $\mathbb{R}$ to $\mathbb{R}$ and the test function $test_{x>0} : \mathbb{R} \to \mathbb{R} + \mathbb{R}$, using composition and sums, the following functions:

   (i)

$$\begin{aligned} test_{x=0} : \mathbb{R} &\longrightarrow \mathbb{R} + \mathbb{R} \\ x &\longmapsto \begin{cases} (x,0) & \text{if } x \neq 0 \\ (x,1) & \text{if } x = 0. \end{cases} \end{aligned}$$

   (ii)

$$\begin{aligned} f : \mathbb{R} &\longrightarrow \mathbb{R} \\ x &\longmapsto \begin{cases} \sin x & \text{if } x \leq 0 \\ \cos x & \text{if } x > 0. \end{cases} \end{aligned}$$

   (iii)

$$\begin{aligned} f : \mathbb{R} &\longrightarrow \mathbb{R} \\ x &\longmapsto \begin{cases} \cos x & \text{if } \cos x \geq 0 \\ 0 & \text{otherwise.} \end{cases} \end{aligned}$$

   (iv)

$$\begin{aligned} f : \mathbb{R} &\longrightarrow \mathbb{R} + \mathbb{R} + \mathbb{R} \\ x &\longmapsto \begin{cases} (x,0) & \text{if } x < 0 \\ (x,1) & \text{if } x = 0 \\ (x,2) & \text{if } x > 0. \end{cases} \end{aligned}$$

In each case sketch a flow chart implementing the function.

11. Consider $f : X_1 \to Y_1$, $g : X_2 \to Y_2$. Show that

$$X_1 + X_2 \xrightarrow{f+1_{X_2}} Y_1 + X_2 \xrightarrow{1_{Y_1}+g} Y_1 + Y_2 = f + g.$$

12. Prove that the following diagram commutes in a category with products:

$$\begin{array}{ccc} X & \xrightarrow{\Delta} & X \times X \\ {\scriptstyle\Delta}\downarrow & & \downarrow{\scriptstyle\Delta \times 1_X} \\ X \times X & \xrightarrow[1_X \times \Delta]{} & X \times X \times X. \end{array}$$

13. Consider $\mathbf{B} = \{0, 1\}$, and the function $f : \mathbf{B}^3 \to \mathbf{B}$ given by

$$f(1,0,0) = 1, \quad f(1,0,1) = 1, \quad f(1,1,1) = 1, \quad f(x,y,z) = 0 \quad \text{otherwise}.$$

Express f in terms of *true*, *false*, $\neg$, *and*, *or* using composition and products. Sketch a circuit implementing the function.

14. Express the function $f : \mathbb{R}^3 \to \mathbb{R}$ given by $f(x,y,z) = x^2 y + 2$, in terms of *add* $: \mathbb{R}^2 \to \mathbb{R}$, *multiply* $: \mathbb{R}^2 \to \mathbb{R}$, and the constants $\mathbb{R}^0 \to \mathbb{R}$, using composition and products.

15. Suppose $X \times Y$ is a product of X and Y with projections $p_1 : X \times Y \to X$, $p_2 : X \times Y \to Y$. Suppose $\alpha : Z \to X \times Y$ is the arrow defined by $p_1 \alpha = f$, $p_2 \alpha = g$.

Show that

$$\alpha = Z \xrightarrow{\Delta} Z \times Z \xrightarrow{f \times g} X \times Y.$$

16. Consider the category with objects $0{\cdot}\mathbb{R}$, $1{\cdot}\mathbb{R}$, $2{\cdot}\mathbb{R}$, ..., and arrows all functions. Construct, using composition and sums, given the continuous functions from $\mathbb{R}$ to $\mathbb{R}$ and the test function $test_{x>0} : \mathbb{R} \to \mathbb{R} + \mathbb{R}$, the following functions:

(i) $test_{-1 \leq x \leq 1} : \mathbb{R} \to \mathbb{R} + \mathbb{R}$;

(ii) $f : \mathbb{R} \to \mathbb{R}$ given by $f(x) = \begin{cases} \cos x & \text{if } -1 \leq x \leq 1, \\ e^x & \text{otherwise.} \end{cases}$

In each case sketch a flow chart implementing the function.

17. In a category with sums:

(i) show that $1_{X+Y} = 1_X + 1_Y$;

(ii) given $f_1 : A_1 \to B_1$, $f_2 : A_2 \to B_2$, $g_1 : B_1 \to C_1$, $g_2 : B_2 \to C_2$, show that $(g_1 + g_2)(f_1 + f_2) = (g_1 f_1 + g_2 f_2)$;

(iii) show that if f, g are isomorphisms then so is $f + g$.

18. Let $\mathbf{C}$ be a finite category in which products of all pairs of objects exist. Show that $\mathbf{C}$ is a preordered set.

Chapter 3

Distributive Categories

It is clear from the last chapter how products and sums are key notions in analysing computation. Products are concerned with operations performed on the data, while sums are concerned with control; that is, decisions on which operations to perform.

It is important to have both products and sums, and to understand how they interact. The main relation between sums and products of *numbers* is the distributive law: $a(b + c) = ab + ac$. The main relation between sums and products of *sets* is also a distributive law.

§1. The Distributive Law

In **Sets** there is a law which relates sums and products. It is called the *distributive law.* Roughly speaking, it says:

(1) $X \times (Y + Z) \cong (X \times Y) + (X \times Z)$;

(2) $X \times O \cong O$.

Remark. It is never precise enough in a category just to say that A is isomorphic to B. It is important to know the specific isomorphism.

Let us see how to state (1) more carefully. There is a canonical arrow

$$X \times Y + X \times Z \xrightarrow{\ \delta\ } X \times (Y + Z)$$

arising as follows. By the defining property of sums, it suffices to give a pair of arrows; take the pair to be as shown:

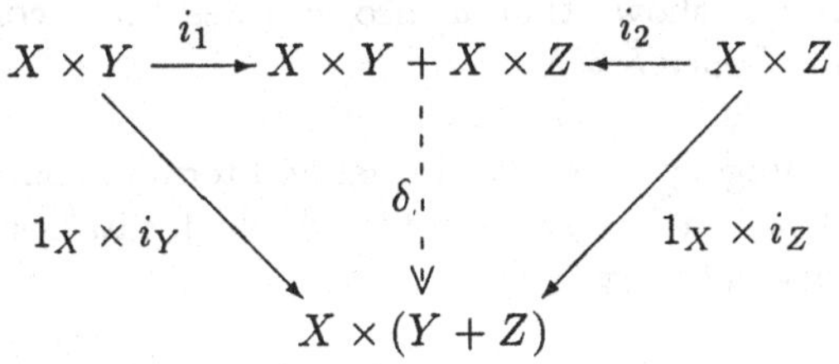

$$\begin{array}{ccccc} X \times Y & \xrightarrow{i_1} & X \times Y + X \times Z & \xleftarrow{i_2} & X \times Z \\ & {}_{1_X \times i_Y}\searrow & \Big\downarrow \delta & \swarrow_{1_X \times i_Z} & \\ & & X \times (Y + Z) & & \end{array}$$

(where the i's are injections).

Axiom 1. The arrow δ is an isomorphism.

Let us see how to state (2) more carefully. There is always an arrow (in fact exactly one)

$$\alpha : O \longrightarrow X \times O,$$

since O is initial.

Axiom 2. The unique arrow $\alpha : O \to X \times O$ is an isomorphism.

Example 1. In **Sets** what is δ? Let us try to guess.

Notice that

$$\begin{aligned}(X \times Y) + (X \times Z) &= \{((x,y),0) : x \in X, y \in Y\} \cup \{((x,z),1) : x \in X, z \in Z\},\\ X \times (Y + Z) &= \{(x,(y,0)) : x \in X, y \in Y\} \cup \{(x,(z,1)) : x \in X, z \in Z\}.\end{aligned}$$

Clearly, we expect δ to be the function:

$$\begin{aligned}((x,y),0) &\mapsto (x,(y,0))\\ ((x,z),1) &\mapsto (x,(z,1)).\end{aligned}$$

This function is certainly a bijection as required.

Let us check whether this function, called $\overline{\delta}$ say, satisfies the definition of δ, namely $\delta i_1 = 1_X \times i_Y$, and $\delta i_2 = 1_X \times i_Z$.

Checking the first of these equations for $\overline{\delta}$:

$$\begin{array}{ccccc} X \times Y & \xrightarrow{i_1} & (X \times Y) + (X \times Z) & \xrightarrow{\overline{\delta}} & X \times (Y + Z) \\ (x,y) & \longmapsto & ((x,y),0) & \longmapsto & (x,(y,0)), \end{array}$$

while

$$\begin{array}{ccc} X \times Y & \xrightarrow{1_X \times i_Y} & X \times (Y + Z) \\ (x,y) & \longmapsto & (x,(y,0)). \end{array}$$

A similar calculation shows that $\overline{\delta}$ also satisfies the second equation of the definition of δ, and hence $\overline{\delta} = \delta$.

Definition. A category which has initial and terminal objects, in which products and sums of pairs of objects exist, and which satisfies Axioms 1 and 2, is called a *distributive* category.

Example 2. We have seen that **Sets** is a distributive category.

Example 3. The category $\mathcal{P}X$ is distributive.

The distributive law is satisfied in $\mathcal{P}X$.

Proof. Axiom 1 says that

$$U \cap (V \cup W) = (U \cap V) \cup (U \cap W).$$

But

$$\begin{aligned} x \in LHS &\Longleftrightarrow x \in U \text{ and } (x \in V \text{ or } x \in W) \\ &\Longleftrightarrow (x \in U \text{ and } x \in V) \text{ or } (x \in U \text{ and } x \in W) \\ &\Longleftrightarrow x \in U \cap V \text{ or } x \in U \cap W \\ &\Longleftrightarrow x \in (U \cap V) \cup (U \cap W) \\ &\Longleftrightarrow x \in RHS. \end{aligned}$$

Axiom 2 just says that $\varnothing = \varnothing \cap U$, which is obvious. ■

Note. In $\mathcal{P}X$ it is also true that

$$U \cup (V \cap W) = (U \cup V) \cap (U \cup W),$$

since

$$\begin{aligned} &(U \cup V) \cap (U \cup W) \\ &\quad = [(U \cup V) \cap U] \cup [(U \cup V) \cap W] \qquad \text{(distributive law)} \\ &\quad = (U \cap U) \cup (U \cap V) \cup (U \cap W) \cup (V \cap W) \text{ (distributive law)} \\ &\quad = U \cup (U \cap V) \cup (U \cap W) \cup (V \cap W) \\ &\quad = U \cup (U \cap W) \cup (V \cap W) \qquad \text{since } (U \geq U \cap V) \\ &\quad = U \cup (V \cap W) \qquad \text{since } (U \geq U \cap W). \end{aligned}$$

In **Sets** it is certainly *not* true that

$$X + (Y \times Z) \cong (X + Y) \times (X + Z).$$

You can check this by comparing the number of elements on each side of the isomorphism. Let the number of elements in X, Y and Z be m, n and p respectively. This would imply that $m + np = (m + n)(m + p)$; and substituting 1 for m, n and p gives $2 = 4$, a contradiction.

Let us use the example of **Sets** to see what kind of arrows can be constructed using composition, products, sums and the distributive law.

§2. Examples

Example 4. Let I denote a one-point set, $\{*\}$. Let $\mathbf{B} = I+I = \{(*,0),(*,1)\}$. We will sometimes identify $\mathbf{B}$ with the set $\{false, true\}$, or with the set $\{0,1\}$. Injections of the sum are the functions we have previously called false and true:

$$\begin{array}{ccccc} I & \xrightarrow{i_1} & \mathbf{B} & \xleftarrow{i_2} & I \\ * & \longmapsto & (*,0) & & \\ & & (*,1) & \longleftarrow & *. \end{array}$$

Question. What functions can be constructed, $\mathbf{B} \to \mathbf{B}$ and $\mathbf{B}^2 \to \mathbf{B}$, using only the constructions available in a distributive category?

The function

$$I+I \xrightarrow{twist_{I,I}} I+I$$

interchanges true and false, and hence is the function $\neg : \mathbf{B} \to \mathbf{B}$.

In a distributive category

$$\mathbf{B}^2 \cong (I+I+I+I).$$

To see this consider the following sequence of isomorphisms:

$$\begin{array}{c} \mathbf{B}^2 = (I+I) \times (I+I) \\ \Big\downarrow \delta^{-1} \\ (I+I) \times I + (I+I) \times I \\ \Big\downarrow \cong \\ (I+I)+(I+I) \\ \Big\downarrow \cong \\ (I+I+I+I). \end{array}$$

So, to construct arrows from $\mathbf{B}^2$ to $\mathbf{B}$, it is sufficient to construct arrows from $I+I+I+I$ to $\mathbf{B}$.

In **Sets** the isomorphism from $\mathbf{B}^2$ to $I+I+I+I$ takes

$$(0,0) = ((*,0),(*,0)) \longmapsto (*,0),$$

$$(1,0) = ((*,1),(*,0)) \longmapsto (*,1),$$

$$(0,1) = ((*,0),(*,1)) \longmapsto (*,2),$$

$$(1,1) = ((*,1),(*,1)) \longmapsto (*,3).$$

The function $\& : \mathbf{B}^2 \to \mathbf{B}$ clearly corresponds, via this isomorphism, to

$$\begin{pmatrix} i_1 \\ i_1 \\ i_1 \\ i_2 \end{pmatrix} = \begin{pmatrix} \mathit{false} \\ \mathit{false} \\ \mathit{false} \\ \mathit{true} \end{pmatrix} : I+I+I+I \to \mathbf{B}.$$

Similarly, all functions $\mathbf{B}^n \to \mathbf{B}$ can be constructed in this way using composition, products, sums and the distributive axioms.

Let us now start with some more functions in **Sets**, and see what we can construct using only the operations of a distributive category; that is, using sums, products, composition, and the distributive law.

We begin with given functions:

$$\begin{aligned} \mathit{add} : \mathsf{IR} \times \mathsf{IR} &\longrightarrow \mathsf{IR} \\ (x,y) &\longmapsto x+y; \end{aligned}$$

$$\begin{aligned} \mathit{multiply} : \mathsf{IR} \times \mathsf{IR} &\longrightarrow \mathsf{IR} \\ (x,y) &\longmapsto xy; \end{aligned}$$

a family of functions, one for each real number r:

$$\begin{aligned} \ulcorner r \urcorner : I &\longrightarrow \mathsf{IR} \\ * &\longmapsto r; \end{aligned}$$

$$\begin{aligned} \mathit{test}_{x<y} : \mathsf{IR} \times \mathsf{IR} &\longrightarrow \mathbf{B} \\ (x,y) &\longmapsto \begin{cases} \mathit{false} & \text{if } x \geq y \\ \mathit{true} & \text{if } x < y; \end{cases} \end{aligned}$$

(Remember that *false* $= (*, 0)$, *true* $= (*, 1)$.)

$$
\begin{aligned}
\mathit{divide}\ : \mathbb{R} \times \mathbb{R} &\longrightarrow I + \mathbb{R} \\
(x, y) &\longmapsto \begin{cases} (*, 0) & \text{if } y = 0 \\ (\frac{x}{y}, 1) & \text{if } y \neq 0. \end{cases}
\end{aligned}
$$

Example 5. Construct the function

$$
\begin{aligned}
\mathit{test}_{x>0}\ : \mathbb{R} &\longrightarrow \mathbb{R} + \mathbb{R} \\
x &\longmapsto \begin{cases} (x, 0) & \text{for } x \leq 0 \\ (x, 1) & \text{for } x > 0, \end{cases}
\end{aligned}
$$

that we used in Chapter 2, §6.

This function can be constructed as the composite of the following arrows:

$$
\begin{array}{ccccc}
\mathbb{R} & \xrightarrow{\cong} & \mathbb{R} \times I & \xrightarrow{\Delta \times \lceil 0 \rceil} & \mathbb{R} \times \mathbb{R} \times \mathbb{R} \\
x & \longmapsto & (x, *) & \longmapsto & (x, x, 0),
\end{array}
$$

$$
\begin{array}{ccccc}
\mathbb{R}^3 & \xrightarrow{1 \times \mathit{twist}} & \mathbb{R}^3 & \xrightarrow{1 \times \mathit{test}_{x<y}} & \mathbb{R} \times \mathbf{B} \\
(x, x, 0) & \longmapsto & (x, 0, x) & \longmapsto & \begin{cases} (x, \mathit{false}) & \text{if } x \leq 0 \\ (x, \mathit{true}) & \text{if } x > 0, \end{cases}
\end{array}
$$

$$
\begin{array}{ccc}
\mathbb{R} \times \mathbf{B} & \xrightarrow{\cong} & (\mathbb{R} \times I) + (\mathbb{R} \times I) \\
(x, \mathit{false}) \text{ if } x \leq 0 & \longmapsto & ((x, *), 0) \text{ if } x \leq 0 \\
(x, \mathit{true}) \text{ if } x > 0 & \longmapsto & ((x, *), 1) \text{ if } x > 0,
\end{array}
$$

$$
\begin{array}{ccc}
(\mathbb{R} \times I) + (\mathbb{R} \times I) & \xrightarrow{\cong} & \mathbb{R} + \mathbb{R} \\
((x, *), 0) \text{ if } x \leq 0 & \longmapsto & (x, 0) \text{ if } x \leq 0 \\
((x, *), 1) \text{ if } x > 0 & \longmapsto & (x, 1) \text{ if } x > 0.
\end{array}
$$

Example 6. We have shown earlier that all polynomials can be constructed just using products.

Example 7. Construct the function

$$\begin{aligned} test_{3<x<4} \ : \mathbb{R} &\longrightarrow \mathbf{B} \\ x &\longmapsto \begin{cases} false & \text{if } x \le 3 \text{ or } x \ge 4 \\ true & \text{if } 3 < x < 4. \end{cases} \end{aligned}$$

First construct

$$test_{3<x} : \mathbb{R} \to \mathbf{B}$$

as the composite:

$$\mathbb{R} \xrightarrow{\cong} I \times \mathbb{R} \xrightarrow{\lceil 3 \rceil \times 1_{\mathbb{R}}} \mathbb{R} \times \mathbb{R} \xrightarrow{test_{x<y}} \mathbf{B}.$$

Then construct $test_{x<4} : \mathbb{R} \to B$ as the composite:

$$\mathbb{R} \xrightarrow{\cong} \mathbb{R} \times I \xrightarrow{1_{\mathbb{R}} \times \lceil 4 \rceil} \mathbb{R} \times \mathbb{R} \xrightarrow{test_{x<y}} \mathbf{B}.$$

Then $test_{3<x<4}$ is the arrow:

$$\mathbb{R} \xrightarrow{\Delta} \mathbb{R} \times \mathbb{R} \xrightarrow{test_{3<x} \times test_{x<4}} \mathbf{B} \times \mathbf{B} \xrightarrow{\&} \mathbf{B}.$$

In other words, we can use boolean operations on tests to produce new tests.

Example 8. Let $t_1, t_2, \ldots, t_n : \mathbb{R} \to \mathbf{B}$ be n tests, and let $P : \mathbf{B}^n \to \mathbf{B}$ be a boolean function. Then we can form:

$$\mathbb{R} \xrightarrow{\Delta_n} \mathbb{R}^n \xrightarrow{t_1 \times t_2 \times \cdots \times t_n} \mathbf{B}^n \xrightarrow{P} \mathbf{B},$$

where

$$\begin{aligned} \mathbb{R} &\xrightarrow{\Delta_n} \mathbb{R}^n \\ x &\longmapsto (x, x, x, \ldots, x), \end{aligned}$$

is obtained by repeated application of $\Delta : \mathbb{R} \to \mathbb{R}^2$.

Example 9. Suppose we have a test

$$test : X \to \mathbf{B}$$

and two functions

$$f : Y \to Z, \qquad g : Y \to Z$$

and we would like to do the function f if the test is false and g if the test is true. That is,

$$\begin{aligned} Y \times X &\longrightarrow Z \\ (y, x) &\longmapsto \begin{cases} f(y) & \text{if } test(x) \text{ is } false; \\ g(y) & \text{if } test(x) \text{ is } true. \end{cases} \end{aligned}$$

This is the function 'if test(x) is true then $z = g(y)$, else $z = f(y)$,' which is fundamental to the control of processes.

This can be constructed as the composite of the following arrows:

$$Y \times X \xrightarrow{1_Y \times test} Y \times \mathbf{B}$$

$$(y, x) \longmapsto \begin{cases} (y, \mathit{false}) & \text{if } test(x) \text{ is } \mathit{false} \\ (y, \mathit{true}) & \text{if } test(x) \text{ is } \mathit{true}, \end{cases}$$

$$Y \times \mathbf{B} \xrightarrow{\cong} (Y \times I) + (Y \times I) \xrightarrow{\cong} Y + Y$$

$$(y, \mathit{false})\ test(x)\ \mathit{false} \longmapsto ((y, *), 0)\ test(x)\ \mathit{false} \longmapsto (y, 0)\ test(x)\ \mathit{false}$$

$$(y, \mathit{true})\ test(x)\ \mathit{true} \longmapsto ((y, *), 1)\ test(x)\ \mathit{true} \longmapsto (y, 1)\ test(x)\ \mathit{true},$$

$$Y + Y \xrightarrow{f + g} Z + Z \xrightarrow{\nabla} Z$$

$$(y, 0)\ test(x)\ \mathit{false} \longmapsto (f(y), 0)\ test(x)\ \mathit{false} \longmapsto f(y)\ test(x)\ \mathit{false}$$

$$(y, 1)\ test(x)\ \mathit{true} \longmapsto (g(y), 1)\ test(x)\ \mathit{true} \longmapsto g(y)\ test(x)\ \mathit{true}.$$

We have now discussed many aspects of the construction of functions used in programming. However, we have not discussed that most fundamental aspect of programming — iteration.

§3. Imperative Programs

Iteration involves a function f with the *same domain as codomain*. Given such a function $f : X \to X$ it makes sense to consider

$$f \circ f : X \to X, \qquad f \circ f \circ f : X \to X, \ \ldots, \qquad f^n : X \to X, \ldots;$$

that is, it makes sense to iterate f.

An example will make this clear.

Example 10. We can construct a function f (from the functions *add*, *multiply*, *divide*, and $test_{x<y}$, using the constructions available in a distributive category) with domain and codomain

$$X = \mathrm{IR} \times \mathrm{IR} \times (I + I),$$

with the following property. If x is a natural number greater than 0, and we repeatedly apply f beginning with the initial value $z = (1, x, 0)$ (that is, we compute z, $f(z)$, $f^2(z)$, ...), then eventually the first coordinate of $f^n(z)$ stabilizes at the value $x!$ (= factorial x). That is,

$$f^n(1, x, 0) = (x!, ?, ?)$$

for all large n. Before constructing the function f let's introduce some nomenclature.

Remark. Such a function f is called an *imperative program* for computing $x!$. The set X is called the ***state space*** of the program; its elements are called ***states***. The initial value z is called the ***initial state*** of the program. Each application of the function f changes the state.

The idea is that we compute $x!$ by successively computing

$$x, \quad x(x-1), \quad x(x-1)(x-2), \ \ldots$$

until the value $x!$ results. When this happens the iteration must *idle*; that is, f does not change the state any further.

At any time in this calculation we need to keep track of three quantities:

(i) the partial product $p = x(x-1)(x-2)\cdots(x-k)$;

(ii) the decreasing factor $d = x - k$ used to calculate the next partial product;

(iii) a flag $t \in I + I$ which indicates whether or not to idle.

The triple (p, d, t) is an element of the set $X = \mathbb{R} \times \mathbb{R} \times (I + I)$, which is the reason for our choice of state space. I claim that the following function $f : X \to X$, when iterated, computes $x!$:

$$f : X \longrightarrow X$$

$$(p, d, t) \longmapsto \begin{cases} (p \cdot d, d-1, 0) & \text{if } d \geq 1 \text{ and } t = 0 \\ (p, d, 1) & \text{if } d < 1 \text{ or } t = 1. \end{cases}$$

Let's check that f applied repeatedly, beginning with the initial state $(1, x, 0)$, does compute $x!$ and then idles. Certainly, while $d > 0$,

$$(1, x, 0) \overset{f}{\longmapsto} (x, x-1, 0) \overset{f}{\longmapsto} (x(x-1), x-2, 0) \overset{f}{\longmapsto} \cdots.$$

After x-iterates of f the state becomes $(x!, 0, 0)$. But $f(x!, 0, 0) = (x!, 0, 1)$, and $f(x!, 0, 1) = (x!, 0, 1)$. Hence $f^n(1, x, 0) = (x!, 0, 1)$ for all $n \geq x + 1$.

Question. How can f be constructed out of the given functions using only the operations of a distributive category?

Notice that, by the distributive law, $X = \mathbb{R}^2 \times (I + I) \cong \mathbb{R}^2 + \mathbb{R}^2$. By the property of sums, to define an arrow out of X (i.e. $X \longrightarrow X$), it suffices to give two functions, $f_0 : \mathbb{R}^2 \to X$, $f_1 : \mathbb{R}^2 \to X$. Notice that f_0 is the function in the case that the flag t is 0; f_1 is the function when the flag t is 1. Hence $f_1(p, d) = (p, d, 1)$; that is, f_1 is the second injection of the sum $\mathbb{R}^2 + \mathbb{R}^2$. The function f_0 is more complicated to construct. The formula for f_0 is:

$$f_0 : \quad \mathbb{R}^2 \longrightarrow \mathbb{R}^2 \times (I + I)$$

$$(p, d) \longmapsto \begin{cases} (p \cdot d, d - 1, 0) & \text{if } d \geq 1 \\ (p, d, 1) & \text{if } d < 1. \end{cases}$$

To construct f_0, first construct $test_{x<1} : \mathbb{R} \to \mathbf{B}$ as the composite

$$\mathbb{R} \cong \mathbb{R} \times \mathbb{R}^0 \xrightarrow{1_{\mathbb{R}} \times \lceil 1 \rceil} \mathbb{R}^2 \xrightarrow{test_{x<y}} \mathbf{B}.$$

Then construct

$$h : \mathbb{R}^2 \longrightarrow \mathbb{R}^2$$

$$(p, d) \longmapsto (p \cdot d, d - 1),$$

as the composite

$$\mathbb{R}^2 \cong \mathbb{R} \times \mathbb{R} \times \mathbb{R}^0 \xrightarrow{1_{\mathbb{R}} \times \Delta \times \lceil -1 \rceil} \mathbb{R}^4 \xrightarrow{mult \times add} \mathbb{R}^2.$$

Then f_0 is the composite of the following:

$$\mathbb{R}^2 \xrightarrow{1_{\mathbb{R}} \times \Delta} \mathbb{R}^3 \xrightarrow{1_{\mathbb{R}^2} \times test_{x<1}} \mathbb{R}^2 \times \mathbf{B},$$

$$\mathbb{R}^2 \times \mathbf{B} \xrightarrow{\cong} \mathbb{R}^2 + \mathbb{R}^2 \xrightarrow{h + 1_{\mathbb{R}^2}} \mathbb{R}^2 + \mathbb{R}^2 \xrightarrow{\cong} \mathbb{R}^2 \times (I + I).$$

We are now in a position to make a general definition of imperative program without input.

Definition. An *imperative program* is a function

$$f : X \to X$$

constructed from a set of given functions (like *add*, *multiply*, *divide*, $test_{x<y}$, and constants) using the constructions available in a distributive category.

The function f is also called the *action* of the imperative program.

A *behaviour* of the imperative program is a sequence of states x, $f(x)$, $f^2(x)$, ... of X; the first state of a behaviour is called the *initial state*.

Another name for behaviour is *orbit*. A state $z \in X$ such that $f(z) = z$ (such as the state $(x!, 0, 1)$ of the last example) is called a *stable state* or a *fixed point* of the program f. A finite sequence of states, x_1, $x_2 = f(x_1)$, $x_3 = f(x_2)$, ..., $x_n = f(x_{n-1})$, such that $f(x_n) = x_1$, is called a *cycle* of length n; a cycle of length one is just a fixed point.

Remark. The definition of imperative program at this stage does not allow input. It allows only an initial state. The definition will be extended in Chapter 5 to allow input to the program.

Example 11. Given a function $g : Y \to Y$ and a test $t : Y \to \mathbf{B}$. Construct an imperative program which does: 'while $t(y)$ is true change the value of y to g of the current value of y, then idle'.

The state space of the program will be $Y \times (I + I)$, and the program itself will be the function:

$$f : Y \times (I+I) \longrightarrow Y \times (I+I)$$

$$(y,t) \longmapsto \begin{cases} (y,0) & \text{if } t=0 \text{ or } test(y) = false \\ (g(y),1) & \text{if } t=1 \text{ and } test(y) = true. \end{cases}$$

The flag value $t = 0$ corresponds to idling.

It is straightforward to check that the program behaves as required.

Let's see how f can be constructed from the given functions using only the operations of a distributive category.

Again, since $Y \times (I + I)$ is isomorphic to $Y + Y$, it suffices to give two arrows f_0, f_1 from Y to $Y+Y$. Now $f_0(y) = (y, 0)$ and hence f_0 is the first injection of $Y+Y$.

The function f_1 is given by:

$$Y \xrightarrow{\quad f_1 \quad} Y+Y$$

$$y \longmapsto \begin{cases} (y,0) & \text{if } test(y) = false \\ (g(y),1) & \text{if } test(y) = true. \end{cases}$$

Hence f_1 is the composite:

$$Y \xrightarrow{\Delta} Y^2 \xrightarrow{1_Y + test} Y \times (I+I) \xrightarrow{\cong} Y+Y \xrightarrow{1_Y + g} Y+Y.$$

Example 12. Any circuit with feedback may be regarded as an imperative program. Consider for example, the following circuit:

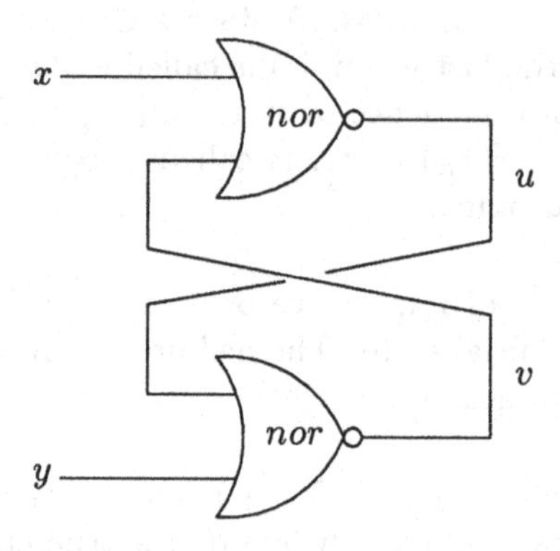

Since this circuit has feedback, we cannot simply consider what happens as we move from left to right through the circuit, as we did in Chapter 2, §3. Instead we have to consider at any moment the state of the whole circuit. At any moment there is a voltage of one volt or zero volts on each of the four wires. Hence the set of all possible states — *the state space* of the circuit — is

$$\mathbf{B}^4 = \{(x, y, u, v);\ \text{where each of } x, y, u, v = 0 \text{ } or \text{ } 1\}.$$

Now we will assume, as the simplest model of the circuit's behaviour, that the circuit changes state in a synchronized way. That is, at each tick of a clock the state of each wire changes according to the nature of the circuit components. For example, when the clock ticks, the new value of u is $\neg(x \text{ } or \text{ } v)$, where x and v are the values before the clock ticks. The function which describes the general change of state is

$$f : \quad \mathbf{B}^4 \longrightarrow \mathbf{B}^4$$

$$(x, y, u, v) \longmapsto (x, y, \neg(x \text{ } or \text{ } v), \neg(y \text{ } or \text{ } u)),$$

which is of course constructible using only the operations of a distributive category.

Let's look at some behaviours of this circuit.

⋆ Starting with initial state $(0,1,0,1)$, the behaviour is

$$(0,1,0,1) \xmapsto{f} (0,1,0,0) \xmapsto{f} (0,1,1,0) \xmapsto{f} (0,1,1,0) \longmapsto \cdots.$$

Notice that the state $(0,1,1,0)$ is a fixed point.

⋆ Starting with initial state $(0,0,0,0)$, the behaviour is

$$(0,0,0,0) \stackrel{f}{\longmapsto} (0,0,1,1) \stackrel{f}{\longmapsto} (0,0,0,0) \stackrel{f}{\longmapsto} (0,0,1,1) \longmapsto \cdots.$$

This behaviour is unstable; a cycle of length 2.

Example 13. Any flowchart with feedback may be regarded as an imperative program. Consider, for example, the following flowchart:

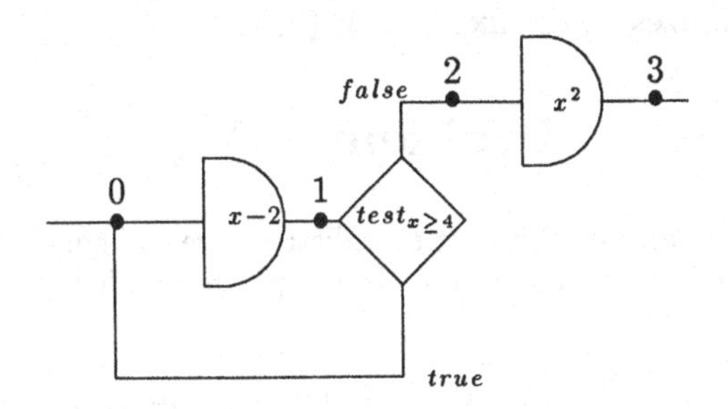

Since this flowchart has feedback, we cannot simply consider what happens as we move from left to right through the flowchart, as we did in Chapter 2, §6. Instead we have to consider at any moment the state of the whole flowchart. At any moment we are in one of four possible positions (denoted 0, 1, 2, and 3) in the flowchart, and we are carrying one real number. Hence the set of all possible states — *the state space* of the flow chart — is

$$\begin{aligned} X &= \mathbb{R} + \mathbb{R} + \mathbb{R} + \mathbb{R} = 4{\bullet}\mathbb{R} \\ &= \{(x,0)\} \cup \{(y,1)\} \cup \{(z,2)\} \cup \{(w,3)\}. \end{aligned}$$

Again we want to consider how the state changes with each tick of the clock. For example, if we are in position 0 carrying the number x, after the clock ticks we will be in position 1 carrying the number $x-2$. The function which describes the general change of state is:

$$f : \mathbb{R} + \mathbb{R} + \mathbb{R} + \mathbb{R} \longrightarrow \mathbb{R} + \mathbb{R} + \mathbb{R} + \mathbb{R}$$

$$\begin{aligned} (x,0) &\longmapsto (x-2,1) \\ (y,1) &\longmapsto \begin{cases} (y,2) & \text{if } y < 4 \\ (y,0) & \text{if } y \geq 4 \end{cases} \\ (z,2) &\longmapsto (z^2,3) \\ (w,3) &\longmapsto (w,3). \end{aligned}$$

It is obvious that this function can be constructed from the given functions *add*, *multiply*, $test_{x<y}$ and constants, using only the constructions available in a distributive category.

Let's consider the behaviour of this flowchart, beginning with initial state $(7,0)$. It is

$$(7,0) \stackrel{f}{\longmapsto} (5,1) \stackrel{f}{\longmapsto} (5,0) \stackrel{f}{\longmapsto} (3,1) \stackrel{f}{\longmapsto}$$
$$(3,2) \stackrel{f}{\longmapsto} (9,3) \stackrel{f}{\longmapsto} (9,3) \stackrel{f}{\longmapsto} \cdots.$$

The behaviour stabilizes at the fixed point $(9,3)$.

Problems 3

1. Suppose that O is an initial object in a distributive category, and there exists an arrow $\alpha : X \to O$. Show that α is an isomorphism and hence X is also an initial object.

2. Given three functions $f, g, h : Y \to Z$ and two tests $t_1, t_2 : X \to \mathbf{B}(= I + I)$ construct, using only the fact that **Sets** is a distributive category, the function $p : X \times Y \to Z$ defined by

'if $t_1(x)$ is true then $z = f(y)$
else if $t_2(x)$ is true then $z = g(y)$
else $z = h(y)$'.

3. Given three tests $t_1, t_2, t_3 : X \to \mathbf{B}$, construct, using only the operations of a distributive category, the test

$$(t_1 \,\&\, t_2)\, or\, (\neg t_1 \,\&\, t_2 \,\&\, t_3) : X \to B.$$

4. Prove that in a distributive category

$$(X \times Y + X \times Y \xrightarrow{\delta} X \times (Y + Y) \xrightarrow{1_X \times \nabla_Y} X \times Y) = \nabla_{X \times Y},$$

where δ is the isomorphism of the distributive law.

5. Construct the following imperative programs, where the given functions are *add*, *multiply*, *divide*, $test_{x<y}$, and the constants $\lceil r \rceil : I \to \mathbb{R}$ $(r \in \mathbb{R})$:

(i) a program which, given n, computes by iteration

$$\sum_{x=1}^{n} x^5;$$

(ii) a program which, given a natural number n, computes whether or not n is prime.

6. Construct, using only the fact that **Sets** is a distributive category, the function $f : \mathbb{R} \to \mathbb{R}$ given by:

$$\text{'if } x < 0.5 \text{ then } f(x) = 2x, \text{ else } f(x) = 2 - 2x\text{'.}$$

(i) Find out what happens by repeatedly applying f to the following initial states: (a) $x = \frac{1}{3}$, (b) $x = \frac{3}{8}$, (c) $x = \frac{1}{5}$, (d) $x = 2$.

(ii) Given the binary expansion of x, what is the binary expansion of $f(x)$?

(iii) Find a point $x \in [0,1]$ whose orbit under f is a cycle of length 17.

(iv) Find a point $x \in [0,1]$ such that the orbit of x under f is dense in $[0,1]$.

7. Construct a function $f : \mathbb{R}^3 \times \mathbf{B} \to \mathbb{R}^3 \times \mathbf{B}$ which, when repeatedly applied to initial state $(1, x, n, 0)$ (n a natural number), eventually stabilizes at $(x^n, x, 0, 1)$ (that is, $f^k(1, x, n, 0) = (x^n, x, 0, 1)$, for all large enough k).

8. Let **A** be a category with a finite number of arrows between each pair of objects.

(i) Suppose that A is an object of category **A** such that $A + A \cong A$. Show that if X is any object, then there is at most one arrow from A to X.

(ii) Suppose the category is distributive and that the terminal object I satisfies $I + I \cong I$. Show that the category **A** is a preordered set.

9. Analyse completely the behaviours of the following:

(i) The circuit,

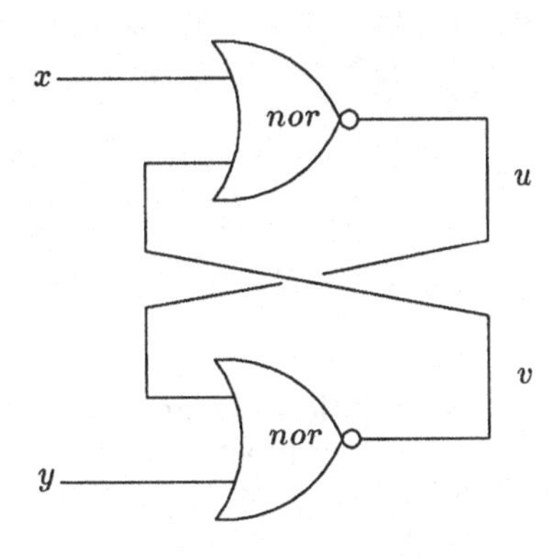

(ii) The flow chart,

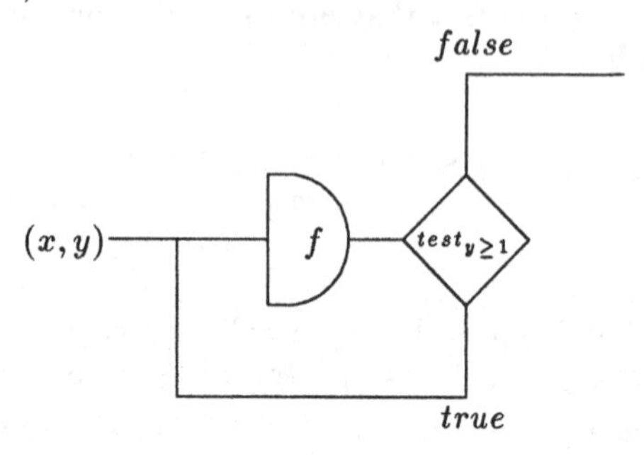

where $f(x,y) = (xy, y-1)$.

10. Construct in **Sets**, using only the operations of a distributive category, the isomorphism:

$$\mathbf{B}^n \longrightarrow (I + I + I + \cdots + I),$$
$$(x_0, x_1, \ldots, x_{n-1}) \longmapsto \left(*, \sum_{i=0}^{n-1} x_i 2^i\right).$$

11. (Robin Cockett.) Show that Axiom 2 for distributive categories is redundant.

12. Find a circuit constructed out of components

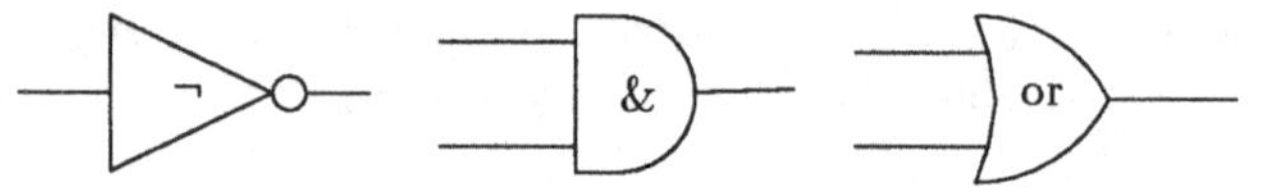

which has a behaviour with a cycle of order 5.

13. (i) Analyse completely the behaviour of the circuit consisting of two *not* gates joined in a circle.

(ii) Find a circuit consisting only of *not* gates which has a behaviour consisting of a cycle of length three.

14. Show that, in a distributive category, the arrow

$$Y \times X + Z \times X \xrightarrow{\begin{pmatrix} i_Y \times 1_X \\ i_Z \times 1_X \end{pmatrix}} (Y + Z) \times X$$

is an isomorphism.

15. (Khalil and Walters.) We say that a program $f : X + U + Y \to X + U + Y$ *idles* on Y if $f i_Y = i_Y$. Suppose another program $g : Y + V + Z \to Y + V + Z$ idles on Z. Show that $(1_{X+U} + g)(f + 1_{V+Z}) : X + W + Z \to X + W + Z$, $(W = U + Y + V)$, is the program whose behaviour, with initial state in X, is first to do f until f idles, and then to do g until g idles.

Chapter 4

Data Types

In the previous chapter we gave examples of simple imperative programs for computing with numbers. This involved the construction of arrows given some basic objects $\mathbb{R}$ and $\mathbf{B}$ and basic arrows like $add : \mathbb{R} \times \mathbb{R} \to \mathbb{R}$ and $test_{x<y} : \mathbb{R} \times \mathbb{R} \to \mathbf{B}$.

Further programming involves the consideration of new data sets (not just $\mathbb{R}$, $\mathbf{B}$, $\mathbb{R} \times \mathbb{R}$, ...), functions between the new data sets, and properties that the new data sets and functions satisfy.

Let us first look more closely at the data sets we have already considered.

§1. Arithmetic

Consider the following functions involving the real numbers:

$$\begin{aligned} add &: \mathbb{R} \times \mathbb{R} \longrightarrow \mathbb{R}, \\ zero &: I \longrightarrow \mathbb{R}, \\ minus &: \mathbb{R} \longrightarrow \mathbb{R}. \end{aligned}$$

So far we have just used such functions to construct new ones using operations like composition and products. But it is also important to be able to express properties that these functions satisfy. This is essential if we wish to prove properties of programs.

The functions we have given above satisfy some well-known properties, known as the axioms of an *abelian group*. For any x, y, z, in $\mathbb{R}$:

$$\begin{gathered} x + 0 = x = 0 + x \quad \text{(identity laws)}, \\ (x + y) + z = x + (y + z) \quad \text{(associative law)}, \\ x + (-x) = 0 = (-x) + x \quad \text{(inverse laws)}, \\ x + y = y + x \quad \text{(commutative law)}. \end{gathered}$$

These properties can be expressed without looking at the elements. In fact, they can be expressed just in terms of properties of products.

★ Let's look at the associative law, for example. It says exactly that the following diagram commutes:

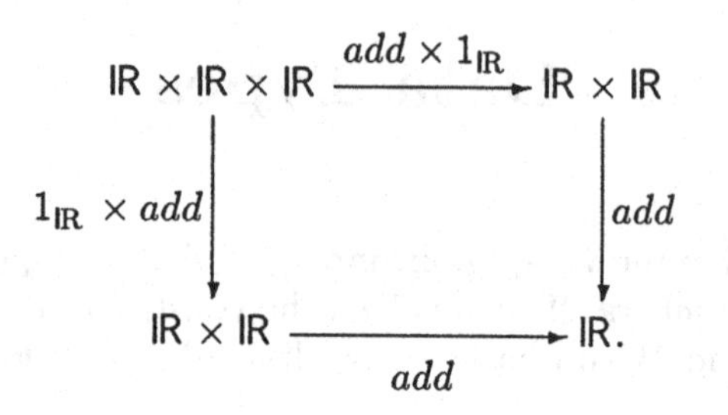

The reason is that if you take a typical element (x, y, z) from $\mathbb{R} \times \mathbb{R} \times \mathbb{R}$, and go around the top of the square, you get

$$\begin{array}{ccccc} \mathbb{R} \times \mathbb{R} \times \mathbb{R} & \xrightarrow{add \times 1_{\mathbb{R}}} & \mathbb{R} \times \mathbb{R} & \xrightarrow{add} & \mathbb{R} \\ (x, y, z) & \longmapsto & (x + y, z) & \longmapsto & (x + y) + z. \end{array}$$

whereas, if you follow the same element around the bottom of the square, you get

$$\begin{array}{ccccc} \mathbb{R} \times \mathbb{R} \times \mathbb{R} & \xrightarrow{1_{\mathbb{R}} \times add} & \mathbb{R} \times \mathbb{R} & \xrightarrow{add} & \mathbb{R} \\ (x, y, z) & \longmapsto & (x, y + z) & \longmapsto & x + (y + z). \end{array}$$

Hence the diagram commutes exactly if $(x + y) + z = x + (y + z)$ for all x, y, z in $\mathbb{R}$.

The other axioms for an abelian group can be expressed similarly.

★ The identity laws say that the following diagram commutes:

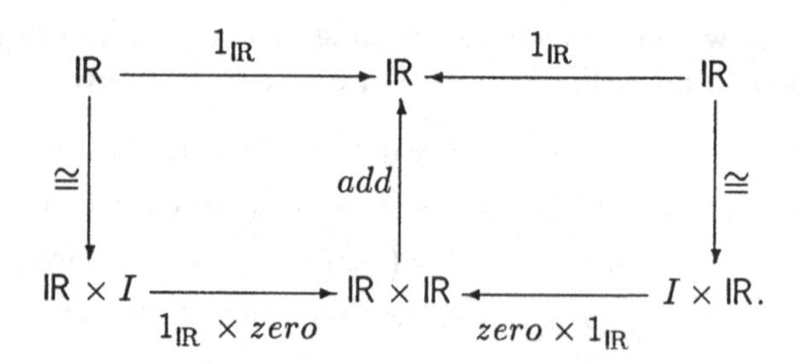

★ The inverse laws say that the following diagram commutes:

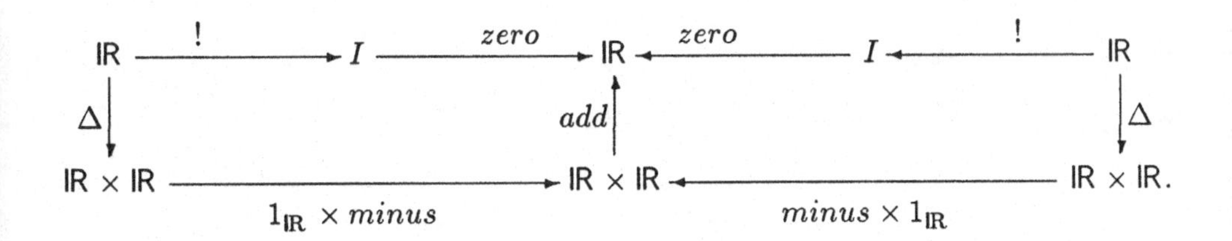

⋆ The commutative law says that the following diagram commutes:

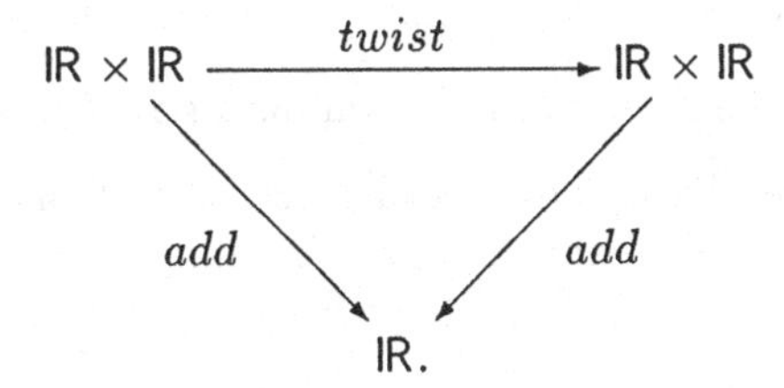

The fact that these commuting diagrams express the axioms stated is easily verified by following elements around the diagram, as we did with the associative law.

So far, I have written down the axioms that say that IR, with *add, zero*, and *minus*, forms an *abelian group*. We can similarly express the fact that IR is a *ring*; that multiplication is associative, and that the distributive law relating multiplication and addition holds.

At the heart of any computer is a ring — the *arithmetic unit*.

The method of defining algebras by giving sets, operations and axioms satisfied by the operations is a familiar one in mathematics. However, computer science has given rise to many new 'algebras' which mathematicians had not considered. These 'algebras' are called *data types*.

A **data type** consists of various sets of data together with operations between them (definable in a distributive category) and equations expressible in a distributive category.

§2. Stacks

Intuitively a *stack* of real numbers is a (vertical) list

$$\begin{array}{c} x_1 \\ x_2 \\ x_3 \\ \cdot \\ \cdot \\ \cdot \\ x_n \end{array}$$

of real numbers. You only have access to the top element of the stack. That is, you can put an extra element on top — this is called *pushing* an element onto the stack; or you can take the top element off the stack — this is called *popping* an element off the stack.

Stacks are one of the most fundamental data structures in computer science.

Let us try to axiomatize this by considering the set S of all stacks of real numbers. For convenience we will write stacks *horizontally* rather than vertically, with the left-hand element being the top element.

The basic operations are:

$$push : \quad \mathbb{R} \times S \longrightarrow S$$

$$(x, x_1 x_2 \cdots x_n) \longmapsto (x x_1 \cdots x_n),$$

and

$$pop : \quad S \longrightarrow \mathbb{R} \times S$$

$$(x_1 x_2 \cdots x_n) \longmapsto (x_1, x_2 \cdots x_n),$$

where x_1 is the top element, and $x_2 \cdots x_n$ is the remaining stack.

Note. This is not quite accurate. There is an empty stack, denoted o, and when you *pop* the empty stack you do not get an element of $\mathbb{R}$.

We met this problem before with division of real numbers where $\frac{x}{y}$ is not defined if $y = 0$. To handle the exceptional case we took division to be a function from $\mathbb{R} \times \mathbb{R}$ to $I + \mathbb{R}$. We do a similar thing with stacks.

We take *pop* to be the function:

$$pop : S \longrightarrow I + \mathbb{R} \times S$$

$$s \longmapsto \begin{cases} * & \text{if } s = o \\ (x_1, x_2 x_3 \cdots x_n) & \text{if } s = x_1 x_2 \cdots x_n. \end{cases}$$

Notation. Notice here, that I have omitted the tag indicating which component of the sum an element is in; I wrote $*$ instead of $(*, 0)$. In future where there is no risk of confusion I shall omit tags.

Question. What other operations are there on S?

The empty stack is a constant of S. That is:

$$\begin{aligned} \lceil o \rceil \ : \ I &\longrightarrow S \\ * &\longmapsto o. \end{aligned}$$

In addition, we also have all the constants $\lceil r \rceil : I \to \mathbb{R}$.

By the property of sums we can combine the two operations $\lceil o \rceil : I \to S$ and *push* : $\mathbb{R} \times S \to S$ into a single operation, which for simplicity we shall also call *push*:

$$\begin{aligned} push \ : \ I + \mathbb{R} \times S &\longrightarrow S \\ * &\longmapsto o \\ (x, o) &\longmapsto x \\ (x, x_1 \cdots x_n) &\longmapsto x x_1 \cdots x_n. \end{aligned}$$

So we have reduced the operations of the set of stacks to two (excepting the constants of $\mathbb{R}$):

$$pop : S \to I + \mathbb{R} \times S,$$
$$push : I + \mathbb{R} \times S \to S.$$

The axioms that these operations satisfy are:

Axiom 1. $\quad pop \cdot push = 1_{I + \mathbb{R} \times S},$

Axiom 2. $\quad push \cdot pop = 1_S.$

That is, *push* and *pop* are inverses of each other. Roughly speaking,

$$S \cong I + \mathbb{R} \times S.$$

Proof. Let us verify the truth of Axioms 1 and 2.

To check Axiom 1, let's see what $pop \cdot push$ does to elements:

$$\begin{array}{ccccc} I + \mathbb{R} \times S & \xrightarrow{push} & S & \xrightarrow{pop} & I + \mathbb{R} \times S \\ * & \longmapsto & o & \longmapsto & * \\ (x, x_1 \cdots x_n) & \longmapsto & x x_1 \cdots x_n & \longmapsto & (x, x_1 \cdots x_n). \end{array}$$

Hence $pop \cdot push = 1_{I+\mathbb{R}\times S}$.

Checking Axiom 2, let's see what $push \cdot pop$ does to elements:

$$\begin{array}{ccccc} S & \xrightarrow{pop} & I+\mathbb{R}\times S & \xrightarrow{push} & S \\ o & \longmapsto & * & \longmapsto & o \\ x_1x_2\cdots x_n & \longmapsto & (x_1, x_2x_3\cdots x_n) & \longmapsto & x_1x_2\cdots x_n. \end{array}$$

Hence $push \cdot pop = 1_S$. ∎

We are now ready for an abstract definition:

Definition. A *type stack* of $\mathbb{R}$, or a *space of stacks* of $\mathbb{R}$, is a set S together with two operations:

$$pop : S \to I + \mathbb{R} \times S,$$
$$push : I + \mathbb{R} \times S \to S.$$

satisfying

$$pop \cdot push = 1_{I+\mathbb{R}\times S},$$
$$push \cdot pop = 1_S.$$

Note. We started with a standard model of these axioms in mind, but now we can look for other examples.

Example 1. (A non-standard type stack.)

Let $S = \{$finite and infinite lists $x_1x_2\cdots$ of reals$\}$.

There are two obvious operations:

$$\begin{array}{rcl} pop : \quad S & \longrightarrow & I+\mathbb{R}\times S \\ o & \longmapsto & * \\ xx_1\cdots & \longmapsto & (x, x_1\cdots), \end{array}$$

and

$$\begin{array}{rcl} push : I+\mathbb{R}\times S & \longrightarrow & S \\ * & \longmapsto & o \\ (x, o) & \longmapsto & x \\ (x, x_1\cdots) & \longmapsto & xx_1\cdots. \end{array}$$

These are clearly inverse. Hence S satisfies the stack space axioms.

Note. So, just from the stack space axioms, we do not know if the stacks are of finite length.

So far I have spoken about stacks of real numbers, but of course we can speak about stacks of elements of any set X. Hence we can define 'type stack-of-X', alternatively called a 'space of stacks of X'.

Definition. A *type stack-of-X* is a set S with two operations :

$$pop : S \to I + X \times S,$$
$$push : I + X \times S \to S,$$

such that

$$push \cdot pop = 1_S,$$
$$pop \cdot push = 1_{I+X\times S}.$$

Example 2. Let $X = \{*\} = I$ and $S = \mathbb{N}$, the set of natural numbers. Then,

$$predecessor : \mathbb{N} \longrightarrow I + I \times \mathbb{N} \cong I + \mathbb{N}$$
$$n \longmapsto \begin{cases} * & \text{if } n = 0 \\ n-1 & \text{if } n > 0, \end{cases}$$

and

$$successor : I + \mathbb{N} \longrightarrow \mathbb{N}$$
$$* \longmapsto 0$$
$$n \longmapsto n+1.$$

are inverses of one another. Hence $\mathbb{N}$ with these operations is a type stack-of-I.

A crazy calculation

Note the following apparently nonsensical calculation. If S is a space of stacks of X then since

$$S \cong I + X \times S$$

we deduce successively that

$$I \times S - X \times S \cong I,$$
$$(I - X) \times S \cong I,$$
$$S \cong I/(I - X),$$
$$S \cong I + X + X^2 + X^3 + \cdots.$$

If S, I, and X were numbers this would be a sensible calculation. Even though this is not the case, the final result has a reasonable interpretation. It says that

S is the disjoint union of I, X, X^2, X^3,.... That is, a stack is an element of one of I, X, X^2, X^3 .... But an element of X^n is an n-tuple of elements of X. So a stack is either the empty stack, or a single element of X, or a pair of elements of X, or a triple of elements of X, et cetera.

Further, the operations of X have a sensible interpretation. The function *push* is the isomorphism

$$I + X \times S \cong I + X \times (I + X + X^2 + \cdots) \xrightarrow{\cong} I + X \times I + X \times X + \cdots \cong S.$$

There is a categorical theory which justifies such crazy calculations, which may be found in [14], [15], and [30]. Let's now see some examples of other operations which are available with stacks, given the two basic operations. But first we introduce some notation.

Notation. From now on we will often denote the identity arrow 1_X by X. So, instead of

$$1_I + 1_X \times pop : I + X \times S \to I + X \times (I + X \times S),$$

we will write simply

$$I + X \times pop : I + X \times S \to I + X \times (I + X \times S),$$

or even $\quad I + Xpop : I + XS \to I + X(I + XS).$

Example 3. The usual operation of pushing an element on a stack is the composite:

$$X \times S \xrightarrow{i_{X\times S}} I + X \times S \xrightarrow{push} S$$

$$(x, s) \longmapsto (x, s) \longmapsto xs.$$

Similarly, the empty stack is:

$$I \xrightarrow{i_I} I + X \times S \xrightarrow{push} S$$

$$* \longmapsto * \longmapsto o.$$

Example 4. Let's now construct an imperative program to compute the depth of a stack, given a type stack S of X, and a number type R.

Take the state space of the program to be $S \times R$. Take the initial state to be $(s, 0)$. Then the following action will, when iterated, compute the depth of the stack, and then idle:

$$S \times R \longrightarrow S \times R$$

$$(x_1 x_2 \cdots x_n, r) \longmapsto (x_2 x_3 \cdots x_n, r + 1)$$

$$(o, r) \longmapsto (o, r).$$

This action is the following composite:

$$SR \xrightarrow{pop\,R} (I+XS)R \xrightarrow{(I+proj)R} (I+S)R \xrightarrow{(\lceil o \rceil + S)R} (S+S)R$$

$$(S+S)R \xrightarrow{\cong} SR+SR \xrightarrow{SR+S\lceil x+1 \rceil} SR+SR \xrightarrow{\nabla} SR.$$

Beginning with initial state (s, o) the program eventually idles at the state $(o, \mathrm{depth}(s))$. A typical behaviour is:

$$(x_1 x_2, 0) \longmapsto (x_2, 1) \longmapsto (o, 2) \longmapsto (o, 2) \longmapsto \cdots.$$

Example 5. Let's see how to construct tests on stacks, by considering the example:

$$\begin{aligned} test\ :\ S &\longrightarrow I+I \\ s &\longmapsto \begin{cases} 0 & \text{if depth}(s) \neq 1 \\ 1 & \text{if depth}(s) = 1. \end{cases} \end{aligned}$$

This test is the composite:

$$S \xrightarrow{pop} (I+XS) \xrightarrow{I+X pop} I+X(I+XS) \xrightarrow{\cong} I+X+X^2S$$

$$I+X+X^2S \xrightarrow{!+!+!} I+I+I \xrightarrow{I+twist} I+I+I \xrightarrow{\nabla+I} I+I.$$

Note. If S is a stack space in **Sets**, then S is infinite, unless $X = 0$, since

$$S \cong I + X \times S,$$

and so, if the number of elements in S is n and the number of elements in X is m, then $n = 1 + mn$, and hence $n > n$.

The existence of stack types is an axiom of infinity. The operations are finitary. An arbitrary amount of data may be stored in a stack without needing to specify an address either for storing or recovering the data. We will see further examples of programming with stacks in §7.

Of course real stack types are bounded; which leads to the possibility of stack overflow. However in most uses of stack types they are treated as potentially infinite data structures.

§3. Arrays

Another way you can store data is to put it in an array.

The data type *array* of X of length n is a type you have for free in a distributive category. It is just the object X^n with no special operations. The operations you want to do on an array are to store information and to retrieve it, but these can be constructed using the properties available in a distributive category. The store operation is:

$$\begin{aligned} store\ : X \times n{\bullet}I \times X^n &\longrightarrow X^n \\ (x, i, a) &\longmapsto a'. \end{aligned}$$

where a' is the array a modified by putting the value x in the ith position. That is,

$$a'[j] = \begin{cases} x & \text{if } j = i, \\ a[j] & \text{if } j \neq i. \end{cases}$$

How can we define *store* just using the properties of a distributive category?

In a distributive category there is an isomorphism

$$\begin{aligned} X \times n{\bullet}I \times X^n \quad &\cong \quad n{\bullet}(X \times X^n) \cong n{\bullet}X^{n+1} \\ (x, i, a) &\longmapsto ((x, a), i), \end{aligned}$$

where $((x,a),i)$ is in the ith component of $n{\bullet}X^{n+1}$. Notice that the i in $((x,a),i)$ is a tag to indicate a component of the sum. The function *store* is this isomorphism composed with a function $\pi : n{\bullet}X^{n+1} \to X^n$. To define π we need to give n arrows from X^{n+1} to X^n. The ith one should be

$$\begin{aligned} X^{n+1} &\longrightarrow X^n \\ (x, a[1], a[2], \ldots, a[n]) &\longmapsto (a[1], a[2], \ldots, a[i-1], x, a[i+1], \ldots, a[n]). \end{aligned}$$

This arrow can be formed as the composite

$$X \times X^n \xrightarrow{swap_{1,i+1}} X \times X^n \xrightarrow{p_2} X^n,$$

where $swap_{1,i+1}$ is that composite of *twist* arrows which interchanges the first and $(i+1)$th components of X^{n+1}, and p_2 is the second projection of the product $X \times X^n$.

The retrieve function is

$$\begin{aligned} read\ : n{\bullet}I \times X^n &\longrightarrow X \\ (i, a) &\longmapsto a[i], \end{aligned}$$

and it is defined as follows. First, define $\alpha : n{\bullet}X^n \to X$ by giving n functions from X^n to X, namely the n projections in order. The function α takes (a, i) to

$a[i]$. Then

$$read : n{\scriptstyle\bullet}I \times X^n \xrightarrow{\cong} n{\scriptstyle\bullet}X^n \xrightarrow{\alpha} X$$

$$(i, a) \longmapsto (a, i) \longmapsto a[i].$$

Note. We have seen earlier another data type which comes free in a distributive category, namely the boolean type, $\mathbf{B} = I + I$. All the boolean functions come for free, and in fact they satisfy the usual laws of boolean algebra.

§4. Binary Trees

Given a set X , a *binary tree* of X is something like the following:

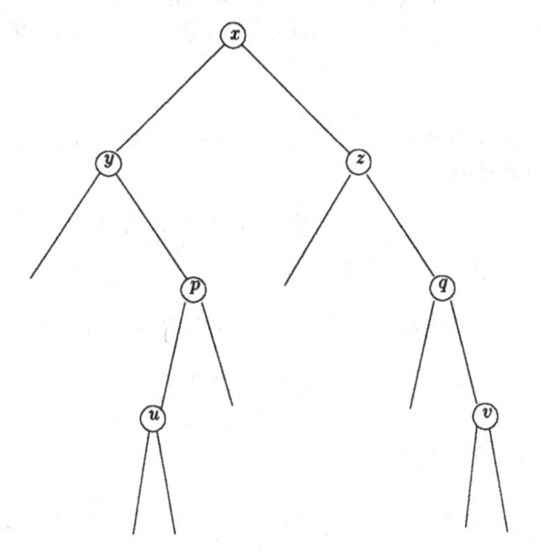

(where x, y, z, p, q, u and v are elements of X). That is, a binary tree has a finite number of nodes which are labelled with, or store, elements of X. If there are any nodes at all, then there is a top node, and below each node there is the possibility of two further nodes. If the tree is not empty, it consists of a top node and two subtrees. If the top node is labelled x and the left and right subtrees are t_1, t_2 then we will denote the tree by t_1xt_2.

Binary trees are useful for hierarchical storage and classification of data. Here is how to axiomatize this structure.

Let T be the set of binary trees of X, with operations:

$$o : I \to T \quad (\text{ the empty tree}),$$

$$make : T \times X \times T \longrightarrow T$$

$$(t_1, x, t_2) \longmapsto t_1 x t_2.$$

These two operations can be joined together, using the property of sums, into a single operation, which we shall again call *make*:

$$make : I + T \times X \times T \longrightarrow T.$$

There is an inverse to *make* which we shall call *break*:

$$break : T \longrightarrow I + T \times X \times T$$

$$t_1 x t_2 \longmapsto (t_1, x, t_2)$$

$$o \longmapsto *.$$

Definition. A type, *binary trees* of X, is an object T with two operations $make : I + T \times X \times T \to T$ and $break : T \to I + T \times X \times T$, which are inverse to one another.

Note. Roughly, the axiom says $T \cong I + T \times X \times T$. So we can make the following crazy calculation:

$$T \cong I + T \times X \times T,$$
$$X \times T^2 - T + I \cong 0.$$

Hence, by the rule for solving quadratic equations,

$$T \cong \frac{I \pm \sqrt{(I - 4X)}}{2X}.$$

But, by the binomial theorem,

$$(I - 4X)^{1/2} \cong I - \binom{\frac{1}{2}}{1} 4X + \binom{\frac{1}{2}}{2} 4^2 X^2 - \binom{\frac{1}{2}}{3} 4^3 X^3 + \cdots.$$

It is not hard to show that, if we take the negative sign in the formula for T above, then using the binomial theorem we get a series expansion for T in which the coefficient of X^n is a positive integer, namely,

$$\frac{1}{n+1}\binom{2n}{n}.$$

So we have

$$T \cong I + X + 2X^2 + 5X^3 + 14X^4 + \cdots + \frac{1}{n+1}\binom{2n}{n} X^n + \cdots.$$

This calculation would make sense if I, X, and T were numbers. However, even when they are sets, the final line has a meaning. We can classify binary trees according to how many 'nodes' there are. The first term in the series corresponds to the trees with 0 nodes: there is just one of them, the empty tree. The second term in the series corresponds to the trees with one node; if $|X|$ is the number of elements of X then there are exactly $|X|$ such trees. The third term in the series corresponds to trees with two nodes; there are two possible shapes for such trees — a top node and a left node, or a top node and a right node. Each of these shapes when labelled gives rise to $|X|^2$ trees, and hence there are $2|X|^2$ trees with two nodes. In general, the number of shapes of trees with n nodes is the nth Catalan number,

$$C_n = \frac{1}{n+1}\binom{2n}{n},$$

and hence, when labelled, there are $C_n|X|^n$ trees with n-nodes, as suggested by our series formula.

§5. Queues

Queues are another important data structure. A queue is similar to a stack, but the operations available are different.

A queue of X is a list like $x_1x_2x_3\cdots x_n$, where we think of x_1 as the *end* of the queue where extra elements can be added, and we think of x_n as the *head* of the queue where elements can be taken off.

Let Q be the set of queues of X. The operations are:

$$\begin{aligned} push\ :\quad & X \times Q \longrightarrow Q \\ & (x, x_1 \cdots x_n) \longmapsto x x_1 \cdots x_n, \\ pop\ :\quad & Q \longrightarrow I + Q \times X \\ & x_1 x_2 \cdots x_n \longmapsto (x_1 \cdots x_{n-1}, x_n) \\ & o \longmapsto *, \end{aligned}$$

and

$$\begin{aligned} empty\ : I & \longrightarrow Q \\ * & \longmapsto o. \end{aligned}$$

Again we can combine *push* and *empty* into a single operation:

$$push : I + X \times Q \to Q.$$

However, for queues, it is not true that *push* and *pop* are inverse. If we pop an element from the head of a queue, and then push it on the end of the queue, the function we get is

$$Q \xrightarrow{pop} I + QX \xrightarrow{\cong} I + XQ \xrightarrow{push} Q$$

$$x_1x_2x_3 \longmapsto (x_1x_2, x_3) \longmapsto (x_3, x_1x_2) \longmapsto x_3x_1x_2,$$

which is clearly not the identity function.

Question. What can be said relating the two operations, *pop* and *push*?

Roughly speaking, $pop \cdot push = push \cdot pop$. But this is not precisely true; in particular, beginning with an empty queue we get a different result by first pushing then popping, than by first popping then pushing.

The precise property that the operations of queues satisfy is that the following diagram commutes:

$$\begin{array}{ccc}
I + X \times Q & \xrightarrow{push} & Q \\
\Big\downarrow{\scriptstyle I + X \times pop} & & \\
I + X \times (I + Q \times X) & & \\
\Big\downarrow{\scriptstyle distributive\ law} & & \Big\downarrow{\scriptstyle pop} \\
I + X + X \times Q \times X & & \\
\Big\downarrow{\scriptstyle distributive\ law} & & \\
I + (I + X \times Q) \times X & \xrightarrow[I + push \times X]{} & I + Q \times X.
\end{array} \qquad (1)$$

Definition. A *type queue* of X is a set Q with operations $push : I + X \times Q \to Q$ and $pop : Q \to I + Q \times X$ satisfying (1).

Let us see what Axiom (1) means, by following elements around the diagram. There are various cases.

Case 1. Taking $* \in I + X \times Q$, and following it around the top, and then the bottom of the diagram we get:

$$I + X \times Q \xrightarrow{push} Q \xrightarrow{pop} I + Q \times X$$

$$* \longmapsto o \longmapsto *,$$

and

$$\begin{array}{ccccccc} I+XQ & \xrightarrow{I+Xpop} & I+X(I+QX) & \xrightarrow{\cong} & I+(I+XQ)X & \xrightarrow{I+pushX} & I+QX \\ * & \longmapsto & * & \longmapsto & * & \longmapsto & *. \end{array}$$

Hence the diagram commutes in this case.

Case 2. Taking $(x, o) \in I + X \times Q$, and following it around the top, and then the bottom of the diagram we get:

$$\begin{array}{ccccc} I+X\times Q & \xrightarrow{push} & Q & \xrightarrow{pop} & I+Q\times X \\ (x,o) & \longmapsto & x & \longmapsto & (o,x), \end{array}$$

and

$$\begin{array}{ccccccc} I+XQ & \xrightarrow{I+Xpop} & I+X(I+QX) & \xrightarrow{\cong} & I+(I+XQ)X & \xrightarrow{I+pushX} & I+QX \\ (x,o) & \longmapsto & (x,*) & \longmapsto & (*,x) & \longmapsto & (o,x). \end{array}$$

Hence the diagram commutes in this case.

Case 3. Taking $(x, x_1x_2\cdots x_n) \in I + X \times Q$, and following it around the top and then the bottom of the diagram we get:

$$\begin{array}{ccccc} I+X\times Q & \xrightarrow{push} & Q & \xrightarrow{pop} & I+Q\times X \\ (x,x_1x_2\cdots x_n) & \longmapsto & xx_1\cdots x_n & \longmapsto & (xx_1\cdots x_{n-1},x_n), \end{array}$$

and

$$\begin{array}{ccccc} I+XQ & \xrightarrow{I+Xpop} & I+X(I+QX) & \xrightarrow{\cong} & I+(I+XQ)X \\ (x,x_1\cdots x_n) & \longmapsto & (x,(x_1\cdots x_{n-1},x_n)) & \longmapsto & ((x,x_1\cdots x_{n-1}),x_n) \end{array}$$

$$\begin{array}{ccc} I+(I+XQ)X & \xrightarrow{I+pushX} & I+QX \\ ((x,x_1\cdots x_{n-1}),x_n) & \longmapsto & (xx_1\cdots x_{n-1},x_n). \end{array}$$

Hence the diagram commutes also in this case.

§6. Pointers

Some commonly occurring data structures consist of some other structure x with a pointer, pointing at a selected element of x. For example, a screen with a cursor is a screen together with a pointer, pointing at one position on the screen.

As an example of this phenomenon, let us consider lists of X with pointer. A typical example is $x_1 x_2 \cdots x_{i-1}[x_i]x_{i+1} \cdots x_n$, the square brackets indicating that the element x_i is selected. The same information is contained in the pair $(i, x_1 \cdots x_n)$, where i gives the address of the selected element. So the set of such lists with n elements, and with a pointer, is $n{\bullet}I \times X^n = \{(i,(x_1,\cdots,x_n)); 1 \leq i \leq n,\ x_i \in X\}$. The set L of all such lists with pointer, as n varies from 1 to ∞, is

$$L = \sum_{n=1}^{\infty} n{\bullet}I \times X^n.$$

Let's now do an apparently illegitimate calculation with this formula:

$$\begin{aligned}
L &\cong \sum_{n=1}^{\infty} n{\bullet}I \times X^n \\
&\cong X\left(\sum_{n=1}^{\infty} n{\bullet}I \times X^{n-1}\right) \\
&\cong X\frac{d}{dX}\left(\sum_{n=0}^{\infty} X^n\right) \\
&\cong X\frac{d}{dX}\left(\frac{1}{I-X}\right) \\
&\cong X\frac{1}{(I-X)^2} = \left(\frac{1}{I-X}\right)X\left(\frac{1}{I-X}\right).
\end{aligned}$$

This suggests defining L as follows:

$$L = S \times X \times S,$$

where S is a stack space ($\cong \frac{1}{(I-X)}$), and taking as operations for L the operations of the stack space S. An element l of L is then a triple (s_1, z, s_2) where s_1 and s_2 are stacks of X, and z is an element of X.

This makes sense if we write the stack s_1 with top element on the right and the stack s_2 with top element on the left (as usual). That is, $s_1 = x_n x_{n-1} \cdots x_1$, say, and $s_2 = y_1 y_2 \cdots y_m$. Then

$$l = (x_n x_{n-1} \cdots x_1, z, y_1 y_2 \cdots y_m),$$

with z being the selected element out of the list of $m+n+1$ elements of X. Since elements are popped to the right from the first stack (rather than to the left), it is convenient to have the *pop* operation on the first stack type as $pop : S \to I + S \times X$ (rather than $pop : S \to I + X \times S$).

Here are some operations you can do with L.

1. Move the pointer to the right.

This is the function

$$SXS \xrightarrow{push \times pop} S(I+XS) \cong S + SXS \xrightarrow{!+SXS} I + SXS$$

$$(s_1, z, y_1 \cdots y_m) \longmapsto (s_1 z, y_1, y_2 \cdots y_m) \longmapsto (s_1 z, y_1, y_2 \cdots y_m)$$

$$(s_1, z, o) \longmapsto (s_1 z, *) \longmapsto *.$$

2. Overwrite z (the selected entry) by some other constant $a : I \to X$.

This is the function

$$SXS \xrightarrow{S!S} SIS \xrightarrow{S \times a \times S} SXS.$$

3. Insert constant a at the pointer, shifting z to the right.

This is the function

$$SXS \xrightarrow{\cong} SIXS \xrightarrow{S \times a \times push} SXS.$$

§7. Turing Machines

We are now going to use the data types we have developed in this chapter to see how arbitrary Turing machines are examples of imperative programs.†

Alan Turing, in 1936, proposed a class of abstract machines which could compute any function from $\mathbb{N}$ to $\mathbb{N}$ which was capable of being computed mechanically.

One of the main elements of a Turing machine is a 'potentially infinite' tape, divided up into squares. A finite number of the squares may be marked with

† This treatment of Turing machines was developed with Wafaa Khalil.

the symbol 1; the remaining squares are 'blank' — we shall think of them as being marked with a 0. At any time, one of the squares is selected as the current square; we call the symbol in that square the *scanned symbol*.

We shall model the tape of the Turing machine using the data type 'list of $I+I$ with pointer'. That is, the set of all tapes T is $S \times X \times S$, where $X = I+I$. Each element of T is a finite list of 1's and 0's. You are to imagine this list extended out to infinity in both directions with blank tape.

The operations we need for the tape are the following:

Move left. The pointer moves one to the left. If the left end of the tape is encountered, an extra square marked with a 0 is added to the left to enable the pointer to move left. This is the composite:

$$SXS \xrightarrow{pop \times push} (I+SX)S \xrightarrow{(o \times 0 + SX)S} (SX+SX) \times S$$

$$(SX+SX) \times S \xrightarrow{\cong} SXS + SXS \xrightarrow{\nabla} SXS.$$

Stay. This is just the identity function $stay = 1_{SXS}$.

Move right. The operation *move right* is defined analogously to *move left*.

Overwrite the scanned symbol with $a \in X$. This function was defined in §6.

In addition to a tape, a Turing machine has a finite set of *internal* states, $Q = \{0, 1, 2, \ldots, (m-1)\} \cong m{\bullet}I$. We shall also need to consider the set of names of movements, $D = \{move\ left,\ stay,\ move\ right\} \cong 3{\bullet}I$.

A particular Turing machine, with *internal* state space Q, is specified by giving a function

$$t : Q \times X \to Q \times D \times X.$$

Suppose the current internal state is q and the current scanned tape symbol is x, and suppose that $t(q,x) = (q', d, x')$. Then the intention is that in the next instant of time the machine will overwrite the current tape symbol with x', and then move in the sense indicated by d, and change internal state to q'.

We will now see that, corresponding to any Turing machine, there is an imperative program built out of the given functions of a stack space, which behaves as the Turing machine is intended to behave.

The state space of the program is the total state space of the Turing machine, including both the tape and the internal states. That is, the state space is

$$Q \times T = m{\bullet}I \times S \times 2{\bullet}I \times S.$$

The action f of the program is the composite:

$$QSXS \xrightarrow{QtwistS} QXSS \xrightarrow{tS^2} QDXSS$$

$$QDXSS \xrightarrow{QDtwistS} QDSXS \xrightarrow{\cong} Q \times 3 \cdot I \times SXS \xrightarrow{Qmove} Q \times SXS,$$

where $move : 3{\bullet}I \times SXS \to SXS$ is defined by three components:

$$move_0 = move\ left, \qquad move_1 = 1_{SXS} = stay, \qquad move_2 = move\ right.$$

It is clear this program behaves as the Turing machine, used to define the program, is intended to behave.

Example 6. We describe a simple Turing machine which moves left, until it encounters a 1 on the tape, and then idles.

The internal state space is $Q = 2{\bullet}I = \{0, 1\}$. The initial internal state is 0. The function $t : QX \to QDX$ which specifies the machine is:

$$\begin{aligned} Q \times X &\longrightarrow Q \times D \times X \\ (0,0) &\longmapsto (0, move\ left, 0) \\ (0,1) &\longmapsto (1, stay, 1) \\ (1,0) &\longmapsto (1, stay, 0) \\ (1,1) &\longmapsto (1, stay, 1). \end{aligned}$$

Remember that the total state space is $Q \times S \times X \times S$. An example of a behaviour, beginning with initial state (0, 01100100, 0, 110) is:

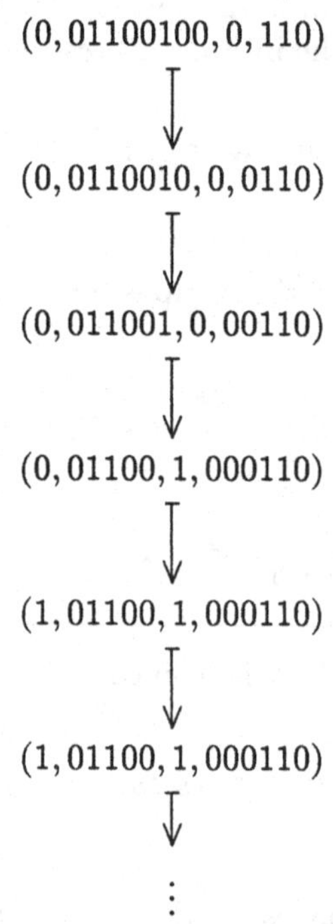

Problems 4

1. Express the distributive law relating addition and multiplication of real numbers in terms of a commuting diagram.

2. Given a stack type S, construct out of the stack operations and the operations of a distributive category the function

$$\begin{array}{rcl} test_o : S & \longrightarrow & B \\ s & \longmapsto & \begin{cases} 0 & \text{if stack } s \text{ is non-empty} \\ 1 & \text{if stack } s \text{ is empty.} \end{cases} \end{array}$$

3. Given a stack type S, construct an imperative program which concatenates two stacks.

4. Given a stack type S, construct out of the stack operations and the operations of a distributive category:

   (i) the function

$$\begin{array}{rcl} X \times S & \longrightarrow & S \\ (x, x_1 x_2 \cdots x_n) & \longmapsto & x x_1 x_2 \cdots x_n. \end{array}$$

(ii) the function

$$\begin{array}{rcl} S & \longrightarrow & S \\ s & \longmapsto & \begin{cases} o & \text{if stack } s = o \\ x_2x_3\ldots x_n & \text{if stack } s = x_1x_2\cdots x_n. \end{cases} \end{array}$$

(iii) the function

$$\begin{array}{rcl} test_{1,2} : S & \longrightarrow & B \\ s & \longmapsto & \begin{cases} 1 & \text{if stack } s \text{ has depth 1 or 2} \\ 0 & \text{otherwise.} \end{cases} \end{array}$$

(iv) the function

$$\begin{array}{rcl} test_{0,1,2\ldots,n} : S & \longrightarrow & B \\ s & \longmapsto & \begin{cases} 1 & \text{if stack } s \text{ has depth } 0,1,2,3,\ldots,n \\ 0 & \text{otherwise .} \end{cases} \end{array}$$

5. Describe a type queue of X ($X \neq \varnothing$) which contains some queues of infinite length.

6. (i) Show that

$$-\frac{1}{2}\binom{\frac{1}{2}}{n+1}(-4)^{n+1}X^n = \frac{1}{n+1}\binom{2n}{n}X^n;$$

(ii) Show directly that the number of binary trees of X with 4 nodes is $14\times(|X|)^4$.

7. A double-ended queue (deque) of X is a list $x_1, x_2, \ldots, x_n$ of elements of X with the allowed operations being:

(i) pushing elements on either end,

(ii) popping elements off either end.

Write down the operations as functions, and suggest axioms for type deque of X.

8. A ternary tree is a tree with branching into three at each node. Define type ternary tree of X. How many ternary trees of X are there with three nodes?

9. One possible view of a file is that it is a list of arrays (of fixed length n) of characters, with a pointer at one character.

If X is the set of characters, describe the data type file. Define, in terms of the basic operations (using the operations of a distributive category), the function which moves the pointer one character forward.

10. Given a type stack S of X, construct, using the operations of a distributive category,

(i) the test

$$test_3 : S \to I + I,$$

which gives the value *true* when the stack has length 3, and the value *false* otherwise;

(ii) the function $S \to I + X^3$, which takes the top three elements of the stack and places them in the array.

11. (i) Write down operations and axioms for the data type, *non-empty stacks of* X;

(ii) Write down operations and axioms for the data type, *stacks of* X *of odd depth*;

(iii) Suppose S is a type stack of odd-depth of X, and R is a type non-empty stack of S. Show that

$$R \cong \frac{X}{I - X - X^2}.$$

Deduce that

$$R \cong X + X^2 + 2X^3 + 3X^4 + \cdots.$$

Interpret this result. What is the general term in the series?

12. (Khalil, Walters.) A *pseudofunction* (or *functional process*) ϕ *from a set* X *to a set* Y, denoted $\phi : X \rightarrow\!\!\!\!+\!\!> Y$, is a function $\phi : X + U + Y \to X + U + Y$, for some set U, satisfying the conditions: (a) (single-valued — ϕ idles on Y) if $y \in Y$ then $\phi(y) = y$, and (b) (fully defined) if $x \in X$ then there exists a natural number n_x such that $\phi^{n_x}(x) \in Y$. Given a pseudofunction $\phi : X \rightarrow\!\!\!\!+\!\!> Y$ there is a corresponding function $\overline{\phi} : X \to Y$ defined by $\overline{\phi}(x) = \phi^{n_x}(x)$, the function obtained by iterating ϕ. Suppose that $\phi : X \rightarrow\!\!\!\!+\!\!> Y$, $\psi : Y \rightarrow\!\!\!\!+\!\!> Z$, and $\theta : X' \rightarrow\!\!\!\!+\!\!> Y'$ are pseudofunctions, and $f : X \to Y$ is a function.

(i) Show that $\lambda = i_2 \nabla_Y (f + 1_Y) : X + Y \to X + Y$ is a pseudofunction from X to Y such that $\overline{\lambda} = f$.

(ii) Show that there exist pseudofunctions $\alpha : X \rightarrow\!\!\!\!+\!\!> Z$, $\beta : X + X' \rightarrow\!\!\!\!+\!\!> Y + Y'$, and $\gamma : X \times X' \rightarrow\!\!\!\!+\!\!> Y \times Y'$ constructed from ϕ, ψ and θ, using the operations of a distributive category, such that

$$\overline{\alpha} = \overline{\psi} \circ \overline{\phi},$$
$$\overline{\beta} = \overline{\phi} + \overline{\theta},$$
$$\overline{\gamma} = \overline{\phi} \times \overline{\theta}.$$

(iii) Given a pseudofunction μ from X to $X + Y$ and a function ord : $X \to \mathbb{N}$ such that if $\mu(x) \in X$ then $\mathrm{ord}(\mu(x)) < \mathrm{ord}(x)$, then construct, using the operations of a distributive category, a pseudofunction $\nu : X \rightarrow\!\!\!\!+\!\!> Y$ such that

$$\overline{\nu}(x) = \overline{\mu}^{m_x}(x) \quad \text{for some } m_x \leq \mathrm{ord}(x) + 1.$$

(iv) Given a pseudofunction $\xi : X \rightarrow\!\!\!\!+\!\!> X$, construct, using the operations of a distributive category, a function $g : X + V \to X + V$ (for some set V) such that if $n_0, n_1, n_2, \cdots$ is the sequence of values of n such that $g^n(x) \in X$ then

$$g^{n_k}(x) = \overline{\xi}^k(x).$$

Chapter 5

Categories of Functors

We have discussed, in Chapter 1, isomorphisms of categories, but not morphisms of categories; that is, general ways of getting from one category to another.

Morphisms of categories are called *functors*.

§1. Functors

Before defining functors, it is useful to introduce some notation. Given a category $\mathbf{A}$ and two objects A_1, A_2 in $\mathbf{A}$ we denote the set of arrows from A_1 to A_2 by

$$\mathrm{Hom}_{\mathbf{A}}(A_1, A_2).$$

Definition. If $\mathbf{A}$ and $\mathbf{B}$ are categories then a *functor* from $\mathbf{A}$ to $\mathbf{B}$ consists of functions

$$F_{\mathrm{obj}} : \mathrm{obj}\,\mathbf{A} \to \mathrm{obj}\,\mathbf{B},$$

and, for each pair of objects A_1, A_2 of $\mathbf{A}$,

$$F_{A_1,A_2} : \mathrm{Hom}_{\mathbf{A}}(A_1, A_2) \to \mathrm{Hom}_{\mathbf{B}}(F(A_1), F(A_2)),$$

satisfying

$$F(1_A) = 1_{FA},$$

$$F(\beta \cdot \alpha) = F\beta \cdot F\alpha \quad \text{if} \quad A_1 \xrightarrow{\alpha} A_2 \xrightarrow{\beta} A_3.$$

Note. We usually denote all the functions F_{obj}, F_{A_1,A_2} by the one symbol F, for simplicity.

Let us try to understand what functors are by looking at examples and different points of view.

Functors are 'homomorphisms' between categories

They are the structure-preserving maps between categories. I would like to point out some special cases.

Example 1. If $\mathbf{A}$ and $\mathbf{B}$ are groups (one object categories, with every arrow invertible), then a functor $F : \mathbf{A} \to \mathbf{B}$ is a function $F : \mathrm{arr}\,\mathbf{A} \to \mathrm{arr}\,\mathbf{B}$, such that $F(\alpha\beta) = F\alpha \cdot F\beta$ and $F1_A = 1_{FA}$. Therefore, F is a group homomorphism.

Example 2. If **A** and **B** are posets, then a functor from **A** to **B** is an order-preserving map.

Note. From this point of view we would expect to have an identity functor $1_{\mathbf{A}} : \mathbf{A} \to \mathbf{A}$ for a category **A**, and there is one. For each A and f in **A** the identity functor is defined by

$$\begin{aligned} 1_{\mathbf{A}} : A &\mapsto A \\ f &\mapsto f. \end{aligned}$$

We also expect to be able to form the composite of two functors,

$$\mathbf{A} \xrightarrow{F} \mathbf{B} \xrightarrow{G} \mathbf{C},$$

and that we can do:

$$\begin{aligned} GF(A) &= G(F(A)), \\ GF(f) &= G(F(f)). \end{aligned}$$

It is easy to check that GF is a functor. Categories and functors now themselves form a category **Cat**. An isomorphism of categories, as defined earlier, is just an isomorphism in **Cat**.

Logical problems arise if we ask whether **Cat** is an *object* of **Cat**. The usual way mathematicians handle this logical problem is to make a distinction between *large* and *small* categories. The objects of **Cat** are small categories, while **Cat** is a large category, and hence **Cat** is not an object of itself. The problem really arose earlier when we described **Sets**. Is the set of objects of **Sets** an object of **Sets**? So we need to distinguish between large and small sets. These distinctions are important in computer science and mathematics, but we will not go further into the matter, since nothing in this book depends essentially upon them.

Functors are constructions

One idea about categories is that they formalise the notion 'type of structure'.

From this point of view, functors are 'constructions' which build, from objects of one category, objects of another.

Example 3. Given a finite set X we can construct a vector space FX with basis X. Take FX to be the set of all formal finite linear combinations of elements in X. This gives the construction:

$$\begin{aligned} \mathbf{Sets} &\to \mathbf{Vect} \\ X &\mapsto FX. \end{aligned}$$

Many natural constructions like this are *functorial*; that is, there is an obvious way to extend the definition to arrows and make F into a functor. In this example, given a function $f : X \to Y$, define Ff by

$$Ff: \; FX \longrightarrow FY$$
$$\sum \lambda_i x_i \longmapsto \sum \lambda_i f(x_i).$$

It is easy to check that Ff is linear; $F1_X = 1_X$, $F(gf) = Fg \cdot Ff$, and so F is a functor.

Often mathematicians describe a construction, say it is functorial, and do not bother to say what the two categories are, or tell you the definition on maps.

Example 4. (An example from computer science.) Given any set X we can construct a new set $Stack(X)$, the set of all stacks of X. This suggests that it may be possible to extend $Stack$ to a functor

$$Stack : \mathbf{Sets} \to \mathbf{Sets}.$$

To do this we need to define $Stack$ on functions; that is, to define $Stack(f) : Stack(X) \to Stack(Y)$, for each function $f : X \to Y$. The obvious definition is:

$$Stack(f) \; : \; Stack(X) \longrightarrow Stack(Y)$$
$$o \longmapsto o$$
$$x_1 x_2 \cdots x_n \longmapsto f(x_1)f(x_2)\cdots f(x_n).$$

Have we succeeded in defining a functor? We need to check the properties $Stack(1_X) = 1_{Stack(X)}$, and $Stack(gf) = Stack(g)Stack(f)$. The first is obvious. Let's check the second:

$$\begin{aligned} Stack(gf)(x_1 x_2 \cdots x_n) &= gf(x_1)gf(x_2)\cdots gf(x_n) \\ &= Stack(g)(f(x_1)\cdots f(x_n)) \\ &= Stack(g)Stack(f)(x_1 \cdots x_n), \end{aligned}$$

as required.

Functors are representations (or models) of categories

The idea here is that a functor, $F : \mathbf{A} \to \mathbf{B}$, is a picture, or model, of the category $\mathbf{A}$ in the category $\mathbf{B}$.

Example 5. Let $\mathbf{B} = \mathbf{Sets}$. I claim that a functor $F : \mathbf{A} \to \mathbf{Sets}$ is a way of picturing $\mathbf{A}$ as consisting of sets and functions; that is where we started, remember?

Example 6. Let $\mathbf{A}$ be the category

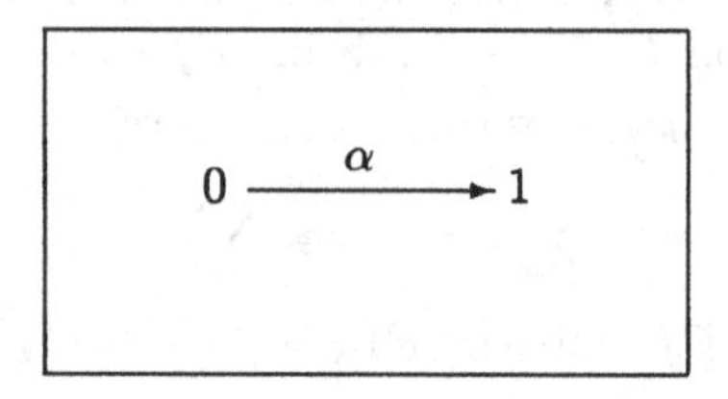

(I have omitted identity arrows.)

To give a functor $F : \mathbf{A} \to \mathbf{Sets}$, we have to give two sets, $F0$ and $F1$, and a function $F0 \overset{F\alpha}{\to} F1$; there is no choice for F on identity arrows. That is, we have to give a representation of $\mathbf{A}$ in terms of sets and functions.

Example 7. If $\mathbf{A}$ is a group, a functor $F : \mathbf{A} \to \mathbf{Sets}$ consists of a set X corresponding to the one object of $\mathbf{A}$, and to each $\alpha \in \mathbf{A}$, a permutation $F\alpha : X \to X$ such that for each α and β in $\mathbf{A}$, $F(\beta\alpha) = F\beta \cdot F\alpha$.

Such a functor is commonly called a *permutation representation* of the group.

Note. Given any category $\mathbf{A}$ and any object $B \in \mathbf{B}$, we can define the *constant functor at* B, denoted $\lceil B \rceil$, from $\mathbf{A}$ to $\mathbf{B}$ as follows:

$$\begin{array}{rrcl} \lceil B \rceil : & \mathbf{A} & \longrightarrow & \mathbf{B} \\ & A & \longmapsto & B \\ & (f : A_1 \to A_2) & \longmapsto & (1_B : B \to B). \end{array}$$

This is not a very good picture of $\mathbf{A}$! All arrows are represented by identity arrows.

Definition. We call a functor $F : \mathbf{A} \to \mathbf{B}$ *faithful* if for each pair of objects A_1, A_2, the function $F : \mathrm{Hom}_{\mathbf{A}}(A_1, A_2) \to \mathrm{Hom}_{\mathbf{B}}(FA_1, FA_2)$ is injective. If, instead, all these functions are surjective we call F *full*.

A functor $F : \mathbf{A} \to \mathbf{B}$ is faithful if, given two arrows $f_1, f_2 : A_1 \to A_2$ such that $Ff_1 = Ff_2$, then $f_1 = f_2$.

A faithful functor F from a group $\mathbf{A}$ into $\mathbf{Sets}$ is a faithful permutation representation of $\mathbf{A}$ (a representation in which different group elements are represented by different permutations).

Example 8. Consider the following category **A**:

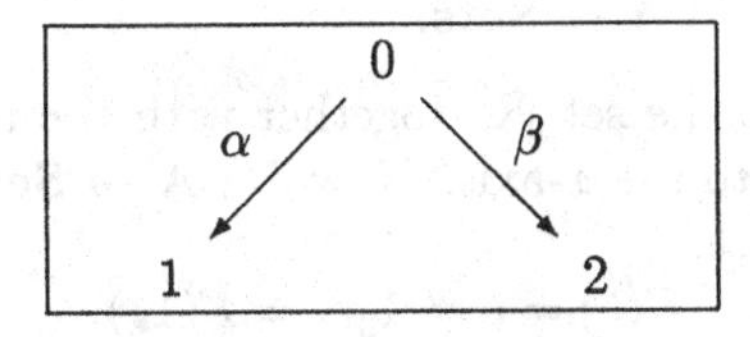

To give a functor from **A** to **Sets** it suffices to give three sets, and two functions, in the shape of **A**; that is, sets and functions like

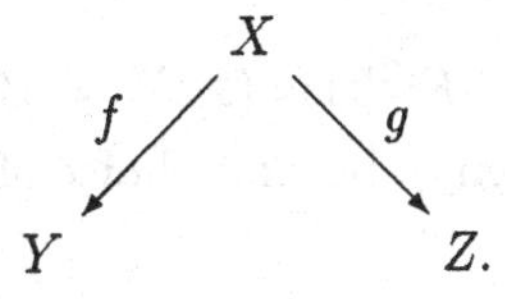

As a special example of this, take the set $X = \{0, 1\}$ and the functions

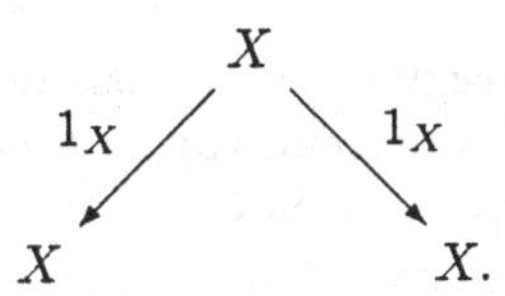

This is the constant functor at X from **A** to **Sets**.

Remark. From this last example we can see that a functor $\mathbf{A} \to \mathbf{B}$ consists of 'several objects and arrows of **B**, taken together as a single entity'. Three sets and two functions constitute a single functor. This is important in computer science, where you often want to consider complex entities consisting of many data types, and functions between them, as a single unified entity.

In order to get more feeling of what a functor is, I would like to do several more examples considering all the functors between two fixed categories **A** and **B**.

Example 9. A functor from $\mathbf{A} = \{0, 1\}$ to **B** is just a pair of objects of **B**.

Example 10. A functor from $\{0, 1, 2, \cdots, n, \cdots\}$ to **B** is just a sequence of objects in **B**.

Example 11. Consider the category **A** generated by one object $*$ and one arrow $e : * \to *$ satisfying $e^2 = e$. A functor from **A** to **Sets** is a set X with an idempotent function α from X to X. That is,

$$F* = X, \qquad Fe = \alpha,$$
$$\alpha = Fe = F(ee) = FeFe = \alpha\alpha.$$

So, any set X, together with the identity function $\alpha = 1_X$, is an example of a (non-faithful) functor from **A** to **Sets**.

A less trivial example is the set $\mathbb{R}^2$ together with the function $\alpha : \mathbb{R}^2 \to \mathbb{R}^2$, the projection of $\mathbb{R}^2$ onto the x-axis. Now $F : \mathbf{A} \to \mathbf{Sets}$ is a faithful functor, since

$$F(e) = \alpha \neq 1_{\mathbb{R}^2} = F(1_*).$$

Example 12. Consider the free monoid **A** on one generator e. A functor $F : \mathbf{A} \to \mathbf{Sets}$ amounts to a set X with an endomorphism. If $F(e) = \alpha$ then we are forced to take

$$F(e^n) = (Fe)^n = \alpha^n.$$

No matter what $F(e)$ is taken to be, this choice of $F(e^n)$ does satisfy the functor axioms since,

$$F(e^n e^m) = F(e^{n+m}) = \alpha^{n+m} = \alpha^n \alpha^m = F(e^n)F(e^m).$$

Remember that an *imperative program* consists of a state space X and a function $\alpha : X \to X$, constructed in a certain way, and hence an imperative program is an example of a functor from **A** to **Sets**.

Example 13. Consider the following category **A**:

$$1 \rightrightarrows 0$$

A functor from **A** to **Sets** consists of two sets X, Y and two parallel functions,

$$X \underset{d_1}{\overset{d_0}{\rightrightarrows}} Y.$$

But this is the same thing as a directed graph. Think of Y as a set of vertices, and X as a set of directed edges. Then for any edge $\alpha \in X$ we have two assigned vertices $d_0\alpha = a$, say, and $d_1\alpha = b$, say. We picture this as $\alpha : a \to b$.

For example, suppose $X = \{\alpha, \beta, \gamma, \delta, \epsilon\}$ and $Y = \{a, b, c, e\}$, and d_0 and d_1 are the functions

$$\begin{array}{llll} d_0 : & \alpha \longmapsto a & d_1 : & \alpha \longmapsto b \\ d_0 : & \beta \longmapsto b & d_1 : & \beta \longmapsto c \\ d_0 : & \gamma \longmapsto b & d_1 : & \gamma \longmapsto c \\ d_0 : & \delta \longmapsto c & d_1 : & \delta \longmapsto a \\ d_0 : & \epsilon \longmapsto c, & d_1 : & \epsilon \longmapsto e. \end{array}$$

We can picture this as the directed graph:

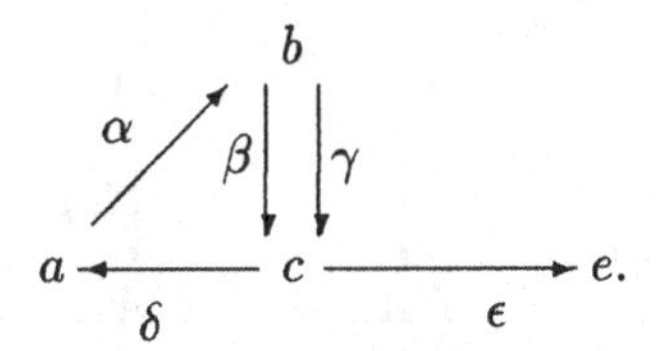

The picture and the two functions $d_0, d_1 : X \to Y$ contain exactly the same information. It is clear how to represent any directed graph by just two sets and two parallel functions.

Example 14. Consider the free monoid $\mathbf{A} = \Sigma^*$ on the alphabet $\Sigma = \{a, b, c, \ldots\}$. A functor $F : \mathbf{A} \to \mathbf{Sets}$ is the same thing as a set X with an endomorphism $f_a : X \to X$ for each letter a in the alphabet Σ.

Certainly for each element $a \in \Sigma$, Fa is an endomorphism of $F(*)$, where $*$ is the one object of $\mathbf{A}$. Write $X = F(*)$ and $f_a = Fa$. Then, if $u = a_1 a_2 a_3 \cdots a_n$ is any arrow in $\mathbf{A}$, the value of F on u is forced to be $f_{a_1} f_{a_2} \cdots f_{a_n}$ since

$$F(u) = F(a_1 a_2 a_3 \cdots a_n) = F(a_1)F(a_2) \cdots F(a_n) = f_{a_1} f_{a_2} \cdots f_{a_n}.$$

So it suffices to give endomorphisms just for the letters of the alphabet. Conversely, any choice of endomorphisms corresponding to the letters of the alphabet is easily seen to give a functor.

Note. Such a thing is a crude model of a computer. Let X be the state space of the computer, and $a, b, c, \ldots$ be the names of inputs. Then $f_a : X \to X$ is the effect of input a on the states. One of the inputs, say c, could be the clock pulse. Other inputs could be inputs from users, interrupts, etc.

Remark. There is a name for a functor from the free monoid on Σ to **Sets**. It is called a *deterministic automaton*. If the state space X is finite then the functor is called a *deterministic finite-state automaton*.

§2. Functor Categories

Given two fixed categories $\mathbf{A}$ and $\mathbf{B}$, the functors from $\mathbf{A}$ to $\mathbf{B}$ actually form a category called $\mathbf{B}^{\mathbf{A}}$, the *functor category* from $\mathbf{A}$ to $\mathbf{B}$.

Definition. Let F, G be functors from $\mathbf{A}$ to $\mathbf{B}$. A *morphism ϕ from F to G* (also called a *natural transformation from F to G*) is a family of arrows of $\mathbf{B}$:

$$\phi_A : FA \to GA \qquad (A \in \mathbf{A}),$$

such that for any arrow $f : A_1 \to A_2$ in $\mathbf{A}$, the following commutes:

$$\begin{array}{ccc} FA_1 & \xrightarrow{\phi_{A_1}} & GA_1 \\ {\scriptstyle Ff}\downarrow & & \downarrow{\scriptstyle Gf} \\ FA_2 & \xrightarrow[\phi_{A_2}]{} & GA_2. \end{array}$$

This commuting diagram is called a *naturality condition.*

That is, ϕ_A is a way of moving from FA to GA compatible with the effect of F and G on arrows of $\mathbf{A}$.

To get a feeling for this, let us look at two examples.

Example 15. Consider the category $\mathbf{A}$:

$$0 \xrightarrow{\alpha} 1$$

A functor F from $\mathbf{A}$ to $\mathbf{B}$ consists of an arrow $F\alpha : F0 \to F1$ in $\mathbf{B}$; similarly, a functor $G : \mathbf{A} \to \mathbf{B}$ consists of an arrow $G\alpha : G0 \to G1$ in $\mathbf{B}$.

A natural transformation ϕ from F to G consists of two arrows (one for each object of $\mathbf{A}$),

$$\phi_0 : F0 \to G0, \qquad \phi_1 : F1 \to G1,$$

satisfying one naturality condition, namely that the following diagram must commute:

$$\begin{array}{ccc} F0 & \xrightarrow{\phi_0} & G0 \\ {\scriptstyle F\alpha}\downarrow & & \downarrow{\scriptstyle G\alpha} \\ F1 & \xrightarrow{\phi_1} & G1. \end{array}$$

So functors from $\mathbf{A}$ to $\mathbf{B}$ are arrows of $\mathbf{B}$, and natural transformations are commutative squares in $\mathbf{B}$.

Example 16. Consider the functor *Stack* : **Sets** $\to$ **Sets**. The following family of functions,

$$reverse_X : Stack(X) \longrightarrow Stack(X) \qquad (X \in \mathbf{Sets})$$

$$x_1 x_2 \cdots x_n \longmapsto x_n \cdots x_2 x_1.$$

is a natural transformation from *Stack* to *Stack*; a fact that is sometimes expressed by computer scientists by saying that *reverse* is a *polymorphic* function. What we have to check is the naturality condition — given a function $f : X \to Y$ the following diagram must commute:

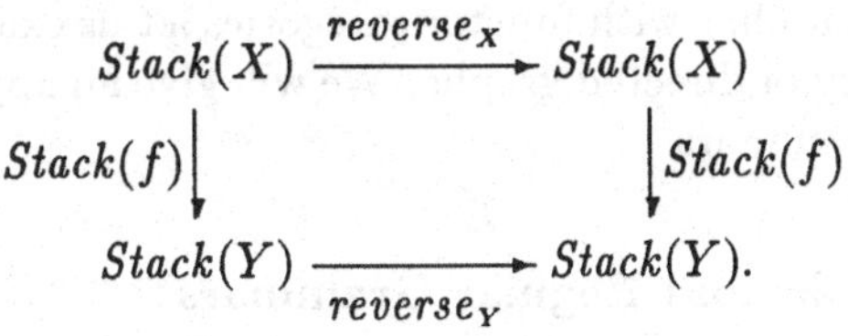

$$\begin{array}{ccc} Stack(X) & \xrightarrow{reverse_X} & Stack(X) \\ {\scriptstyle Stack(f)}\downarrow & & \downarrow{\scriptstyle Stack(f)} \\ Stack(Y) & \xrightarrow[reverse_Y]{} & Stack(Y). \end{array}$$

To check this, take an element $x_1 x_2 \cdots x_n$ from $Stack(X)$ and follow it both ways around the diagram. Going around the top of the diagram we get:

$$x_1 x_2 \cdots x_n \longmapsto x_n \cdots x_2 x_1 \longmapsto f(x_n) \cdots f(x_2) f(x_1).$$

Going round the bottom of the diagram we get:

$$x_1 x_2 \cdots x_n \longmapsto f(x_1) f(x_2) \cdots f(x_n) \longmapsto f(x_n) \cdots f(x_2) f(x_1).$$

So both ways round the diagram yield the same result — the diagram commutes.

Remark. Given natural transformations $\alpha : F \to G$, $\beta : G \to H$, we can form a composite,

$$\beta \cdot \alpha : F \to H,$$

as follows:

$$FA \xrightarrow{(\beta \cdot \alpha)_A} HA \;=\; FA \xrightarrow{\alpha_A} GA \xrightarrow{\beta_A} HA.$$

It is easy to check the naturality of $\beta \cdot \alpha$. Consider the diagram:

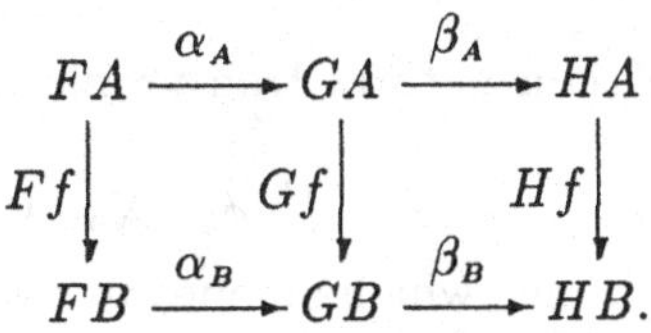

$$\begin{array}{ccccc} FA & \xrightarrow{\alpha_A} & GA & \xrightarrow{\beta_A} & HA \\ {\scriptstyle Ff}\downarrow & & {\scriptstyle Gf}\downarrow & & {\scriptstyle Hf}\downarrow \\ FB & \xrightarrow{\alpha_B} & GB & \xrightarrow{\beta_B} & HB. \end{array}$$

The left and right squares commute since α and β are natural. Hence, the outside rectangle commutes — that is, $\beta \cdot \alpha$ is natural.

It is obvious that the composition is associative, and that there is an identity natural transformation $(1_F)_A = 1_{FA} : FA \to FA$.

Definition. Given categories **A** and **B**, the *functor category*, denoted by $\mathbf{B}^{\mathbf{A}}$, is defined as follows: the objects of $\mathbf{B}^{\mathbf{A}}$ are functors $\mathbf{A} \to \mathbf{B}$; the arrows are natural transformations $F \to G : \mathbf{A} \to \mathbf{B}$; and composition is composition of natural transformations.

In order to become familiar with functor categories let us examine an example in detail — the category of directed graphs. We will give an application of directed graphs to regular grammars.

§3. Directed Graphs and Regular Grammars

The category $\mathbf{Sets}^{\mathbf{A}}$ with **A** being the category

$$1 \rightrightarrows 0$$

is called the *category of directed graphs*, and is sometimes denoted **Grphs**.

An object X of $\mathbf{Sets}^{\mathbf{A}}$ is a functor $\mathbf{A} \to \mathbf{Sets}$. That is X is a pair of sets X_1, X_0 with two functions:

$$X_1 \underset{d_1}{\overset{d_0}{\rightrightarrows}} X_0.$$

The set X_1 is called the set of edges, or arrows, of the graph; the set X_0 is called the set of vertices, or objects, of the graph; d_0 is the domain function, d_1 is the codomain function. We will use the same names d_0, d_1 for the domain and codomain functions of any graph.

Notation. If $\alpha \in X_1$ and $d_0\alpha = x$, $d_1\alpha = y$, we write $\alpha : x \to y$.

Question. What is a morphism of directed graphs (that is, a morphism in $\mathbf{Sets}^{\mathbf{A}}$)?

A morphism $\phi : X \to Y$ is a natural transformation; it consists of a pair of functions,

$$\phi_1 : X_1 \to Y_1, \qquad \phi_0 : X_0 \to Y_0,$$

satisfying naturality conditions, which amount to two commuting diagrams:

$$\begin{array}{ccc} X_1 & \xrightarrow{\phi_1} & Y_1 \\ {\scriptstyle d_0}\downarrow & & \downarrow{\scriptstyle d_0} \\ X_0 & \xrightarrow[\phi_0]{} & Y_0, \end{array} \qquad \begin{array}{ccc} X_1 & \xrightarrow{\phi_1} & Y_1 \\ {\scriptstyle d_1}\downarrow & & \downarrow{\scriptstyle d_1} \\ X_0 & \xrightarrow[\phi_0]{} & Y_0. \end{array}$$

That is, the naturality conditions consist of the two equations:

$$\phi_0 d_0 = d_0 \phi_1,$$
$$\phi_0 d_1 = d_1 \phi_1.$$

In terms of our picture of directed graphs, what is a graph morphism?

Note that ϕ_0 is a function from the objects of X to the objects of Y; and ϕ_1 is a function from the arrows of X to the arrows of Y.

The first of the naturality conditions says that if $\alpha : x_1 \to x_2$ in X, and $\phi_1(\alpha) : y_1 \to y_2$ in Y then

$$y_1 = d_0(\phi_1(\alpha)) = \phi_0(d_0(\alpha)) = \phi_0(x_1).$$

The second of the naturality conditions says that

$$y_2 = d_1(\phi_1(\alpha)) = \phi_0(d_1(\alpha)) = \phi_0(x_2).$$

So the two naturality conditions together say exactly that if $\alpha : x_1 \to x_2$ then $\phi_1(\alpha) : \phi_0(x_1) \to \phi_0(x_2)$.

Note. We often write the same name for ϕ_0 and ϕ_1, calling them both ϕ. Using this convention, a graph morphism from X to Y consists of a function ϕ from the objects of X to the objects of Y, and a function ϕ from the arrows of X to the arrows of Y such that if $\alpha : x_1 \to x_2$ in X then $\phi(\alpha) : \phi(x_1) \to \phi(x_2)$ in Y.

Let's now look at some examples of graph morphisms.

Example 17. If X is the graph

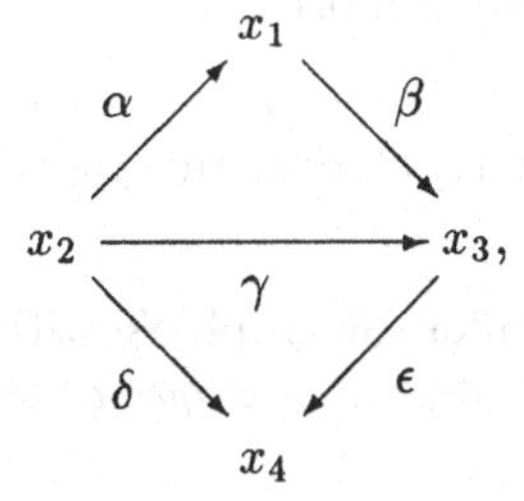

and Y is the graph

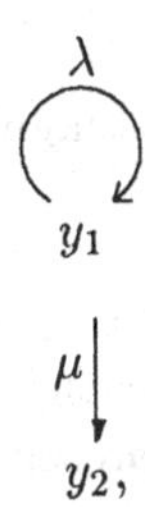

then ϕ, defined as follows, is a graph morphism from X to Y:

$$\begin{aligned}
&\phi(x_1) = \phi(x_2) = \phi(x_3) = y_1, \\
&\phi(x_4) = y_2, \\
&\phi(\alpha) = \phi(\beta) = \phi(\gamma) = \lambda, \\
&\phi(\delta) = \phi(\epsilon) = \mu.
\end{aligned}$$

Example 18. If X is any graph, and I is the graph with one object $*$ and one arrow $\lambda : * \to *$ then there is a unique morphism ϕ from X to I:

$$\begin{aligned}
\phi(x) &= * \quad (\text{for all nodes } \ x \in X), \\
\phi(\alpha) &= \lambda \quad (\text{for all edges } \ \alpha \in X).
\end{aligned}$$

So I is the terminal directed graph.

Example 19. If O is the empty graph and X is any graph, then there is a unique morphism from O to X, and hence O is the initial directed graph.

Remark. In fact, the category of directed graphs shares, with all categories of the form $\mathbf{Sets}^{\mathbf{A}}$, the property that it is a distributive category.

Example 20. An isomorphism in the category of directed graphs is a graph morphism $\phi : X \to Y$ for which ϕ_0, ϕ_1 are both bijections.

Then ϕ_0, ϕ_1 have inverses $\phi_0^{-1} : Y_0 \to X_0$, $\phi_1^{-1} : Y_1 \to X_1$, and the pair of functions ϕ_0^{-1}, ϕ_1^{-1} constitute a morphism of graphs $\phi^{-1} : Y \to X$ inverse to ϕ.

A class of languages of great importance in computer science are the *regular languages*. We will analyse regular languages in this section using graph morphisms.

Let Σ be an alphabet. Consider the graph S_Σ with one object $*$, and with arrows being the elements of Σ *together with a special arrow* ϵ, called the *null symbol.*

Definition. A *regular grammar* is a graph morphism,

$$\phi : X \to S_\Sigma,$$

where X is a finite graph with two distinguished objects J (the beginning object) and K (the end object).

Remark. Notice that every object of X must go to the one object of S_Σ. Further, there is no restriction where the arrows go to under ϕ. Hence, a graph morphism $\phi : X \to S_\Sigma$ may be represented by sketching X and labelling the edges of X with the elements of $\Sigma \cup \{\epsilon\}$ which they go to under ϕ. In other words, a graph morphism from X to S_Σ is a *labelled graph*.

Remark. The notion of regular grammar given above is very close to (but not quite the same as) the notion of *non-deterministic finite-state automaton*. It is called a grammar here because it allows you to generate the words in the language, and also because of the connections with context-free grammars given in Chapter 6.

Example 21. Suppose $\Sigma = \{a, b\}$. The following labelled graph is a regular grammar:

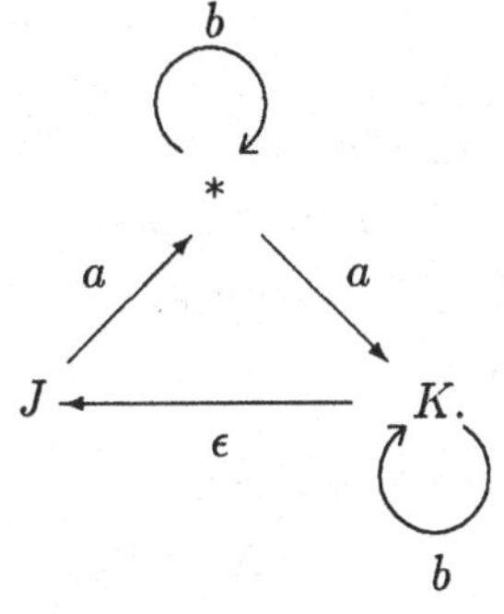

The image of each arrow of the graph in $\Sigma \cup \{\epsilon\}$ is indicated by its label.

Note. A morphism of graphs $\phi : X \to Y$ induces a functor

$$\mathcal{F}\phi : \mathcal{F}X \to \mathcal{F}Y,$$

where $\mathcal{F}X$ and $\mathcal{F}Y$ are the free categories on the graphs X and Y respectively; $\mathcal{F}\phi$ is defined as follows. Suppose

$$x_1 \xrightarrow{\alpha_1} x_2 \xrightarrow{\alpha_2} \cdots \xrightarrow{\alpha_n} x_{n+1}$$

is a path in X; that is, an arrow from x_1 to x_{n+1} in $\mathcal{F}X$. Then

$$\mathcal{F}\phi : (\alpha_n \cdots \alpha_2\alpha_1) \mapsto \phi\alpha_n \cdots \phi\alpha_2\phi\alpha_1.$$

It is easy to see that $\mathcal{F}\phi$ is a functor; it takes concatenation of paths to concatenation of paths.

Example 22. Consider the graph morphism,

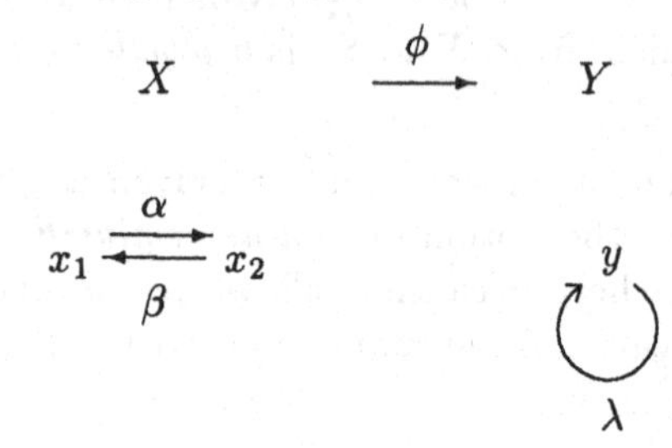

where

$$\phi : \alpha \longmapsto \lambda$$
$$\beta \longmapsto \lambda.$$

Then

$$\mathcal{F}\phi : (\alpha\beta\alpha\beta\alpha\beta\alpha : x_1 \to x_2) \longmapsto (\lambda^7 : y \to y).$$

More generally, $\mathcal{F}\phi$ gives the length of a path,

$$\mathcal{F}\phi : w \mapsto \lambda^n,$$

where n is the length of w.

Example 23. Given a regular grammar

$$\phi : X \to S_\Sigma,$$

then $\mathcal{F}\phi$ takes a path to an element of $(\Sigma \cup \{\epsilon\})^*$ since this is the free category on S_Σ.

Example 24. Consider the grammar

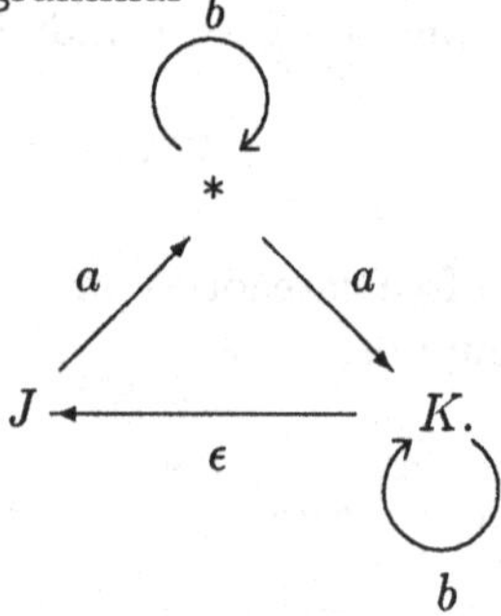

Then $\mathcal{F}\phi$ takes the path

$$J \xrightarrow{a} * \xrightarrow{b} * \xrightarrow{b} * \xrightarrow{a} K \xrightarrow{\epsilon} J \xrightarrow{a} * \xrightarrow{b} * \xrightarrow{b} * \xrightarrow{b} K$$

to the word

$$bbba\epsilon abba.$$

Note. Given a word in $(\Sigma \cup \{\epsilon\})^*$, we can get a word in Σ^* by just equating ϵ to the identity (that is by omitting ϵ's).

Definition. The subset of Σ^* obtained from a regular grammar by taking all paths from J to K and applying $\mathcal{F}\phi$ and then omitting ϵ's is called the *regular language* generated by the grammar.

Example 25. Suppose $\Sigma = \{a, b, c\}$. Then $\{a, b\}$ is a regular language.

Clearly,

$$J \underset{b}{\overset{a}{\rightrightarrows}} K$$

is a grammar for this language.

Example 26. Suppose $\Sigma = \{a\}$. Then $\{a^3, a^4, a^5, \ldots\}$ is a regular language.

Clearly the following is a grammar generating this language:

$$J \xrightarrow{a} * \xrightarrow{a} * \xrightarrow{a} K. \quad (\text{with a loop } a \text{ at } K)$$

Example 27. Suppose $\Sigma = \{a, b\}$. Then $\{1, a, a^2, \ldots, b, b^2, \ldots\}$ is a regular language.

Clearly,

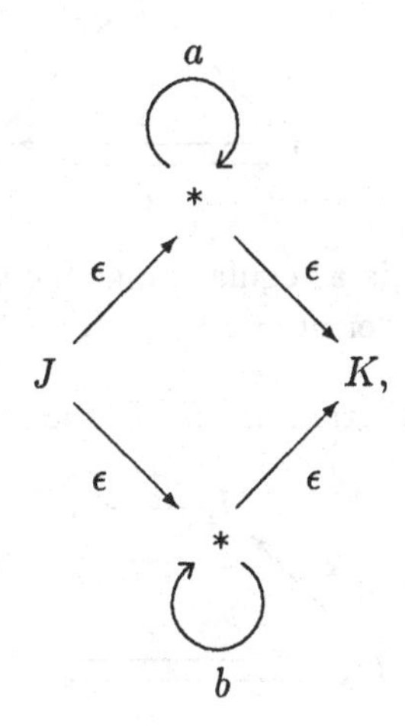

is a grammar for this language.

Example 28. Given two regular languages $U, V \subseteq \Sigma^*$, then the union $U \cup V$ is also a regular language.

If

$$J_1 \xrightarrow{U} K_1$$

denotes a grammar for U and

$$J_2 \xrightarrow{V} K_2$$

denotes a grammar for V then, clearly,

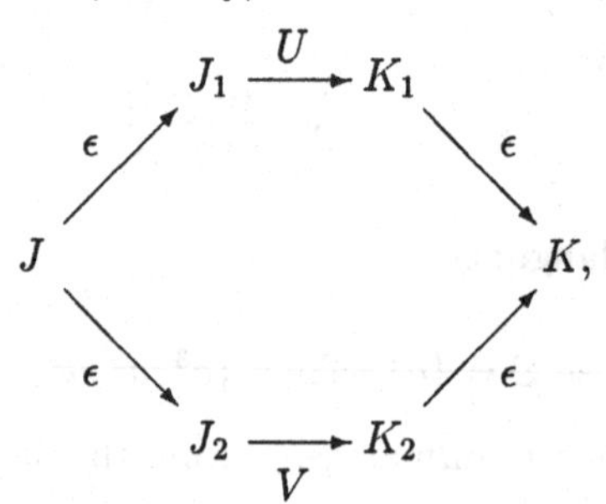

is a grammar for $U \cup V$.

Example 29. Suppose $\Sigma = \{a, b\}$. Then

$$U = \{1, ab, abab, ababab, \ldots, (ab)^n, \ldots\}$$

is a regular language.

The grammar for U is

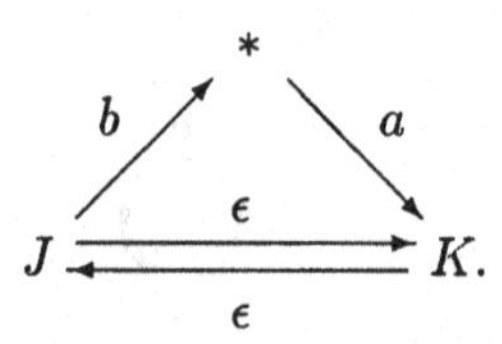

Example 30. If $U \subseteq \Sigma^*$ is a regular language then so is U^*, the set obtained by concatenating any number of words in U.

If $J_1 \xrightarrow{U} K_1$ represents a grammar for U then

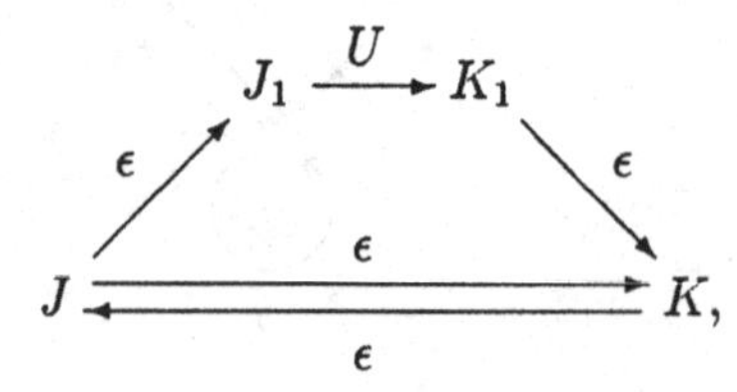

is a grammar for U^*.

Example 31. If U is a language and V is a language, then so is

$$UV = \{uv : u \in U, v \in V\}.$$

If

$$J_1 \xrightarrow{U} K_1$$

represents a grammar for U and

$$J_2 \xrightarrow{V} K_2$$

represents a grammar for V then

$$J \xrightarrow{\epsilon} J_1 \xrightarrow{V} K_1 \xrightarrow{\epsilon} J_2 \xrightarrow{U} K_2 \xrightarrow{\epsilon} K$$

is a grammar for UV.

Question. Are there any subsets of Σ^* which are not regular languages?

Example 32. Consider $\Sigma = \{a, b\}$. Then $U = \{a^k b a^k;\ k = 0, 1, 2, \ldots\}$ is *not* a regular language.

The idea is that to construct a word in a regular language does not require any memory other than the graph morphism and the current place in the graph; that is, it requires a fixed, finite amount of memory. Whereas in U, constructing $a^k b a^k$ requires remembering k; unbounded memory is required.

Proof. Suppose $\phi : X \to S_\Sigma$ is a grammar defining U. Suppose the number of objects in graph X is n, and that k is greater than n.

Now $a^k b a^k$ is the image of a path in X. Part of that path lands on the first factor a^k. That part of the path is something like:

$$x_1 \xrightarrow{a} x_2 \xrightarrow{\epsilon} x_3 \xrightarrow{a} x_4 \xrightarrow{\epsilon} x_5 \xrightarrow{a} \cdots \xrightarrow{\epsilon} x_{l-1} \xrightarrow{a} x_l.$$

Look at the objects at the beginning of the a's. There are $k > n$ such objects but there are only n objects in the graph. Hence at least two of the objects at the beginning of a's must be the same. That is, there must be a loop in the path:

$$\begin{array}{ccccc} & & x_{i+1} \longrightarrow \cdots \longrightarrow x_j & & \\ & & {\scriptstyle a}\nwarrow \quad \swarrow & & \\ x_1 \xrightarrow{a} x_2 \xrightarrow{\epsilon} \cdots \longrightarrow & & x_i & & \longrightarrow \cdots \xrightarrow{a} x_l. \end{array}$$

But this means we get a new path in X by repeating the loop. The new path will go to

$$a^k b a^{k+m}$$

if m is the number of a's in the loop ($m \geq 1$). This is a contradiction because $a^k ba^{k+m}$ is not of the right form to be in U. ∎

Remark. I have shown that any singleton (one-element) subset of Σ is a regular language, and that regular languages are closed under operations,

$$U^*, \qquad UV, \qquad U \cup V.$$

These operations on subsets are called *regular operations*. Any expression formed by repeated use of regular operations, beginning with singleton subsets, is called a *regular expression*.

3.1 Theorem. (Kleene) A subset of Σ^* is a regular language if and only if it can be described by a regular expression; that is, if and only if it can be obtained from singleton subsets of Σ by applying a finite number of operations U^*, UV and $U \cup V$.

Example 33. Consider the grammar

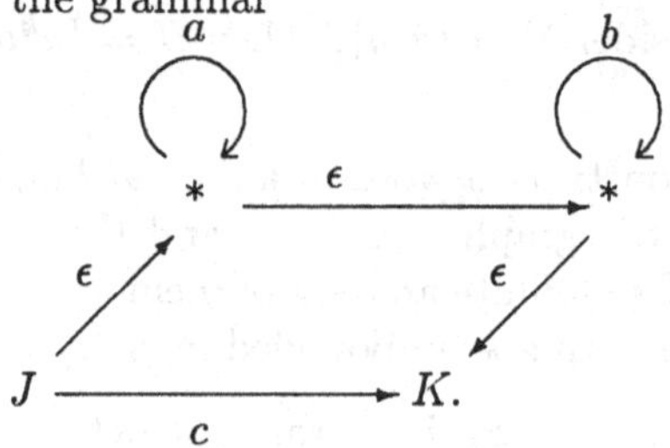

A little thought shows that the language generated by this grammar is:

$$U = \{b^k a^l; k, l = 0, 1, 2, \cdots\} \cup \{c\}.$$

Clearly, $U = \{b\}^*\{a\}^* \cup \{c\}$.

To simplify the notation, we will denote one-element subsets by the element contained in them. So we will denote the regular language of this example by $U = b^* a^* \cup c$.

Proof. We have shown that any regular expression describes a regular language. It only remains to prove that any regular language can be so obtained.

First notice that we can always find a grammar for a regular language without any null symbols ϵ, provided that, instead of one beginning object and one end object, we allow one beginning object and a finite set of end objects. Given a grammar with null symbols we can modify it as follows: if there is a path from x to y consisting of null symbols and one $a \in \Sigma$, put a new edge $a : x \to y$ (unless one already exists); if there is a path $x \to K$, K the end object, consisting only consisting only of null symbols of null symbols then call x also an end object; finally, remove all edges with null symbols. This results in a new grammar describing the same language, containing no null symbols.

Example 34. Applying this procedure to the grammar (with beginning J and end K)

we get a new grammar with no null symbols,

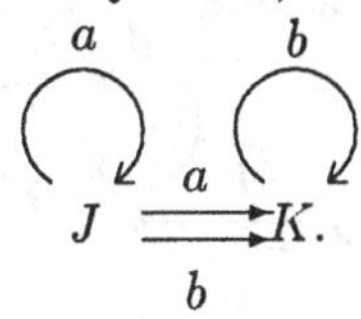

but now with *two* end objects J and K.

The language generated by either of these grammars is

$$\{b^l a^k; l, k = 0, 1, 2, \ldots\}.$$

Resuming the proof, we can now assume that the grammar has no null symbols. We can also assume that it has only one end object, because the language obtained from several end objects is just a union of the sublanguages obtained by taking each of the end objects separately. So if each of these sublanguages is given by a regular expression, then so is the whole language.

Consider a grammar $\phi : X \to S_\Sigma$, with no null symbols, and with one beginning object J, and one end object K. If x, y are objects of X, let $U_{x,y}$ denote the set of labelled edges from x to y.

We will successively modify the graph X by removing objects, but always keeping the same paths from J to K. At each stage the sets $U_{x,y}$ will change, but will always be given by regular expressions.

Consider an object $z \in X$ with $z \neq J, K$. Paths going through z come in from another object, circle around z, and then go out to another object (perhaps repeatedly). So we get the same paths from J to K if we omit z, but augment the edges from x to y (for all pairs x, $y \neq z$) by $U_{z,y}(U_{z,z})^* U_{x,z}$.

Note. The graph may become infinite, but this doesn't affect the argument.

We repeatedly remove objects in this way until we obtain the graph

$$U_{J,J} \circlearrowright J \underset{U_{K,J}}{\overset{U_{J,K}}{\rightleftarrows}} K \circlearrowleft U_{K,K}.$$

Then the set of paths from J to K, and hence the language described by the grammar is

$$U_{K,K}^* U_{J,K} \left(U_{J,J} \cup U_{K,J} U_{K,K}^* U_{J,K}\right)^* .$$

■

Example 35. Consider the grammar

$$J \xrightarrow{a} x \underset{c}{\overset{b}{\rightleftarrows}} z \xrightarrow{e} y \xrightarrow{f} K, \quad \text{with a loop } d \text{ at } z.$$

Removing the vertex z and modifying the sets of arrows by the rule given, we obtain the graph

$$J \xrightarrow{a} x \xrightarrow{ed^*b} y \xrightarrow{f} K, \quad \text{with a loop } cd^*b \text{ at } x.$$

Next, omitting vertex y, we get the graph

$$J \xrightarrow{a} x \xrightarrow{fed^*b} K, \quad \text{with a loop } cd^*b \text{ at } x.$$

Finally, omitting x we get the graph

$$J \xrightarrow{fed^*b(cd^*b)^*a} K.$$

Hence the language given by the grammar is

$$fed^*b(cd^*b)^*a.$$

§4. Automata and Imperative Programs with Input

Let Σ be an alphabet and consider functors from the free monoid on Σ to **Sets**. We have seen earlier that such a functor amounts to a set X (the state space) and functions $f_a : X \to X$ (for each $a \in \Sigma$).

If the state space is finite, the functor is called a deterministic finite-state automaton or machine, and the elements of Σ are called atomic inputs. We can sketch all the information in the automaton by drawing a labelled graph with vertices, the states of X, and arrows as follows: if $f_a(x) = y$ put an arrow from x to y labelled with a. The arrow represents the fact that input a changes the state from x to y. Since f_a is a function, this graph has the following characteristic property; that given x and a there is a unique arrow out of x labelled with a.

We can think about languages in a new way. Instead of giving a grammar, that is, a way of producing words, we could give an automaton which recognizes whether or not a word is in the language.

Definition. A *finite-state recognizer* is a finite-state automaton with one specified start state J and a finite set $K_1, K_2, \ldots$ of specified end states.

A recognizer defines a subset U of Σ^* as follows:

$$a_n a_{n-1} \cdots a_1 \in U \qquad \text{if} \qquad f_{a_n} \cdots f_{a_2} f_{a_1}(J) = K_i$$

for some end state K_i.

4.1 Theorem. The set $U \subseteq \Sigma^*$ is recognized by finite-state recognizer if and only if U is a regular language.

Proof. A recognizer is a special type of regular grammar and hence any set recognized by an automaton is a regular language.

Conversely, given a grammar X (without null characters), we will show how to construct an automaton which recognizes the same language as that generated by the grammar.

Take the states of the automaton to be the subsets of the vertices of X. Put an arrow $a : Y_1 \to Y_2$ if $Y_2 = \{y_2 : \exists y_1 \in Y_1 \text{ and } \exists a : y_1 \to y_2 \text{ in the grammar}\}$.

Given Y_1 there is a unique arrow a out of Y_1; that is, we have defined a finite-state machine. I still have to specify the start and end states. Take the start state to be $\{J\}$, where J is the start object of the grammar; take the end states to be all subsets containing at least one end object of the grammar.

It is straightforward to check that this machine recognizes the same language as the grammar generates.

Example 36. Consider the grammar

$$a \circlearrowright J \overset{a}{\underset{b}{\rightrightarrows}} K \circlearrowleft b,$$

with beginning object J, and end objects J, K. The language generated by this grammar is

$$\{b^n a^m; m, n = 0, 1, 2, \ldots\}.$$

Let's now construct a finite-state machine which recognizes this language. The states are subsets of the objects of the grammar; that is,

$$\varnothing, \qquad \{J\}, \qquad \{K\}, \qquad \{J, K\}.$$

Further, $a : Y \to Z$ is in the machine if

$$Z = \{z; \exists y \in Y \text{ and } \exists a : y \to z, \text{ in the grammar}\}.$$

We sketch the machine below:

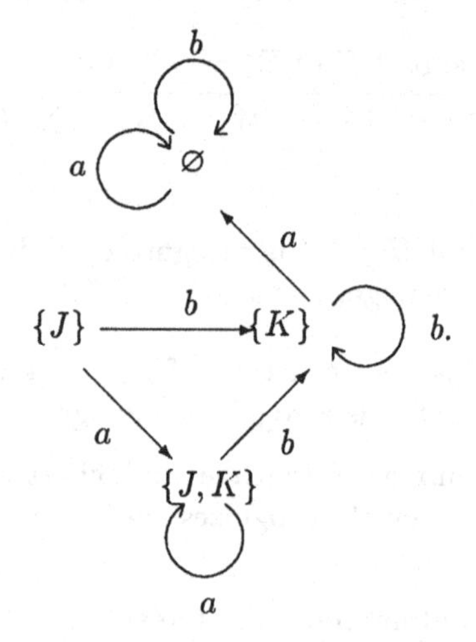

The start state is $\{J\}$. The end states are $\{J\}$, $\{K\}$, and $\{J, K\}$.

Imperative programs with input

Earlier we discussed isolated imperative programs. An isolated imperative program was a state space X and a function $f : X \to X$ constructed out of some given functions using the operations available in a distributive category.

Definition. Given an alphabet Σ, an *imperative program with input from* Σ is a functor $\Sigma^* \to$ **Sets**, constructed out of given functions using the operations available in a distributive category. That is, it is a set X (the state space) and functions $f_a : X \to X$ $(a \in \Sigma)$ constructed from given functions in the appropriate way.

A *behaviour* of an imperative program consists of the effect of a sequence of inputs on an initial state,

$$x_0 \xmapsto{f_{a_1}} x_1 \xmapsto{f_{a_2}} x_2 \xmapsto{f_{a_3}} \cdots,$$

where $f_{a_i}(x_{i-1}) = x_i$.

Example 37. Suppose the given functions are *add*, *multiply*, and $test_{x \leq y} : \mathsf{IR} \times \mathsf{IR} \to \mathbf{B}$. Construct an imperative program which accepts as input a natural number, then calculates $n!$, then accepts another natural number, and so on.

Take the state space to be $X = \mathsf{IR} \times \mathsf{IR} \times (I + I)$, and the alphabet of inputs to be $\Sigma = \{clock\} \cup \mathsf{IN}$. Notice that *clock* is a single symbol, and that there are an infinite number of symbols in IN.

We have to give functions from X to X for each input letter; that is, f_{clock} and f_n for each $n \in \mathsf{IN}$.

Denote a typical element of X by (p, d, t). The idea is that when $t = 0$ the clock input is enabled and the calculation takes place; the number inputs are disabled. Conversely, when $t = 1$ the clock input is disabled (no calculation takes place); the number inputs are enabled — that is, we can enter a number.

A suitable clock function is

$$\begin{aligned} f_{clock} \; : \mathsf{IR}^2 \times (I+I) &\longrightarrow \mathsf{IR}^2 \times (I+I) \\ (p,d,0) &\longmapsto \begin{cases} (p \cdot d, d-1, 0) & \text{if } d \geq 1 \\ (p,d,1) & \text{if } d < 1 \end{cases} \\ (p,d,1) &\longmapsto (p,d,1). \end{aligned}$$

We have seen in Chapter 3, §3, that if the initial state is $(1, n, 0)$ then repeated clock inputs lead to the eventual state being $(n!, 0, 1)$. The value of t is 0 until this result is reached.

Now let's look at f_n ($n \in \mathsf{IN}$). We would like it to be the case that if $t = 0$, then f_n is the identity function. When $t = 1$ we would like f_n to change the state to $(1, n, 0)$, the initial state of the computation of $n!$. So we would like f_n to be

$$\begin{aligned} f_n \; : \mathsf{IR}^2 \times (I+I) &\longrightarrow \mathsf{IR}^2 \times (I+I) \\ (p,d,0) &\longmapsto (p,d,0) \\ (p,d,1) &\longmapsto (1,n,0). \end{aligned}$$

It is clear that f_{clock} and f_n ($n \in \mathsf{IN}$) are all constructible from the given functions using the operations of a distributive category, and hence we have defined an imperative program.

Further, it is clear that the behaviour is as follows. While $t = 0$, any clock input results in a step of the factorial computation, and any number input has no effect; when the factorial computation is complete a clock input changes t to 1. While $t = 1$, any clock input has no effect; any number input initializes the factorial calculation, changing t to 0.

Example 38. Consider two programs: the first with input alphabet $\Sigma_1 = \{a\}$, state space X and action $f_a : X \to X$; the second with input alphabet $\Sigma_2 = \{b\}$, state space Y and action $f_b : Y \to Y$. Think of this as modelling two different machines with two different users.

Now, consider two new programs with alphabet $\Sigma = \Sigma_1 \cup \Sigma_2$. Each of these new programs may be thought of as a single machine with two users. The actions corresponding to alphabet Σ_1 are the actions available to the first user; those corresponding to alphabet Σ_2 are those available to the second user.

Program 1 has state space $X \times Y$ and actions

$$g_a = f_a \times 1_Y : X \times Y \to X \times Y,$$
$$g_b = 1_X \times f_b : X \times Y \to X \times Y.$$

Program 2 has state space $X + Y$ and actions

$$h_a = f_a + 1_Y : X + Y \to X + Y,$$
$$h_b = 1_X + f_b : X + Y \to X + Y.$$

The difference between these two programs is fundamental in computer science.

Program 1 allows the two users to work independently of each other. At any time, g_a changes the state which is of interest to the first user; g_b does the same for the second user.

With Program 2 however, the two users are in total conflict. If the initial state belongs to the first component of $X + Y$ then every input from the first user has effect; no input of the second user has any effect. If the initial state belongs to the second component then the roles are reversed.

Remark. In our analysis of imperative programs we have in effect described a programming language where the allowable operations are those of a distributive category. If G is the graph of given functions we call this language IMP(G). Wafaa Khalil has shown how to write a surprisingly simple interpreter for IMP(G) in IMP(H), where H is a certain graph extending G.

§5. The Specification of Functions

An important development in programming languages is the move towards programming by *specification* of goals or functions, as distinct from imperative programming. Often the specification actually contains the means for the goal to be computed. This is the idea behind logic and functional languages.

Example 39. The function

$$f : \mathbb{N} \longrightarrow \mathbb{N}$$
$$x \longmapsto 2x,$$

is specified (even without knowing multiplication or addition of numbers) by the equations

$$f(0) = 0,$$
$$f(x+1) = f(x) + 1 + 1.$$

Not only do these equations specify f, they also describe how to compute f. For example,

$$\begin{aligned} f(0+1+1+1) &= f(0+1+1)+1+1 \\ &= f(0+1)+1+1+1+1 \\ &= f(0)+1+1+1+1+1+1 \\ &= 0+1+1+1+1+1+1. \end{aligned}$$

In fact, what is really going on here is that the specification is a set of generators and relations for a category which contains the arrow f. More precisely, the specification above consists of two graphs, one which specifies the data and one which specifies the function.

⋆ The data graph *Data* has two objects I and N and two arrows

$$0 : I \to N, \qquad s : N \to N.$$

You should think of the symbol 0 as the number 0, and s as the successor function. The arrows in the free category on this graph from I to N are of the form $s^n 0$ and hence may be identified with natural numbers; the natural number n is the nth successor of 0.

⋆ The function graph *Function* contains *Data*, but has one extra arrow $f : N \to N$.

As well as these two graphs, the specification contains a finite set, *Equation*, of equations between paths in the function graph. In this example *Equation* consists of

$$fs = ssf, \qquad f0 = 0.$$

Definition. A *functional specification* consists of two graphs,

$$Data \subseteq Function,$$

and a set, *Equation*, of equations between paths in *Function*. Further *Data* has three specified objects, I, J, K; *Function* has a specified arrow $f : J \to K$.

A functional specification determines a relation

$$\overline{f} : Paths_{Data}(I, J) \to Paths_{Data}(I, K)$$

as follows: $\overline{f}(\pi) = \sigma$ if $f\pi = \sigma$ is deducible in *Function* from the equations in *Equation*.

Example 40. In Example 39, $J = K = N$. The relation specified is

$$\overline{f} : Paths(I, N) \longrightarrow Paths(I, N)$$

$$s^n 0 \longmapsto s^m 0,$$

if $fs^n 0 = s^m 0$ is deducible from $fs = ssf$ and $f0 = 0$. It is clear that the function specified is

$$\overline{f} : s^n 0 \mapsto s^{2n} 0.$$

Note. Although the idea I began with was the specification of *functions*, there is no guarantee that the relation $\overline{f}$ associated with a specification is actually a function. It may be partially defined, or even multiple-valued. In fact, Robbie Gates has shown that the partial functions specifiable from the natural numbers to the natural numbers are precisely the *partial recursive functions*.

We'll now do two examples involving specification of functions defined on lists of elements from the alphabet $\Sigma = \{a_1, a_2, a_3, \ldots\}$.

Example 41. Consider the data graph *Data* with three objects I, L, and N and arrows

$$0 : I \to N, \qquad s : N \to N,$$
$$o : I \to L, \qquad a_1, a_2, a_3, \ldots : L \to L.$$

Then a path from I to N is a natural number $s^n 0$, and a path from I to L is a list $a_1 a_2 \cdots a_n o$ of elements from Σ; think of o as the empty list, and each letter a as appending a letter to the list.

Consider the function graph *Function* consisting of *Data* together with one extra arrow $length : L \to N$. Consider also *Equation* consisting of:

$$length \cdot a_i = s \cdot length \qquad (a_i \in \Sigma),$$
$$length \cdot o = 0.$$

(The first of these equations says that if you append an element to a list, and then calculate the length, you get the same result as first calculating the length, and then adding one.) Take the specified objects to be I, L and N, and the specified arrow to be *length*. The function specified,

$$\overline{length} : Paths(I,L) \to Paths(I,N),$$

gives the length of a list. Here is a typical computation:

$$\begin{aligned} length \cdot a_1 \cdot a_3 \cdot a_3 \cdot a_2 \cdot o &= s \cdot length \cdot a_3 \cdot a_3 \cdot a_2 \cdot o \\ &= s \cdot s \cdot length \cdot a_3 \cdot a_2 \cdot o \\ &= s \cdot s \cdot s \cdot length \cdot a_2 \cdot o \\ &= s \cdot s \cdot s \cdot s \cdot length \cdot o \\ &= s \cdot s \cdot s \cdot s \cdot 0 = s^4 0. \end{aligned}$$

Example 42. We now assume that the alphabet Σ is ordered, say $a_1 < a_2 < a_3 < \cdots$. Consider data graph *Data* consisting of two objects I and L and arrows $o : I \to L$, $a_1, a_2, a_3, \ldots : L \to L$.

Consider the function graph *Function* with the same objects and arrows as *Data* supplemented by two arrows, $transfer : L \to L$ and $sort : L \to L$. The idea we have in mind is that *sort* is the function which sorts lists, and *transfer* is the function which alters a list in the following way: it takes the leftmost element of a list and moves it to the left of the first element which is larger or the same.

Consider set *Equation* of equations consisting of

$$\begin{aligned} sort \cdot o &= o, \\ sort \cdot a &= transfer \cdot a \cdot sort \qquad (a \in \Sigma), \\ transfer \cdot o &= o, \\ transfer \cdot a \cdot o &= a \cdot o, \\ transfer \cdot a_i \cdot a_j &= a_i \cdot a_j \qquad (a_i \le a_j \in \Sigma), \\ transfer \cdot a_i \cdot a_j &= a_j \cdot transfer \cdot a_i \qquad (a_i > a_j). \end{aligned}$$

Take the specified objects to be I, L and L, and the specified arrow to be *sort*. The function specified,

$$\overline{sort} : Paths(I,L) \to Paths(I,L),$$

sorts a list into ascending order.

Here is a typical computation:

$$
\begin{aligned}
&sort \cdot a_2 \cdot a_1 \cdot a_3 \cdot a_1 \cdot o = \\
&\quad = transfer \cdot a_2 \cdot sort \cdot a_1 \cdot a_3 \cdot a_1 \cdot o \\
&\quad = transfer \cdot a_2 \cdot transfer \cdot a_1 \cdot sort \cdot a_3 \cdot a_1 \cdot o \\
&\quad = transfer \cdot a_2 \cdot transfer \cdot a_1 \cdot transfer \cdot a_3 \cdot sort \cdot a_1 \cdot o \\
&\quad = transfer \cdot a_2 \cdot transfer \cdot a_1 \cdot transfer \cdot a_3 \cdot transfer \cdot a_1 \cdot sort \cdot o \\
&\quad = transfer \cdot a_2 \cdot transfer \cdot a_1 \cdot transfer \cdot a_3 \cdot transfer \cdot a_1 \cdot o \\
&\quad = transfer \cdot a_2 \cdot transfer \cdot a_1 \cdot transfer \cdot a_3 \cdot a_1 \cdot o \\
&\quad = transfer \cdot a_2 \cdot transfer \cdot a_1 \cdot a_1 \cdot transfer \cdot a_3 \cdot o \\
&\quad = transfer \cdot a_2 \cdot transfer \cdot a_1 \cdot a_1 \cdot a_3 \cdot o \\
&\quad = transfer \cdot a_2 \cdot a_1 \cdot a_1 \cdot a_3 \cdot o \\
&\quad = a_1 \cdot transfer \cdot a_2 \cdot a_1 \cdot a_3 \cdot o \\
&\quad = a_1 \cdot a_1 \cdot transfer \cdot a_2 \cdot a_3 \cdot o \\
&\quad = a_1 \cdot a_1 \cdot a_2 \cdot a_3 \cdot o.
\end{aligned}
$$

§6. What Does *Free* Mean?

The concepts that have been introduced so far in this book are: category, product, sum, distributive law, functor, natural transformation, and *free*. These were all defined precisely, except for the last concept. In terms of these concepts we have been able to describe notions like: grammar, graph, language, machine, imperative program, functional specification, circuit, flowchart, and data types.

Let me now show how the concept of *free* has a precise definition. It turns out to be one of the central concepts of category theory (as it has been a key idea in this book).

We will take as our main example the free monoid on an alphabet A.

Definition. Given a functor

$$\mathbf{A} \xleftarrow{U} \mathbf{B}$$

and an object $A \in \mathbf{A}$. An object $FA \in \mathbf{B}$ is said to be *free on* A if there is an arrow $\eta_A : A \to UFA$ such that for any arrow $\alpha : A \to UB$ $(B \in \mathbf{B})$ there is a unique arrow $\beta : FA \to B$ in $\mathbf{B}$ such that $U\beta \cdot \eta_A = \alpha$.

Diagrammatically

$$\mathbf{A} \xleftarrow{\;U\;} \mathbf{B}$$

$$\begin{array}{ccc} A \xrightarrow{\eta_A} UFA & & FA \\ {\scriptstyle\alpha}\searrow \quad \downarrow{\scriptstyle U\beta} & & \downarrow{\scriptstyle \exists!\beta} \\ UB & & B. \end{array}$$

Note. This axiom is called a ***universal property***. The arrow η_A is called a ***universal arrow***.

Example 43. Suppose $\mathbf{A}$ = **Sets** and $\mathbf{B}$ = **Monoids**, the category of monoids and monoid homomorphisms (= functors). Consider

$$\mathbf{Sets} \xleftarrow{\;U\;} \mathbf{Monoids}$$

where U : **Monoids** $\to$ **Sets** is the 'forgetful functor'; that is, if M is a monoid, then $U(M)$ is the underlying set of arrows of M, and if f is a monoid homomorphism then $U(f)$ is the underlying function between sets of arrows.

Given a set A, let FA be the free monoid on A; that is $FA = A^*$, the monoid of words in A. Clearly $A \subseteq UFA$; that is, letters are special words. This inclusion function is

$$\eta_A \;:\; A \xrightarrow{\;\subseteq\;} UFA.$$

Given any other monoid B and a function $\alpha : A \to UB$ we can define a monoid morphism $\beta : FA \to B$ as follows:

$$\begin{array}{rcl} \beta & : & FA \longrightarrow B \\ & & a_1 a_2 \cdots a_n \longmapsto \alpha(a_1)\alpha(a_2)\cdots\alpha(a_n). \end{array}$$

We must first check that β is a monoid morphism:

$$\begin{aligned} \beta((a_1 a_2 \cdots a_n)\cdot(a_1' a_2' \cdots a_m')) &= \beta(a_1 a_2 \cdots a_n a_1' a_2' \cdots a_m') \\ &= \alpha(a_1)\cdots\alpha(a_m') \\ &= (\alpha(a_1)\cdots\alpha(a_n))(\alpha(a_1')\cdots\alpha(a_m')) \\ &= \beta(a_1 \cdots a_n)\beta(a_1' \cdots a_m'). \end{aligned}$$

Finally, we must check the uniqueness of $\beta : FA \to B$. Suppose $\gamma : FA \to B$ is a monoid morphism such that $U\gamma \cdot \eta_A = \alpha = U\beta \cdot \eta_A$. That is, $\gamma a = \beta a = \alpha a$ for

$a \in A$. We want to show that $\gamma(a_1 \cdots a_n) = \beta(a_1 \cdots a_n)$. Since γ is a monoid morphism,

$$\begin{aligned}\gamma(a_1 \cdots a_n) &= \gamma a_1 \cdot \gamma a_2 \cdots \gamma a_n \\ &= \alpha a_1 \cdot \alpha a_2 \cdots \alpha a_n \\ &= \beta(a_1 \cdots a_n).\end{aligned}$$

One simple proposition regarding free objects — the universal property of FA determines FA up to isomorphism.

6.1 Proposition. Consider $U : \mathbf{B} \to \mathbf{A}$. Suppose FA, $F'A$ are both free on A. Then $FA \cong F'A$.

Proof. There exist arrows $\eta_A : A \to UFA$, $\eta'_A : A \to UF'A$ satisfying the universal property.

First use the universal property of FA. Corresponding to the arrow $\eta'_A : A \to UF'A$, there is a unique arrow $\beta' : FA \to F'A$ such that $U\beta' \cdot \eta_A = \eta'_A$.

Next use the universal property of $F'A$. Corresponding to the arrow $\eta_A : A \to UFA$, there is a unique arrow $\beta : F'A \to FA$ such that $U\beta \cdot \eta'_A = \eta_A$.

Then,

$$U(\beta\beta')\eta_A = U\beta U\beta' \cdot \eta_A = U\beta \cdot \eta'_A = \eta_A = U1_{F'A} \cdot \eta_A.$$

Hence the uniqueness part of the universal property of FA implies that

$$\beta\beta' = 1_{FA}.$$

By symmetry,

$$\beta'\beta = 1_{F'A},$$

and hence β is an isomorphism between FA and $F'A$. ∎

Example 44. Consider $\mathbf{B} = \mathbf{Vect}$, $\mathbf{A} = \mathbf{Sets}$, and

$$\mathbf{Sets} \xleftarrow{U} \mathbf{Vect},$$

the forgetful functor.

Given a finite set $X = \{x_1, x_2, \ldots, x_n\}$, the free vector space on X is

$$FX = \{\sum_{i=1}^{n} \lambda_i x_i : \lambda_i \in \mathbb{R}\},$$

the set of finite formal linear combinations of elements of X.

The elements of X are special elements of FX, so we have an inclusion function:

$$\eta_X : X \longrightarrow UFX$$

$$x \longmapsto x.$$

The elements of X certainly form a basis for FX. The universal property is the well-known property of vector spaces, that a linear map $FX \to V$ is given precisely by a function $X \to U(V)$; that is, it is given by where the basis vectors go.

Example 45. The free category on a graph satisfies the universal property relative to the functor

$$\mathbf{Grphs} \xleftarrow{U} \mathbf{Cat},$$

which takes a category to its underlying graph, and a functor to its underlying graph morphism.

Example 46. The definition of sum of two objects in $\mathbf{B}$ is a special case of the notion of free.

Let $\mathbf{A} = \mathbf{B} \times \mathbf{B}$, and let $U : \mathbf{B} \to \mathbf{A}$ be the functor which takes B to (B, B) and $f : B_1 \to B_2$ to $(f, f) : (B_1, B_1) \to (B_2, B_2)$; that is, the *diagonal functor*.

Now, consider an object (B_1, B_2) of $\mathbf{A} = \mathbf{B} \times \mathbf{B}$. A free object on (B_1, B_2) is an object S of $\mathbf{B}$, with an arrow $(i_1, i_2) : (B_1, B_2) \to US = (S, S)$ satisfying the universal property.

The universal property says that for any object $B \in \mathbf{B}$ and any arrow

$$(\mu_1, \mu_2) : (B_1, B_2) \to (B, B) = UB,$$

there is a unique arrow $\beta : S \to B$ such that

$$(\beta, \beta)(i_1, i_2) = (\mu_1, \mu_2).$$

That is, given any pair of arrows $\mu_1 : B_1 \to B$, $\mu_2 : B_2 \to B$, there is a unique arrow $\beta : S \to B$ such that $\beta i_1 = \mu_1$ and $\beta i_2 = \mu_2$.

This is exactly the universal property of sums. That is, S with injections i_1, i_2 is the sum of B_1 and B_2.

§7. Adjoint Functors

Consider functor $U : \mathbf{B} \to \mathbf{A}$. Suppose for each object A of $\mathbf{A}$, a free object FA, with universal arrow η_A, exists. Then the construction FA can be made into a functor from $\mathbf{A}$ to $\mathbf{B}$ as follows. Given $f : A_1 \to A_2$ then Ff is the unique arrow from FA_1 to FA_2 such that $UFf \cdot \eta_{A_1} = \eta_{A_2} f : A_1 \to UFA_2$; Ff exists by the universal property of FA_1. If $g : A_2 \to A_3$ then

$$\begin{aligned} U(FgFf)\eta_{A_1} &= UFgUFf \cdot \eta_{A_1} \\ &= UFg \cdot \eta_{A_2} \cdot f \\ &= \eta_{A_3} \cdot gf \\ &= UF(gf)\eta_{A_1}. \end{aligned}$$

The uniqueness part of the universal property of FA_1 then ensures that $FgFf = F(gf)$. Hence F is a functor.

Note. The defining equation of Ff is an instance of the condition for the family η_A $(A \in \mathbf{A})$ to be a natural transformation from $1_{\mathbf{A}}$ to UF.

Definition. Consider functor $U : \mathbf{B} \to \mathbf{A}$. If for each $A \in \mathbf{A}$, FA is free on A with universal arrow η_A, then the functor $F : \mathbf{A} \to \mathbf{B}$ defined on arrows so that

$$UFf \cdot \eta_{A_1} = \eta_{A_2} \cdot f$$

is called the *left adjoint* of U. The functor U is called the *right adjoint* of F. The pair U, F is called an *adjunction*. The natural transformation $\eta : 1_{\mathbf{A}} \to UF$ is called the *unit* of the adjunction.

There is a symmetry between the left and right adjoints which is not apparent in this definition. In the next few paragraphs we will develop this symmetry.

If F is left adjoint to U with unit η, then define $\epsilon_B : FUB \to B$ to be the unique arrow such that

$$U(\epsilon_B)\eta_{UB} = 1_{UB}.$$

The family of arrows ϵ_B $(B \in \mathbf{B})$ forms a natural transformation from FU to $1_{\mathbf{B}}$. To see this notice that for $g : B_1 \to B_2$,

$$\begin{aligned} U(\epsilon_{B_2}FUg)\eta_{UB_1} &= U\epsilon_{B_2}UFUg \cdot \eta_{UB_1} \\ &= U\epsilon_{B_2} \cdot \eta_{UB_2} \cdot Ug \\ &= Ug \\ &= Ug \cdot U\epsilon_{B_1} \cdot \eta_{UB_1} \\ &= U(g \cdot \epsilon_{B_1})\eta_{UB_1}. \end{aligned}$$

The uniqueness part of the universal property now assures us that $\epsilon_{B_2} \cdot FUg = g \cdot \epsilon_{B_1}$, and hence that ϵ is natural from FU to $1_{\mathbf{B}}$.

We call the natural transformation ϵ the *counit* of the adjunction. We have already, from the defining property of ϵ, that

$$U\epsilon_B \cdot \eta_{UB} = 1_{UB};$$

but there is a second equation relating the unit and counit, namely

$$\epsilon_{FA} \cdot F\eta_A = 1_{FA}.$$

This follows from the uniqueness part of the universal condition, after the following calculation:

$$\begin{aligned} U(\epsilon_{FA} \cdot F\eta_A)\eta_A &= U(\epsilon_{FA})UF\eta_A \cdot \eta_A \\ &= U(\epsilon_{FA})(\eta_{UFA})\eta_A \\ &= 1_{UFA} \cdot \eta_A \\ &= \eta_A \\ &= U(1_{FA})\eta_A. \end{aligned}$$

The next proposition shows that an adjunction can be characterized as a pair of functors and a pair of natural transformations satisfying these two equations.

7.1 Proposition. Suppose $U : \mathbf{B} \to \mathbf{A}$, $F : \mathbf{A} \to \mathbf{B}$ are functors, and $\eta : 1_{\mathbf{A}} \to UF$, $\epsilon : FU \to 1_{\mathbf{B}}$ are natural transformations satisfying

$$\begin{aligned} U\epsilon_B \cdot \eta_{UB} &= 1_{UB} \qquad (B \in \mathbf{B}), \\ \epsilon_{FA} \cdot F\eta_A &= 1_{FA} \qquad (A \in \mathbf{A}). \end{aligned}$$

Then F is left adjoint to U, with unit η and counit ϵ.

Proof. The essential thing to check is the universal property. Given $\mu : A \to UB$, the arrow $\epsilon_B \cdot F\mu : FA \to B$ satisfies

$$\begin{aligned} U(\epsilon_B \cdot F\mu)\eta_A &= U(\epsilon_B)(UF\mu)\eta_A \\ &= U(\epsilon_B)\eta_{UB} \cdot \mu \\ &= \mu. \end{aligned}$$

This is the existence part of the universal property. To check the uniqueness part, suppose $U\beta \cdot \eta_A = \mu$. Then,

$$\begin{aligned} \epsilon_B \cdot F\mu &= \epsilon_B \cdot FU\beta \cdot F\eta_A \\ &= \beta \cdot \epsilon_{FA} \cdot F\eta_A \\ &= \beta. \end{aligned}$$

■

The symmetry of an adjunction now allows us to deduce that UB is *cofree* on B, in the sense that UB, with $\epsilon_B : FUB \to B$, satisfies the following *couniversal property*: given any $\nu : FA \to B$ there is a unique $\alpha : A \to UB$ such that $\epsilon_B \cdot F\alpha = \nu$.

Problems 5

1. Consider the graph

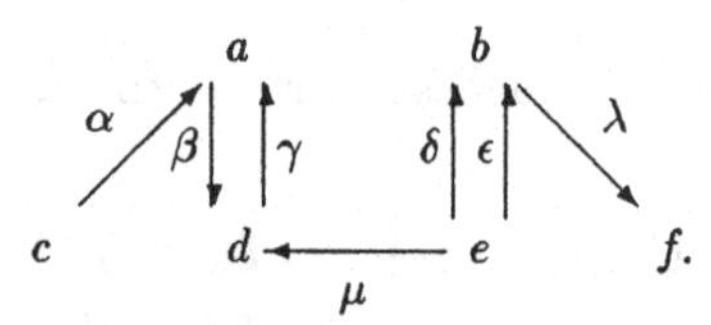

Express this graph as a functor from the category

$$\boxed{\;0 \rightrightarrows 1\;}$$

to **Sets**.

2. (i) Let **G** be the cyclic group of order n. Find a faithful functor $\mathbf{G} \to \mathbf{Sets}$.

(ii) Let **G** be any group. Find a faithful functor from **G** to **Sets**.

3. Consider $\mathcal{P}X$, the set of all subsets of the set X. Show how to make $\mathcal{P}$ into a functor $\mathcal{P} : \mathbf{Sets} \to \mathbf{Sets}$ by defining $\mathcal{P}f$ for each function $f : X \to Y$ appropriately.

4. Show that a functor $F : \mathbf{A} \to \mathbf{B}$ with an inverse $F^{-1} : \mathbf{B} \to \mathbf{A}$ (i.e. $F^{-1}F = 1_{\mathbf{A}}$, $FF^{-1} = 1_{\mathbf{B}}$) is exactly an isomorphism of categories as defined in Chapter 1.

5. Suppose **A** is a category with products, and $A \in \mathbf{A}$. Show that

$$\mathbf{A} \xrightarrow{\;F\;} \mathbf{A}$$

$$X \longmapsto A \times X$$

$$(f : X \to Y) \longmapsto 1_A \times f,$$

is a functor.

6. Consider the functor *Stack* from **Sets** to **Sets**. Let N be the constant functor $N : \mathbf{Sets} \to \mathbf{Sets}$ with $N(X) = \mathbb{N}$. Show that

$$depth : Stack(X) \to N(X)$$

is a natural transformation from *Stack* to N.

7. Show that the family of functions

$$pop_X \;:\; Stack(X) \to I + X \times Stack(X) \qquad (X \in \mathbf{Sets})$$

is a natural transformation (a key fact behind the justification of the crazy calculations). That is, show that for any function $f : X \to Y$ the following diagram commutes:

$$\begin{array}{ccc} Stack(X) & \xrightarrow{\;pop_X\;} & I + X \times Stack(X) \\ {\scriptstyle Stack(f)}\downarrow & & \downarrow{\scriptstyle I + f \times Stack(f)} \\ Stack(Y) & \xrightarrow[\;pop_Y\;]{} & I + Y \times Stack(Y). \end{array}$$

8. Find regular grammars which produce the following languages:

(i) $\{a^n; n \geq 2\}$.

(ii) $\{a^m b^n; m \geq 2, n \geq 3\}$.

(iii) $\{a, b, ab^2\}$.

(iv) Sequences of digits with optional + or − signs.

(v) Same as (iv) but with leading zeros suppressed.

(vi) $\{a, aba, ababa, abababa, \ldots\}$.

(vii) The words in a, b, containing at least one a.

9. Show that any finite subset of Σ^* is a regular language.

10. Let $\Sigma = \{(,)\}$. Consider the subset U of Σ^* consisting of all well-formed bracketings (e.g. $(()())((())) \in U$). Show that U is *not* a regular language.

11. Show that $U = \{a^p : p \text{ prime}\}$ is not a regular language.

12. Consider the regular grammars:

(i)

(ii)

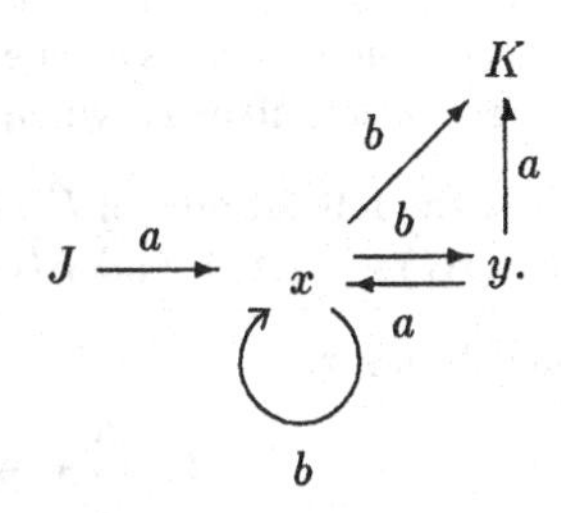

In each case use the method of Kleene's theorem to express the corresponding language as a regular expression.

13. Suppose that $\mathbf{A}$, $\mathbf{B}$ are categories, $F, G : \mathbf{A} \to \mathbf{B}$ are functors, and $\alpha : F \to G$ is a natural transformation. Suppose further that α_A has an inverse $(\alpha_A)^{-1} : GA \to FA$ for each A in $\mathbf{A}$. Show that the family $(\alpha_A)^{-1}$, $(A \in \mathbf{A})$, is a natural transformation from G to F. Show that α has an inverse in $\mathbf{B}^{\mathbf{A}}$.

14. Consider the regular grammar:

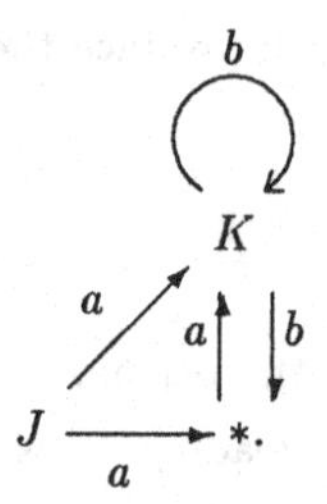

Construct a recognizer for the language generated by this grammar.

15. Determine all the regular languages with alphabet $\Sigma = \{a\}$.

16. Write functional specifications for the following functions:

(i) $f : \mathbb{N} \to \mathbb{N}; f(x) = 3x + 1$.

(ii) $f : \mathbb{N} \to \mathbb{N}; f(x) = \begin{cases} 1 & \text{if } x \text{ odd} \\ 0 & \text{if } x \text{ even.} \end{cases}$

(iii) $f : L \to L$, ($L =$ lists of elements of $\{a_1, a_2, \ldots, a_n\}$), defined by

$$f(x_1 x_2 \cdots x_n) = x_1 x_1 x_2 x_2 \cdots x_n x_n.$$

(iv) $f : L \to L$ defined by

$$f(x_1 x_2 \cdots x_n) = x_1 x_2 \ldots x_n x_1 x_2 \cdots x_n.$$

(v) $f : L \to L$ defined by

$$f(x_1 x_2 \cdots x_n) = x_n x_{n-1} \cdots x_1.$$

17. Given two imperative programs

(i) $\Sigma_1 = \{a\}$; $f_a : X \times C \to X \times C$,

(ii) $\Sigma_2 = \{b\}$; $g_b : C \times Y \to C \times Y$,

whose state spaces have a factor in common. Construct an imperative program on alphabet $\Sigma = \{a, b, c\}$ such that c switches control between a and b, and when a has control the program acts like (i), when b has control it acts like (ii).

18. Suppose $F : \mathbf{A} \to \mathbf{B}$ is the left adjoint of $U : \mathbf{B} \to \mathbf{A}$, and that $\mathbf{A}$ has sums. Show that $F(A_1 + A_2) \cong F(A_1) + F(A_2)$, and $F(O) \cong O$.

19. Consider the diagonal functor:

$$\mathbf{A} \xrightarrow{\Delta} \mathbf{A} \times \mathbf{A}$$

$$A \longmapsto (A, A)$$

$$f \longmapsto (f, f).$$

Show that a cofree object exists on (A_1, A_2) in $\mathbf{A} \times \mathbf{A}$, relative to Δ, if and only if $A_1 \times A_2$ exists in $\mathbf{A}$.

20. Show that if $F : \mathbf{A} \to \mathbf{B}$ is left adjoint to $U : \mathbf{B} \to \mathbf{A}$ and $G : \mathbf{B} \to \mathbf{C}$ is left adjoint to $V : \mathbf{C} \to \mathbf{B}$, then $GF : \mathbf{A} \to \mathbf{C}$ is left adjoint to $UV : \mathbf{C} \to \mathbf{A}$.

Chapter 6

More About Products

This chapter is about free categories with products. We will look at applications to functional specification and context-free grammars. We have seen in Chapter 2 the relevance of categories with products to circuits.

We end the chapter with some brief remarks on cartesian closed categories, and the lambda calculus.

§1. The Free Category with Products

What can we build a free category with products out of? That is, what do we take for generators? Remember that the generators of a category form a graph.

The answer is that we can start with some objects

$$A,\ B,\ C, \ldots,\ X,\ Y,\ Z$$

and some arrows; but the arrows are not just arrows between the objects. The arrows have domains which are (intended to be) products of objects, and codomains which are objects.

Example 1.

$$X \times Y \xrightarrow{f} Z \qquad\qquad X \times X \xrightarrow{g} X$$

Such a thing, a set of objects and a set of arrows, with domains being words in objects, and codomains being single objects, is called a *multigraph*.

Example 2. The following is a multigraph:

- Two objects X, L.
- Four arrows:

$$I \overset{a}{\underset{b}{\rightrightarrows}} X, \qquad I \xrightarrow{o} L, \qquad X \times L \xrightarrow{cons} L.$$

Note. The domain of an arrow in a multigraph may be the empty word in the objects, which we have denoted as I. Arrows of the form $f : XYZ \to W$ are called *function symbols* of three variables; arrows of the form $a : I \to X$ are called *constants*.

Example 3. Given any circuit, for example

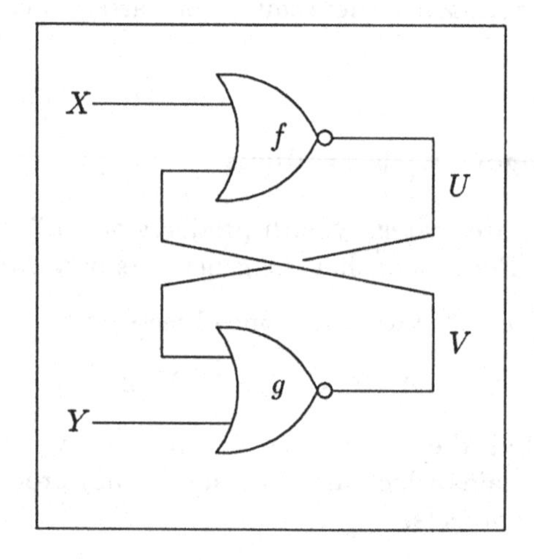

there is an associated multigraph. Name the wires and components as shown. Then:

$$X \times V \xrightarrow{f} U \qquad\qquad U \times Y \xrightarrow{g} V$$

This multigraph makes sense: the component f is a function of two variables. If X, Y, U, V denote the state space of each wire, then f acts on $X \times V$ and produces an output in U

Now let us consider how to build the free category with products out of a multigraph.

Description of free category $\mathcal{F}_\times G$ with products on a multigraph G

Given a multigraph

$$G = \{ \text{ Objects } : X, Y, Z, \ldots \text{ ; } \quad \text{Arrows } : f : X_1X_2 \cdots X_n \to Y, \ \ldots\}.$$

Take a sequence of symbols $x_1, x_2, \ldots$ called variables.

The objects of $\mathcal{F}_\times G$ are the words in objects of G. The arrows of $\mathcal{F}_\times G$ are defined inductively by the following rules:

Rule 1. x_i is an arrow from $Y_1Y_2 \cdots Y_n \to Y_i$ provided $i \leq n$.

Rule 2. If $c : I \to X$ is a constant of G, then for any object Y of $\mathcal{F}_\times G$, $c : Y \to X$ is an arrow of $\mathcal{F}_\times G$.

Rule 3. Given n arrows

$$\alpha_i : X_1X_2 \cdots X_m \to Y_i \quad (i = 1, 2, \cdots, n) \text{ in } \mathcal{F}_\times G,$$

and a function symbol $f : Y_1Y_2 \cdots Y_n \to Z \ \in G$, then

$$f(\alpha_1, \alpha_2, \ldots, \alpha_n) : X_1X_2 \cdots X_m \to Z$$

is an arrow of $\mathcal{F}_\times G$.

The arrows in $\mathcal{F}_\times G$ with codomain a single object are exactly those produced by successive use of Rules (1), (2), and (3). They are sometimes called *terms*.

Arrows in $\mathcal{F}_\times G$ with codomain a product, that is, of the form

$$X_1X_2 \cdots X_m \to Y_1Y_2 \cdots Y_n,$$

are just n-tuples of arrows $X_1X_2 \cdots X_m \to Y_i$ $(i = 1, 2, \ldots, n)$ in $\mathcal{F}_\times G$. That is, if $\alpha_i : X_1X_2 \cdots X_m \to Y_i$ $(i = 1, 2, \ldots, n)$ are arrows resulting from Rules (1), (2), and (3), then

$$\alpha_1, \alpha_2, \cdots, \alpha_n : X_1X_2 \cdots X_m \to Y_1Y_2 \cdots Y_n$$

is an arrow of $\mathcal{F}_\times G$.

We omit the definition of composition in $\mathcal{F}_\times G$, and the justification of the fact that $\mathcal{F}_\times G$ does indeed have products. Composition is *substitution* of terms; see [27] for details.

Example 4. Given $G = \{a, b : I \to X, \ o : I \to L, \ cons : X \times L \to L\}$, what are the arrows in $\mathcal{F}_\times G$ from I to L?

They are the arrows built up inductively using Rules (1), (2), and (3).

By Rule (2), $I \xrightarrow{o} L$ is an arrow. The only other way to get arrows from I to L is to first have a pair of arrows $I \xrightarrow{\alpha} X$, $I \xrightarrow{\beta} L$ and

$$cons(\alpha, \beta) : I \to L. \tag{1}$$

How can we get arrows into X? There are only two; $a, b : I \to X$. There is no way of producing new ones. So, at the beginning, the only arrows $I \to L$ produced by (1) are

$$cons(a, o) : I \to L, \qquad \text{and} \qquad cons(b, o) : I \to L,$$

built from $a : I \to X,\ o : I \to L$ and $b : I \to X,\ o : I \to L$, respectively.

We can now repeat the process (1). From

$$b : I \to X, \qquad cons(a, o) : I \to L$$

we get

$$cons(b, cons(a, o)) : I \to L.$$

It is clear that the arrows from I to L in $\mathcal{F}_\times G$ are of the form:

$$cons(a, cons(a, cons(b, cons(a, \ldots, cons(b, o) \ldots)))).$$

Such a thing is called a *list* whose elements belong to $\{a, b\}$. So we have a new idea of what a list is. The symbol *cons* is called the list constructor; *cons* appends a new element to the list.

Note. This view of lists is fundamental in list-processing languages. Throughout this book we have been talking about lists in different guises. The list constructor *cons* we have just described is essentially the function *push* of stacks; only the context is different.

Example 5. Suppose G is the multigraph with one object R, one constant $e : I \to R$, and one function symbol $m : R \times R \to R$.

Question. What are the arrows from $R^2 \to R$ in $\mathcal{F}_\times G$?

From Rule (1), $x_1 : R^2 \to R$, $x_2 : R^2 \to R$ are arrows. Intuitively, the arrow x_1 is the first projection, and x_2 the second projection of the product.

From Rule (2), $e : R^2 \to R$ is an arrow of $\mathcal{F}_\times G$. To build up new arrows we must use Rule (3). That is, we must have two arrows $\alpha, \beta : R^2 \to R$ and then form $m(\alpha, \beta)$.

For example:

$$\begin{aligned} m(x_1,x_1) &: R^2 \to R, \\ m(x_1,x_2) &: R^2 \to R, \qquad (2) \\ m(e,x_1) &: R^2 \to R, \\ m(e,e) &: R^2 \to R, \\ m(x_2,x_1) &: R^2 \to R. \qquad (3) \end{aligned}$$

These arrows have intuitive meanings. Let $R = \mathbb{R}$ and $m =$ multiplication, then we may interpret (2) and (3) as:

$$\mathbb{R}^2 \longrightarrow \mathbb{R}$$

$$(x_1,x_2) \longmapsto x_1x_2, \qquad (*)$$

$$(x_1,x_2) \longmapsto x_2x_1. \qquad (**)$$

The commutative law for multiplication says that $(*) = (**)$.

Remember, however, that our construction is purely formal.

Given these arrows $R^2 \to R$ involving one m, we can now build up arrows $R^2 \to R$ involving two m's, using Rule (3). For example, $m(e, m(x_1,x_1)) : R^2 \to R$, and so on. It is clear that arrows $R^n \to R$ in $\mathcal{F}_\times G$ are all expressions built up from the variables $x_1, x_2, \ldots, x_n$, and the constant e by repeated application of m.

The associative law for m is an equation between such arrows, namely

$$m(x_1, m(x_2,x_3)) = m(m(x_1,x_2),x_3) : R^3 \to R.$$

The construction I have just described occurs throughout computer science and mathematics: in functional programming, with languages like Lisp, ML, Miranda; in logic programming, with languages like Prolog; in context-free grammars; in term rewrite systems; in logic; and in universal algebra.

§2. Functional Specification with Products

In this section we extend the ideas of functional specification given in Chapter 5, §5, to categories with products.

Definition. A *functional specification*, using products, consists of two multigraphs, a data multigraph *Data*, and a function multigraph *Function*,

$$Data \subseteq Function,$$

together with three specified objects I, J, K of $\mathcal{F}_\times \mathit{Data}$, and a specified arrow f from J to K in $\mathcal{F}_\times \mathit{Function}$. In addition, a functional specification has a finite set, *Equation*, of equations between arrows of $\mathcal{F}_\times \mathit{Function}$.

The relation

$$\overline{f} : \mathrm{Hom}_{\mathcal{F}_\times \mathit{Data}}(I, J) \to \mathrm{Hom}_{\mathcal{F}_\times \mathit{Function}}(I, K)$$

determined by the specification is

$$\begin{array}{rcl} \overline{f} : \mathrm{Hom}_{\mathcal{F}_\times \mathit{Data}}(I, J) & \longrightarrow & \mathrm{Hom}_{\mathcal{F}_\times \mathit{Function}}(I, K) \\ \phi & \longmapsto & \sigma, \end{array}$$

if $f\phi = \sigma$ is provable from the equations.

Example 6. Let's see how to give a functional specification of the addition of natural numbers.

The multigraph *Data* is

$$0 : I \longrightarrow N, \qquad s : N \longrightarrow N.$$

The specified objects are $I = I$, $J = N^2$, and $K = N$.

The multigraph *Function* is

$$0 : I \longrightarrow N, \qquad s : N \longrightarrow N,$$

$$\mathit{add} : N^2 \longrightarrow N.$$

The specified arrow is $\mathit{add} : N^2 \to N$.

The set *Equation* of equations is

$$\begin{aligned} \mathit{add}(s(x_1), x_2) &= s(\mathit{add}(x_1, x_2)), \\ \mathit{add}(0, x_2) &= x_2. \end{aligned}$$

Note. If you think of s as the successor function, then these equations constitute a recursive definition of addition.

The specification contains the means for calculating the sum of two numbers. For example,

$$\begin{aligned} \mathit{add}(s^3 0, s^2 0) &= s \cdot \mathit{add}(s^2 0, s^2 0) \\ &= ss \cdot \mathit{add}(s0, s^2 0) \\ &= sss \cdot \mathit{add}(0, s^2 0) \\ &= s^5 0. \end{aligned}$$

Example 7. We next give a functional specification of the multiplication of numbers.

The multigraph *Data* is

$$0 : I \longrightarrow N, \qquad s : N \longrightarrow N.$$

The specified objects are $I = I$, $J = N^2$, and $K = N$.

The multigraph *Function* is

$$o : I \longrightarrow N, \qquad s : N \longrightarrow N,$$
$$add : N^2 \longrightarrow N, \qquad multiply : N^2 \longrightarrow N.$$

The specified arrow is $multiply : N^2 \to N$.

The set, *Equation*, of equations, is

$$\begin{aligned} add(s(x_1), x_2) &= s(add(x_1, x_2)), \\ add(0, x_2) &= x_2, \\ multiply(s(x_1), x_2) &= add(multiply(x_1, x_2), x_2), \\ multiply(0, x_2) &= 0. \end{aligned}$$

Let's see a calculation based on this specification:

$$\begin{aligned} multiply(s^2 0, s^2 0) &= add(multiply(s0, s^2 0), s^2 0) \\ &= add(add(multiply(0, s^2 0), s^2 0), s^2 0) \\ &= add(add(0, s^2 0), s^2 0) \\ &= add(s^2 0, s^2 0) \\ &= \cdots = s^4 0. \end{aligned}$$

Example 8. We will now extend the above examples to specify the function *factorial*.

The multigraph, *Data*, is the same as in the previous two examples. The specified objects are $I = I$, $J = N$ and $K = N$.

The multigraph, *Function*, contains the corresponding multigraph for specifying *multiply* and has one additional arrow:

$$factorial : N \longrightarrow N.$$

The specified arrow is $factorial : N \to N$.

The set, *Equation*, of equations, contains those for *multiply*, and has two additional equations:

$$factorial(s(x_1)) = multiply(s(x_1), factorial(x_1)),$$
$$factorial(0) = s(0).$$

It is easy to see that the function specified is

$$factorial(s^n 0) = s^{n!} 0.$$

Example 9. Let us develop next a specification for the function which concatenates *lists* of elements from the alphabet $\{a_1, a_2, \ldots, a_n\}$.

The multigraph *Data* is:

$$o : I \longrightarrow L, \qquad cons : A \times L \longrightarrow L,$$
$$a_1, a_2, \ldots, a_n : I \longrightarrow A.$$

The specified objects are $I = I$, $J = L^2$ and $K = L$.

Note. Arrows from I to L in the free category with products on this multigraph are expressions of the form

$$cons(a_{i_1}, cons(a_{i_2}, \ldots));$$

that is, the arrows are lists. Arrows from I to L^2 are pairs of lists.

The multigraph, *Function*, is defined by:

$$o : I \longrightarrow L, \qquad cons : A \times L \longrightarrow L,$$
$$a_1, a_2, \ldots, a_n : I \longrightarrow A, \qquad concatenate : L^2 \longrightarrow L.$$

The specified arrow is $concatenate : L^2 \to L$.

The set, *Equation*, of equations, is:

$$concatenate(cons(x, l_1), l_2) = cons(x, concatenate(l_1, l_2)),$$
$$concatenate(o, l) = l.$$

Let's see a calculation based on this specification:

$$\begin{aligned} &concatenate(cons(a, cons(b, o)), cons(c, cons(d, o))) \\ &\quad = cons(a, concatenate(cons(b, o), cons(c, cons(d, o)))) \\ &\quad = cons(a, cons(b, concatenate(o, cons(c, cons(d, o))))) \\ &\quad = cons(a, cons(b, cons(c, cons(d, o)))). \end{aligned}$$

§3. Context-free Languages

Definition. A **context-free grammar** on an alphabet Σ is a finite multigraph, with some of the letters of Σ being constants (that is, arrows with domain I), and with one specified object E. The function symbols, other than the letters of Σ, which occur in the multigraph are called *productions* of the grammar.

Consider the arrows from I to E in the free category with products on the grammar. For each such arrow we can find a word in Σ^* by just taking the letters of the alphabet which occur in the arrow, in the order in which they occur in the arrow. The set of all words so obtained is called the *context-free language* generated by the grammar. An arrow from which a particular word is obtained is called the *parse tree* of the word; it is usually drawn as a tree rather than as a term.

Example 10. Let $\Sigma = \{a, b\}$. Consider the multigraph

$$a : I \to E, \qquad a : I \to X, \qquad b : I \to X, \qquad \alpha : XE \to E.$$

Then $\alpha(a, \alpha(b, \alpha(b, \alpha(b, a)))) : I \to E$ is an arrow in the free category with products on this multigraph. The word corresponding to this arrow is *abbba* — just remove all brackets, commas, and α's. It is clear that the language produced by this grammar is $(a \cup b)^* a$.

Example 11. Let $\Sigma = \{a, b\}$. Consider the multigraph

$$\alpha : I \to E, \qquad a : I \to X, \qquad b : I \to Y, \qquad \beta : YE \to E, \qquad \gamma : EX \to E.$$

Then $\beta(b, \gamma(\gamma(\beta(b, \beta(b, \alpha)), a), a)) : I \to E$ is an arrow in the free category with products on this multigraph. The word corresponding to this arrow is *bbbaa* — just remove all brackets, commas, and α's, β's, and γ's. It is clear that the language produced by this grammar is $b^* a^*$.

Example 12. Any regular language is also a context-free language. We leave the proof to the reader.

However, there are languages which are context-free but not regular.

Example 13. Let $\Sigma = \{a, b\}$; then $U = \{a^n b^n;\ n = 0, 1, 2, \ldots\}$ is context-free but not regular.

Consider the multigraph

$$a : I \to A, \qquad b : I \to B, \qquad \alpha : I \to E, \qquad \beta : AEB \to E.$$

The arrows from I to E in the free category with products on this multigraph are:

$$\alpha : I \to E,$$
$$\beta(a, \alpha, b) : I \to E,$$
$$\beta(a, \beta(a, \alpha, b), b) : I \to E,$$
$$\beta(a, \beta(a, \beta(a, \alpha, b), b), b) : I \to E,$$
$$\vdots$$

So the language is $\{a^n b^n; n = 0, 1, 2, \ldots\}$.

Example 14. Consider the alphabet $\{a, b, [,], +, \times\}$, and the multigraph with constants

$$[: I \to L, \quad]: I \to R, \quad + : I \to B, \quad \times : I \to B, \quad a : I \to E, \quad b : I \to E,$$

and function symbol

$$\alpha : LEBER \to E.$$

Note. It is useful to think of each of the objects as a set of words of a particular type — L is the set of left brackets, R is the set of right brackets, B is the set of binary operation symbols, and E is the set of all expressions. Then α, the production of the grammar, is a function producing words of type indicated by the codomain from tuples of words, one for each domain type. The parse tree tells you exactly how the word has been produced.

In the above example, α produces an expression from a left bracket, an expression, a binary operation symbol, an expression, and a right bracket.

A more or less typical arrow from I to E, in the free category with products on this multigraph, is:

$$\alpha([, a, \times, \alpha([, \alpha([, b, \times, a,]), +, b,]),]).$$

The word corresponding to this arrow is

$$[a \times [[b \times a] + b]].$$

It is clear that the language generated by this grammar is a set of arithmetic expressions.

§4. Natural Numbers and Cartesian Closed Categories

We have discussed the specification of functions both in plain categories, and in categories with products. It is clear that the more structure the categories have, the easier it is to specify functions. We will discuss two important extra structures a category may admit, namely the existence of a *natural numbers object*, and the existence of *exponential objects*.

A natural numbers object

Definition. Suppose $\mathbf{A}$ is a category with products. Then a *natural numbers object* in $\mathbf{A}$ is an object N, together with two arrows $0 : I \to N$, $s : N \to N$, which satisfy the following universal property: given any objects A, B of $\mathbf{A}$ and arrows $a : B \to A$, $f : A \to A$, there is a unique arrow $g : B \times N \to A$ such that both $g(1_B \times 0) = a$ and $g(1_B \times s) = fg$. Diagrammatically,

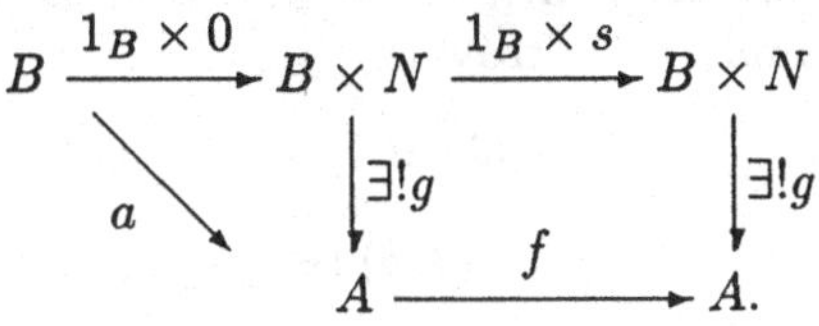

$$\begin{array}{ccccc} B & \xrightarrow{1_B \times 0} & B \times N & \xrightarrow{1_B \times s} & B \times N \\ & \searrow^{a} & \downarrow{\exists! g} & & \downarrow{\exists! g} \\ & & A & \xrightarrow{f} & A. \end{array}$$

Example 15. In the category **Sets** the usual natural numbers $\mathbb{N}$, with the constant function at 0, and the successor function $s : \mathbb{N} \to \mathbb{N}$, is a natural numbers objects. Given functions $a : B \to A$ and $f : A \to A$ the function $g : B \times N \to A$ must satisfy

$$g(b, 0) = a(b) \quad \text{and} \quad g(b, n+1) = f(g(b, n)).$$

But these equations are the recursive definition of a function

$$\begin{aligned} g(b,0) &= a(b), \\ g(b,1) &= f(g(b,0)) = f(a(b)), \\ g(b,2) &= f(g(b,1)) = f^2(a(b)), \\ g(b,3) &= f(g(b,2)) = f^3(a(b)), \\ &\vdots \end{aligned}$$

Cartesian closed categories

Definition. Suppose $\mathbf{A}$ is a category with products and B is an object of $\mathbf{A}$. Consider the functor

$$\begin{aligned} \mathbf{A} &\xrightarrow{F} \mathbf{A} \\ A &\longmapsto A \times B \\ (f : A \to A') &\longmapsto f \times 1_B. \end{aligned}$$

We say that **A** is *cartesian closed*, or has *exponential objects*, if F has a right adjoint U. We then denote $U(C)$ by C^B.

Remember from Chapter 5, §7, that the existence of a right adjoint is equivalent to the existence of a cofree object C^B on each $C \in \mathbf{A}$, with couniversal arrow $\epsilon_C : C^B \times B \to C$. The couniversal property is that, given any $\alpha : A \times B \to C$, there exists a unique $\beta : A \to C^B$ such that

$$\epsilon_C(\beta \times 1_B) = \alpha.$$

Example 16. As usual, **Sets** is the first example. Exponential objects do exist in **Sets**; if B and C are sets, then $C^B = \{f : B \to C\}$, the set of all functions from B to C. The couniversal arrow is

$$\begin{aligned} \epsilon_C \ : C^B \times B &\longrightarrow C \\ (f, b) &\longmapsto f(b). \end{aligned}$$

The function ϵ_C is called *evaluation*, since its effect is to evaluate a function at an element of its domain.

Let's check the universal property. Consider a function $\alpha : A \times B \to C$; then we can define a function $\beta : A \to C^B$ by

$$\begin{aligned} A &\xrightarrow{\ \beta\ } C^B \\ a &\longmapsto (b \mapsto \alpha(a, b)). \end{aligned}$$

Then

$$\begin{aligned} A \times B &\xrightarrow{\ \beta \times 1_B\ } C^B \times B \xrightarrow{\ \epsilon_C\ } C \\ (a, b) &\longmapsto ((b' \mapsto \alpha(a, b')), b) \longmapsto \alpha(a, b). \end{aligned}$$

Hence, $\epsilon_C(\beta \times 1_B) = \alpha$. It is clear that this equation determines β in terms of α and hence the universal property is satisfied.

Remark. The importance of cartesian closedness is that it allows the discussion of functions which act on functions. Another calculus designed for such higher-order operations is the *lambda calculus*. The lambda calculus takes different basic operations to achieve essentially the same result as cartesian closed categories. One of the operations is the same. The operation of forming a function $A \to C^B$ from a function $A \times B \to C$ — which we have just described above — is called *lambda abstraction*, and is one of the two basic operations of the lambda calculus. However, instead of composition, the lambda calculus uses *application*, which in cartesian closed terms is the operation

$$(f : X \to C^B,\ g : X \to B) \longmapsto (X \xrightarrow{(f,g)} C^B \times B \xrightarrow{\epsilon_C} B).$$

Problems 6

1. Consider the following multigraphs G. In each case describe the arrows in the free category with products $\mathcal{F}_\times G$ with the specified domain and codomain.

(i) Three objects A, E, B; three constants $a : I \to A$, $b : I \to B$, $e : I \to E$; one function symbol $m : AEB \to E$; find the arrows from I to E.

(ii) Three objects E, S, P; constants $p_i : I \to P$, $s_j : I \to S$ $(i = 1, 2, \ldots, m; j = 1, 2, \ldots, n)$; function symbol $m : SP \to E$; find the arrows from I to E.

(iii) One object X; no function symbols or constants; find the arrows from X^m to X^n.

2. Describe a multigraph G, containing objects X and *Lol*, such that the arrows from I to *Lol* in $\mathcal{F}_\times G$ are lists of lists of constants $I \to X$.

3. Describe context-free grammars on the alphabet $\Sigma = \{a, b, c\}$ which generate the following languages:

(i) $\{a, ab, b^2\}$;

(ii) $\{a^{3n}; n = 0, 1, 2, \ldots\}$;

(iii) $\{a^n b^n c; n = 0, 1, 2, 3, \ldots\}$.

4. Show that a regular language is context-free.

5. Write a functional specification with products for the function which reverses lists.

6. Write a functional specification with products for the function which sorts lists of $\{a_1, a_2 \cdots a_n; a_1 < a_2 < \cdots a_n\}$ into ascending order.

7. Write a functional specification with products for the function which gives the length of a list.

8. Write a functional specification, with products, for the function which flattens lists of lists into simple lists.

9. Suppose $\mathbf{A}$ is a category with products, and a natural numbers object N. Show how to define arrows, *add* : $N \times N \to N$ and *multiply* : $N \times N \to N$, which agree with the usual addition and multiplication in the case that $\mathbf{A} = \mathbf{Sets}$.

10. Suppose that $\mathbf{A}$ is a cartesian closed category with sums. Show that $\mathbf{A}$ is a distributive category.

11. (i) Suppose $F : \mathbf{A} \to \mathbf{B}$ is left adjoint to $U : \mathbf{B} \to \mathbf{A}$. Show that for each $A \in \mathbf{A}$, $B \in \mathbf{B}$ there is a bijection

$$\mathrm{Hom}_{\mathbf{B}}(F(A), B) \xrightarrow{\cong} \mathrm{Hom}_{\mathbf{A}}(A, U(B)).$$

(Notice the analogy with adjoint linear transformations. Notice also, as an aid to memory, that in this formula the left adjoint occurs on the left of the Hom, the right adjoint on the right.)

(ii) Suppose $\mathbf{A}$ is cartesian closed. Show that for any three objects A_1, A_2, A_3 of $\mathbf{A}$ there is a bijection

$$\mathrm{Hom}_{\mathbf{A}}(A_1 \times A_2, A_3) \xrightarrow{\cong} \mathrm{Hom}_{\mathbf{A}}(A_1, A_3^{A_2}).$$

Chapter 7

Computational Category Theory

In this chapter we describe briefly two procedures for computing with categories. The first is a special case of the Knuth–Bendix procedure for determining, in a category given by generators and relations, whether or not two paths are equal.

The second is a procedure for computing left Kan extensions, developed from the Todd–Coxeter procedure, by Sean Carmody and the author.

§1. The Knuth–Bendix Procedure

Consider a category **A** given by generators and relations. Suppose the generators form a finite graph G, and suppose there is a finite set E of relations. The question we would like to consider is: given two paths in G with the same domain and codomain, are they the same arrow in **A**? If u and v are the same arrow in **A** we write $u \sim v$.

Example 1. Consider graph G with objects A, B, and C, and arrows $f : A \to A$, $g : A \to A$, $h : B \to A$, $k : B \to B$ and $m : C \to B$. Consider relations $E = \{fhk = gh,\ m = kkm\}$. Together G and E define a category **A**. We would like an algorithm for determining whether or not two paths in G are the same arrow in **A**. For example, is $fffghkkkm = ffghkm$ in **A**?

The Knuth–Bendix procedure is sometimes successful in producing such an algorithm. The idea is to put an order on the paths in G, and to find rules for reducing paths, while keeping the same arrow in **A**. Ideally, two paths are the same in **A** if they reduce to the same path.

Ordering paths

Take an order on the arrows of the graph G. Then we can order the paths between each pair of objects of G as follows:

- if the length of u is greater than the length of v then we say $u > v$;
- if $u = a_1 a_2 \cdots a_n$ and $v = b_1 b_2 \cdots b_n$ (a's and b's arrows in G) then $u > v$ if $a_1 = b_1$, $a_2 = b_2$, $\ldots$, $a_i = b_i$, but $a_{i+1} > b_{i+1}$, for some i.

Observe a couple of obvious properties of this order. Firstly, if $w : A \to B$, $v_1, v_2 : B \to C$ and $u : C \to D$ are paths in G then $v_1 > v_2$ implies that

$uv_1w > uv_2w$. Secondly, between any two objects A and B of G any descending chain $v_1 > v_2 > v_3 > \cdots$ is finite.

Now, using the order on paths, each of the equations in E can be written with the left-hand path, u say, of the equation being greater than the right-hand path, say v. We call an equation written in this way a *reduction*, and we denote it $u \Rightarrow v$.

Example 2. In the example given above let us take the order on the arrows of G to be $f > g > h > k > m$. Then $fhk > gh$, $kkm > m$ and $ffhkk > fghkk$. The equations written as reductions become

$$fhk \Rightarrow gh, \qquad kkm \Rightarrow m.$$

The reduction process

Given any path u in G we may now be able to apply the reductions of E repeatedly, obtaining a strictly decreasing sequence $u > u_1 > u_2 > \cdots > u_n = v$, while keeping $u \sim u_1 \sim u_2 \sim \cdots \sim u_n = v$. This is done by applying the reductions of E to subpaths. If u can be reduced to v in this way we write

$$u \Rightarrow^* v,$$

and we call v a *descendent* of u.

Example 3. In the example we are following

$$fgfg(fhk)kkkm > fgfg(gh)kkkm = fgfgghk(kkm) > fgfgghk(m).$$

So, in this example $fgfgfhkkkm \Rightarrow^* fgfgghkm$.

Note. There may be several ways, or none, to reduce a given path. At each stage we may have a choice as to which reduction to use, and on which subpath to use it. We have observed above that any sequence of reductions will eventually yield an *irreducible* path. A desirable situation would be that any sequence of reductions applied to a path yields the same irreducible path. We give a name to this situation.

Definition. A set E of reductions is called *confluent* if each path u has a unique irreducible descendent, v say. Then v is called the *normal form* of u.

1.1 Proposition. Suppose E is a confluent set of reductions. Then $u \sim v$ (that is, $u = v$ in $\mathbf{A}$) if and only if u and v have the same normal form.

Proof. If u and v have the same normal form w then $u \sim w \sim v$ and hence $u \sim v$.

Conversely, if $u \sim v$, then there is a sequence of paths $u_1, u_2, u_3, \ldots, u_n$ such that

$$u \sim u_1 \sim u_2 \sim \cdots \sim u_n = v,$$

and $u_i \Rightarrow^* u_{i+1}$ or $u_{i+1} \Rightarrow^* u_i$ $(i = 1, 2, 3, \ldots, n-1)$.

But it is clear that if $u_i \Rightarrow^* u_j$ then u_i and u_j have the same normal form — any descendent of u_j is a descendent of u_i. Hence u and v have the same normal form. ∎

Example 4. The example we are following is *not* a confluent set of reductions. The paths $fhkkm$ can be reduced to two different irreducible paths:

$$(fhk)km \Rightarrow^* (gh)km$$

and

$$fh(kkm) \Rightarrow^* fh(m).$$

But both $ghkm$ and fhm are irreducible.

1.2 Proposition. A set E of reductions is confluent if and only if for each pair of reductions $u_1 \Rightarrow v_1$, $u_2 \Rightarrow v_2$ in E the following hold:

(Subpath Rule.) If $u_1 = xu_2y$ for paths x and y then there exists a path z such that $v_1 \Rightarrow^* z$ and $xv_2y \Rightarrow^* z$;

(Overlap Rule.) If $u_1 = xy$ and $u_2 = yz$ for some paths x, y, z (and hence $xu_2 = u_1z$), then there exists a path w such that $xv_2 \Rightarrow^* w$ and $v_1z \Rightarrow^* w$.

Proof. Certainly confluent sets of reductions satisfy these two properties — in each case, take the common descendent to be the common normal form.

Conversely, suppose the Subpath and Overlap Rules are satisfied. Suppose that E is not confluent, and choose a path w, minimal with the property that it can be reduced to two different irreducible paths p and q. The first step $u_1 \Rightarrow v_1$ in the sequence of reductions used to get from w to p must be different from the first reduction $u_2 \Rightarrow v_2$ used to get from w to q, since otherwise we could have chosen a smaller w. Further, if after the first step the two paths we obtain are w_1 and w_2 then w_1 and w_2 have no common descendent. Having a common descendent would imply that they have a common irreducible descendent. But by the minimality of w, both w_1 and w_2 have a unique irreducible descendent. This implies, since p is a descendent of w_1 and q is a descendent of w_2, that $p = q$, a contradiction.

There must be some overlap between the first pair u_1 and u_2 of subpaths replaced. If there were none we could replace u_2 after replacing u_1, and conversely, and hence obtain a common descendent of w_1 and w_2. But the fact that there is common overlap between u_1 and u_2 (or that one is a subpath of the other) means, by the Overlap and Subpath Properties, that w_1 and w_2 have a common descendent, a contradiction. ■

Note. Checking whether or not a set E of reductions is confluent is a finite process. You just need to check the left-hand sides of each pair of reductions to see if there is overlap or if one is a subpath of another. If there is overlap between u_1 and u_2, that is $u_1 = xy$, $u_2 = yz$, then reduce $v_1 z$ and xv_2 to an irreducible form. If u_2 is a subpath of u_1, that is $u_1 = xu_2y$, then reduce v_1 and xv_2y to an irreducible form. If, for every pair of reductions with some form of overlap, the irreducible forms so obtained are the same then the set E is confluent. If in any case the irreducible forms are different then the set E is not confluent.

The Knuth–Bendix procedure

The Knuth–Bendix procedure applied to a set E of equations between paths in a graph G consists first in checking the set E for confluence as described above. If it is not confluent, then from either an overlap or a subpath situation we will obtain a pair of irreducible paths $p \neq q$ with $p \sim q$, since they are both descendents of a single path. With respect to the order on paths, either $p > q$ or $q > p$. In the first case add to the set E the reduction $p \Rightarrow q$; in the second case add $q \Rightarrow p$. Adding $p = q$ to the relations does not change the category $\mathbf{A}$ given by the generators and relations, since we know that $p = q$ is a consequence of the existing relations.

We repeat this process, checking whether the new set of reductions is confluent, and adding an extra reduction if necessary. The Knuth–Bendix procedure is said to terminate if, after a finite number of steps, a confluent set of reductions is achieved. We then have an algorithm for determining whether or not two paths are the same in $\mathbf{A}$. Reduce both paths to normal form; the paths are the same in $\mathbf{A}$ if and only if the normal forms are the same.

Note. During the process of adding to the set of reductions it may happen that existing reductions become redundant and hence may be omitted.

Example 5. Consider the example described above — graph G with objects A, B, and C, and arrows $f : A \to A$, $g : A \to A$, $h : B \to A$, $k : B \to B$, and $m : C \to B$; and reductions

$$E = \{fhk \Rightarrow gh, \quad kkm \Rightarrow m\}.$$

We have seen that E is not confluent since $fhkkm$ may be reduced to two different irreducible forms $ghkm$ and fhm, with $ghkm > fhm$. However, adding

$ghkm \Rightarrow fhm$ to the set of reductions does produce a confluent set of reductions

$$fhk \Rightarrow gh, \qquad kkm \Rightarrow m, \qquad ghkm \Rightarrow fhm.$$

We can now test whether $fffghkkkm = ffghkm$ in $\mathbf{A}$, by reducing both sides of the equation to normal form as follows:

$$fffghk(kkm) \Rightarrow fffghk(m) = fff(ghkm) \Rightarrow fff(fhm) \quad \text{and}$$
$$ff(ghkm) \Rightarrow ff(fhm).$$

Therefore, $fffghkkkm \neq ffghkm$ in $\mathbf{A}$.

§2. Computing Left Kan extensions

The *Todd–Coxeter procedure* ([10]) for the enumeration of cosets of a subgroup in a group, has long been a powerful tool in Computational Group Theory. The underlying procedure is, however, not specific to group theory. Here we describe a generalization — the generalized Todd–Coxeter procedure — which relates to a construction in category theory known as the *left Kan extension*. The enumeration of cosets then becomes a special case of this generalized procedure, which may also be used for a great variety of other purposes. One example, which we shall illustrate here, includes listing the arrows of a category given generators and relations.

We omit proof of the correctness and termination of the procedure. Details may be found in the references [7], [8].

Definition. Given functors $F : \mathbf{A} \to \mathbf{B}$ and $X : \mathbf{A} \to \mathbf{C}$, a *left Kan extension* of X along F consists of a functor $L : \mathbf{B} \to \mathbf{C}$ (sometimes denoted $\mathrm{Lan}_F X$) and a natural transformation $\epsilon : X \to LF$, with the universal property that for each $M : \mathbf{B} \to \mathbf{C}$ and $\alpha : X \to MF$, α factors through ϵ as $\alpha = \sigma F \cdot \epsilon$ for a unique $\sigma : L \to M$.

Remark. When $\mathbf{B}$ is the category with one object and one arrow, the functor L is essentially an object of $\mathbf{C}$. In this important case L is called the *colimit* of X. We have already seen a special kind of colimit; if $\mathbf{A}$ is the category with two objects A_1, A_2 and two arrows, then a functor $X : \mathbf{A} \to \mathbf{C}$ amounts to two objects $X(A_1)$, $X(A_2)$ of $\mathbf{C}$, and the colimit of X is $X(A_1) + X(A_2)$.

We will be interested here only in the case when $\mathbf{C} = \mathbf{Sets}$. We now give an explicit formulation of the left Kan extension for this case.

2.1 Theorem. Given functors $F : \mathbf{A} \to \mathbf{B}$ and $X : \mathbf{A} \to \mathbf{Sets}$, where $\mathbf{A}$ and $\mathbf{B}$ are finitely generated categories, the left Kan extension, L, of X along F is given as follows:

- on objects

$$LB = \Big(\sum_{A \in \mathbf{A}} \mathbf{B}(FA, B) \times XA\Big)/\!\sim, \qquad \text{for } B \in \mathbf{B},$$

where $\sim$ is the smallest equivalence relation such that for all $f : A \to A'$ in $\mathbf{A}$, $g : FA' \to B$ in $\mathbf{B}$, $x \in XA$;

$$(gFf, x) \sim (g, Xf(x)); \tag{1}$$

- on arrows

$$Lh: LB \to LB': [g, x] \longmapsto [hg, x], \qquad \text{for } h: B \to B' \text{ in } \mathbf{B},$$

where we denote the equivalence class of (g, x) by $[g, x]$.

Proof. Since for all $f: A \to A'$ in $\mathbf{A}$, $g: FA' \to B$ in $\mathbf{B}$, $x \in XA$,

$$[hgFf, x] = [hg, Xf(x)] \quad \text{by (1)},$$

it follows that the map $(g, x) \mapsto [hg, x]$ respects (1), so L is well-defined. Functoriality of L follows directly from associativity of composition in $\mathbf{B}$.

We define

$$\begin{aligned} \epsilon_A: XA &\to LFA \\ x &\longmapsto [1_{FA}, x]. \end{aligned}$$

Setting $g = 1_{FA'}$ in (1) gives

$$\begin{aligned} [Ff, x] &= [1_{FA'}, Xf(x)], \\ \text{so} \quad LFf \cdot \epsilon_A(x) &= \epsilon_{A'} Xf(x). \end{aligned}$$

for all $f: A \to A'$ in $\mathbf{A}$, $x \in XA$. Hence $\epsilon: X \to LF$ is a natural transformation.

Given any other functor $M: \mathbf{B} \to \mathbf{Set}$ and natural transformation $\alpha: X \to MF$, define:

$$\sigma_B: LB \to MB: [g, x] \longmapsto Mg \cdot \alpha_A(x).$$

Since for all $f: A \to A'$ in $\mathbf{A}$, $g: FA' \to B$ in $\mathbf{B}$, $x \in XA$,

$$\begin{aligned} M(gFf)\alpha_A(x) &= MgMFf \cdot \alpha_A(x) \\ &= Mg \cdot \alpha_{A'}(Xf(x)) \quad \text{(by naturality of } \alpha), \end{aligned}$$

it follows that the map $(g, x) \mapsto Mg \cdot \alpha_A(x)$ respects (1), so σ_B is well defined.

Now for all $h: B \to B'$ in $\mathbf{B}$ and $[g, x] \in LB$,

$$\begin{aligned} Mh \cdot \sigma_B[g, x] &= MhMg \cdot \alpha_A(x) \\ &= M(hg)\alpha_A(x) \qquad \text{(by functoriality of } M\text{)} \\ &= \sigma_{B'}[hg, x] \\ &= \sigma_{B'} Lh[g, x], \end{aligned}$$

so $\sigma: L \to M$ is a natural transformation.

Finally,

$$\begin{aligned} (\sigma F \cdot \epsilon)_A(x) &= (\sigma F)_A \epsilon_A(x) \\ &= \sigma_{FA}([1_{FA}, x]) \\ &= M(1_{FA})\alpha(x) \quad \text{(by definition of } \sigma\text{)} \\ &= \alpha_A(x); \end{aligned}$$

thus we have the required property that α factors as

$$\alpha = \sigma F \cdot \epsilon.$$

Further, this σ is unique, since

$$\alpha = \sigma F \cdot \epsilon \Rightarrow \sigma_{FA}([1_{FA}, x]) = \alpha_A(x)$$

and given $g : FA \to B$ in $\mathbf{B}$, by the naturality of σ,

$$\sigma_B Lg([1_{FA}, x]) = Mg \cdot \sigma_{FA}([1_{FA}, x]).$$

Thus,

$$\sigma_B([g, x]) = Mg \cdot \alpha_A(x)$$

as given above. ■

Note. **A** and **B** are required to be generated by a finite graph to ensure that the sum in the expression for L is actually meaningful.

We now give two examples of left Kan extensions. We will use one of them later to provide an illustration of the use of the procedure.

Example 6. (Categories.) Consider a category **B**. Let $\mathbf{A} = \text{obj } \mathbf{B}$ be the category whose objects are those of **B** and with only identity arrows. Let $F : \mathbf{A} \to \mathbf{B}$ be the inclusion of obj **B** in **B**. Let $X : \mathbf{A} \to \mathbf{Sets}$ be the constant functor at a one-point set.

Then the left Kan extension gives the arrows of the category **B**. More precisely,

$$L(B) = \sum_{B' \in \mathbf{B}} \mathbf{B}(B', B).$$

This clearly comes directly from the above theorem. Here ϵ maps the one-point set to the identity arrows.

Note. It is easy to see that L is a faithful representation of the category **B** in **Sets**.

Example 7. (Cosets of a Group.) Let **B** be a group G, considered as a category with one object $*$, and let **A** be a subgroup H of G, also considered as a category with one object $*$. Let $F : \mathbf{A} \to \mathbf{B}$ be the inclusion of H in G. Let X be the constant functor at a one-point set.

Then the left Kan extension gives the cosets of H in G. That is, $L* = G/H$, and

$$Lg: G/H \to G/H: xH \longmapsto gxH.$$

This follows from the above theorem, since the expression for $L*$ reduces to $G/\!\sim$, where $gh \sim g$ for all $h \in H$. However,

$$\begin{aligned} g_1 H = g_2 H &\iff g_2^{-1} g_1 \in H \\ &\iff g_2^{-1} g_1 = h \quad \text{for some } h \in H \\ &\iff g_1 = g_2 h \quad \text{for some } h \in H. \end{aligned}$$

Thus the partitioning of G into cosets is, in this instance, precisely the equivalence relation expressed by (1). Also, ϵ_* maps the one-point set to the coset H itself. It is this example which provides the connection to the original Todd–Coxeter procedure.

The general procedure

We now describe the generalized Todd–Coxeter procedure. In full generality, the description is somewhat complicated, since there is a substantial amount of information to contend with. We will do one simple example to clarify the processes involved.

Specification

We now specify precisely the input data that the generalized Todd–Coxeter procedure requires, and the resulting output it produces if it terminates.

Input

Category **A**: objects and generating arrows, i.e.: a finite graph G_A.

Category **B**: objects and generating arrows, i.e.: a finite graph G_B.

Relations $\mathcal{R}$: a set of 'relations' between the generating arrows of **B**. More precisely, a finite set of pairs of arrows with matching domain and codomain in the free category $\mathcal{F}G_B$ on the generators of **B**. If $(f_1, f_2) \in \mathcal{R}$, we say $f_1 = f_2$ in $\mathcal{R}$.

Functor X: a collection of finite sets XA, for each $A \in \mathbf{A}$ (for simplicity, these sets will always be specified as $[n] = \{1, \ldots, n\}$), and functions $Xf : XA_1 \to XA_2$, for each generator $f : A_1 \to A_2$ in **A**.

Functor F: a map from the objects of **A** to the objects of **B**, and a map from the arrows of G_A to the arrows of $\mathcal{F}G_B$; that, is each generator of **A** maps to a path in the generators of **B**.

Output

Left Kan extension $L: \mathbf{B} \to \mathbf{Set}$ (given on generating arrows).

Natural transformation $\epsilon: X \to LF$.

The procedure will terminate if and only if LB is finite for each $B \in \mathbf{B}$.

Terminology

Tables

These extend the basic multiplication and relation tables of the traditional Todd–Coxeter algorithm. In the general case, there are four types of tables. The first two types contain information on sets and partial functions which are generated during the course of the procedure, while the last two types are used to impose relations between the elements of the sets generated. We describe the tables as they are at the beginning of the algorithm, initialized with all the input data.

(i) (ϵ-tables.) For all $A \in \mathbf{A}$ these are tables of the form

ϵ_A

$XA \to LFA$	
1	
2	
$\vdots$	
n	

where in this case, $XA = [n]$. When the procedure terminates these tables will give the components of the natural transformation ϵ.

(ii) (L-tables.) These tables are perhaps best thought of as a collection of tables for each $B \in \mathbf{B}$, generators $g_i: B \to B_i$ in $\mathbf{B}$:

Lg_i	
$LB \to$	LB_i

But for convenience we will compress these to

	Lg_1	Lg_2		Lg_n
LB	LB_1	LB_2	$\cdots$	LB_n

for all $B \in \mathbf{B}$, where $\{g_1, \ldots, g_n\} = \{g \text{ in } \mathbf{B} \mid \operatorname{dom} g = B\}$. When the procedure terminates, these tables give the effect of the functor L on objects and generating arrows of $\mathbf{B}$.

(iii) (Relation tables.) For each relation $g_n \cdots g_1 = h_m \cdots h_1: B_1 \to B_2$ in $\mathcal{R}$,

Lg_1		Lg_n	Lh_1		Lh_m
$LB_1 \to$	$\cdots \to$	LB_2	$LB_1 \to$	$\cdots \to$	LB_2
	$\cdots$			$\cdots$	

(iv) (Naturality tables.) For all generators $f: A_1 \to A_2$ in $\mathbf{A}$, if $Ff = g_n \cdots g_1$

Xf	ϵ_{A_2}		ϵ_{A_1}	Lg_1		Lg_n
$XA_1 \to$	$XA_2 \to$	LFA_1	$XA_1 \to$	$LFA_1 \to$	$\cdots$	$\to LFA_2$
1	5		1			
2	3		2		$\cdots$	
$\vdots$	$\vdots$		$\vdots$			
n	2		n			

Here, for the purpose of illustration, we have taken $XA_1 = [n]$ and
$Xf\colon 1 \mapsto 5,\ 2 \mapsto 3,\ \dots,\ n \mapsto 2$.

Note. Tables (i) and (iv) will be of fixed length, determined by the sizes of the XA, while in general, Tables (ii) and (iii) will vary in length over the course of the algorithm.

Undefined elements

Undefined elements are unfilled entries in tables (i) or (ii) in rows which have elements appearing in the left-hand column. For example:

ϵ_A

XA	$\to LFA$
1	□
2	
⋮	
n	

or

	Lg_1	Lg_2		Lg_n
LB	LB_1	LB_2	$\cdots$	LB_n
1	3	4	$\cdots$	7
2	□			

Here we say that $\epsilon_A(1)$ and $Lg_1(2)$ are undefined. Note that initially there will always be some undefined entries, and that these will all be in the ϵ-tables.

Coincidences

Coincidences consist of two *different* elements which are to be made equal, and may occur in either of two ways. Firstly they may appear in tables (iii) or (iv), when two elements appear in the same row of a table, one at the end of the left-hand side, the other at the end of the right-hand side. For example:

Lg_1	Lg_n		Lh_1	Lh_n	
$LB_1 \to$	$\cdots \to$	LB_2	$LB_1 \to$	$\cdots \to$	LB_2
1		3	1		3
2	$\cdots$	$\underline{4}$	2	$\cdots$	$\underline{6}$
3			3		

Here we have a coincidence, namely 4 and 6. We denote such a coincidence by $4 — 6$. The second way coincidences may occur is in 'dealing with coincidences' (discussed in more detail below). In this case they arise in the L-tables when two different elements occur in the same column of two rows which are already coincidences themselves. For example, if we have a coincidence of 1 and 2, and have the table

	Lg_1	Lg_2		Lg_n
LB	LB_1	LB_2	$\cdots$	LB_n
1	3	<u>4</u>		7
2	3	<u>5</u>		7
$\vdots$				

then there is the further coincidence of 4 and 5.

The Procedure

We have shown that the left Kan extension is given on objects as the quotient of

$$\sum_{A \in \mathbf{A}} \mathbf{B}(FA, B) \times XA$$

by an equivalence relation. The generalized Todd–Coxeter procedure essentially enumerates the elements of the closely related set

$$\sum_{A \in \mathbf{A}} \mathcal{F}G_{\mathbf{B}}(FA, B) \times XA$$

and periodically employs a sub-procedure to impose both the equivalence relation described in the theorem, and the relations between generating arrows of **B**.

The general procedure is given by

```
initialize tables
while there are undefined elements
    (
    define new elements
    fill in consequences
    while there are coincidences
        (
        deal with coincidences
        fill in consequences
        )
    )
```

Above we described how to *initialize tables*, and explained the terms *undefined elements* and *coincidences*. It remains to describe the procedures *filling in consequences, defining new elements* and *dealing with coincidences*.

Filling in consequences

It has been noted that the tables of type (i) and (ii) represent partial functions between the various sets XA and LB. When we *fill in consequences* we use these partial functions to fill all possible entries in the type (iii) and (iv) tables.

Defining new elements

Given an undefined element in a column headed by, say LB_1, we define a new element of LB_1, adding to LB_1 the first integer not already in LB_1 and placing this firstly in the unfilled position, secondly in the left-hand column of the LB_1-table, and thirdly in the left-hand columns of each side of each type (iii) table which begins with LB_1. We clarify this with an example.

Example 8. Suppose we have tables

	Lg_1	Lg_2		Lg_n
LB	LB_1	LB_2	$\cdots$	LB_n
1	2	4	$\cdots$	7
2	□			

Lg	
$LB_1 \to LB_2$	
1	3
2	

and

Lg_1	Lg_n		Lh_1	Lh_n	
$LB_1 \to \cdots \to LB_2$			$LB_1 \to \cdots \to LB_2$		
1		3	1		3
2		5	2		5

Then we define a new element for $Lg_1(2)$ and these tables become:

	Lg_1	Lg_2		Lg_n
LB	LB_1	LB_2	$\cdots$	LB_n
1	2	4	$\cdots$	7
2	3			

Lg	
$LB_1 \rightarrow$	LB_2
1	3
2	
3	

and

Lg_1	Lg_n		Lh_1	Lh_n	
$LB_1 \rightarrow$	$\cdots \rightarrow$	LB_2	$LB_1 \rightarrow$	$\cdots \rightarrow$	LB_2
1		3	1		3
2		5	2		5
3			3		

It is also essential to clarify which new elements to define and when to define them. In this step of the procedure, we may define any number of new elements (though at least one must be defined), and the only necessary guiding principle in choosing which ones to define is that for each $x \in XA$ and $g = g_n \cdots g_1$ in $\mathcal{F}G_B$ the element $Lg_n \cdots Lg_1 \epsilon_A(x)$ would be defined after a finite number of steps of the procedure (if it does not terminate first, of course). A typical systematic method is to firstly define elements in the ϵ-tables, and then to work row by row across the L-tables.

Dealing with coincidences

We take a coincidence, say $x — y$, where $x, y \in LB$, from the list of current coincidences. We then add to the list of any coincidences arising from the L-tables as a result of the $x — y$ coincidence in the manner described above. Next, replace every occurrence of, say, y as an element of LB by x in the tables and the coincidence list (traditionally the smaller of the two replaces the larger, but this is not essential). Finally, for appearances' sake, we generally relabel the elements of LB so as to obtain a set of consecutive integers once more.

A Calculation Example

We now consider the left Kan extension of X along obj $\mathbf{B} \rightarrow \mathbf{B}$, where X takes objects to one-point sets. Here LB consists of all the arrows into B. Thus the generalized procedure may be used to enumerate the arrows of a category given by generators and relations.

We again consider a simple example.

Example 9. Categories. We specify the category $\mathbf{B}$ as:

- objects: A, B, C;
- arrows: $\alpha : A \rightarrow B$, $\beta : B \rightarrow C$, $\gamma : C \rightarrow A$;
- relations: $\gamma\beta\alpha = 1_A$, $\alpha\gamma\beta = 1_B$, $\beta\alpha\gamma = 1_C$.

There are no tables of type (iv). In the tables which follow, notice the way the treatment of identities in relations essentially as empty words in the generators.

So we have initially

(i)

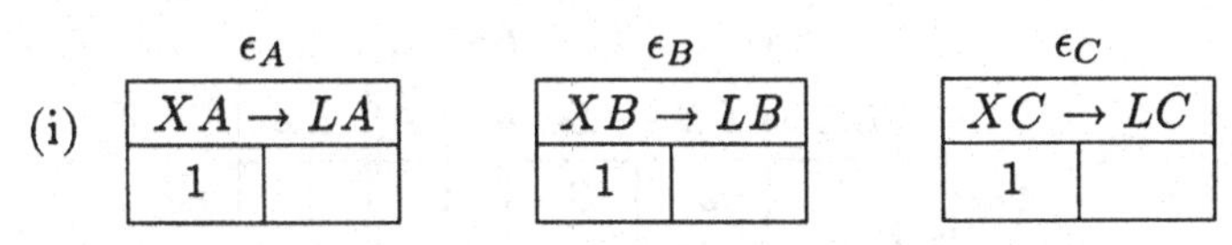

ϵ_A

$XA \to LA$	
1	

ϵ_B

$XB \to LB$	
1	

ϵ_C

$XC \to LC$	
1	

(ii)

$L\alpha$

$LA \to LB$	

$L\beta$

$LB \to LC$	

$L\gamma$

$LC \to LA$	

(iii)

LA	$\xrightarrow{L\alpha}$ LB	$\xrightarrow{L\beta}$ LC	$\xrightarrow{L\gamma}$ LA	LA

LB	$\xrightarrow{L\beta}$ LC	$\xrightarrow{L\gamma}$ LA	$\xrightarrow{L\alpha}$ LB	LB

LC	$\xrightarrow{L\gamma}$ LA	$\xrightarrow{L\alpha}$ LB	$\xrightarrow{L\beta}$ LC	LC

We begin defining elements until we obtain

(i)

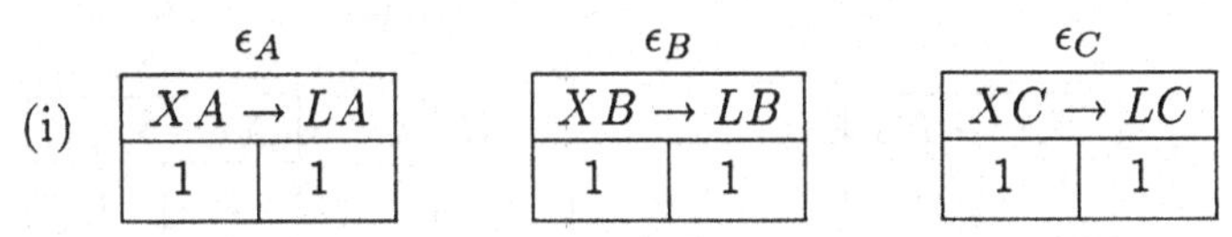

ϵ_A

$XA \to LA$	
1	1

ϵ_B

$XB \to LB$	
1	1

ϵ_C

$XC \to LC$	
1	1

(ii)

$L\alpha$

$LA \to LB$	
1	2
2	3
3	4
4	

$L\beta$

$LB \to LC$	
1	2
2	3
3	4
4	

$L\gamma$

$LC \to LA$	
1	2
2	3
3	4
4	

(iii)

$L\alpha$ $L\beta$ $L\gamma$

$LA \to$	$LB \to$	$LC \to$	LA	LA
1	2	3	$\underline{4}$	$\underline{1}$
2	3	4		2
3	4			3
4				4

$L\beta$ $L\gamma$ $L\alpha$

$LB \to$	$LC \to$	$LA \to$	LB	LB
1	2	3	$\underline{4}$	$\underline{1}$
2	3	4		2
3	4			3
4				4

$L\gamma$ $L\alpha$ $L\beta$

$LC \to$	$LA \to$	$LB \to$	LC	LC
1	2	3	$\underline{4}$	$\underline{1}$
2	3	4		2
3	4			3
4				4

This results in coincidences 1 — 4 in each of LA, LB, and LC. We now deal with these coincidences, which produce no further coincidences.

(i)

ϵ_A

$XA \to$	LA
1	1

ϵ_B

$XB \to$	LB
1	1

ϵ_C

$XC \to$	LC
1	1

(ii)

$L\alpha$

$LA \to$	LB
1	2
2	3
3	1

$L\beta$

$LB \to$	LC
1	2
2	3
3	1

$L\gamma$

$LC \to$	LA
1	2
2	3
3	1

(iii)

$L\alpha$	$L\beta$	$L\gamma$		
$LA \to$	$LB \to$	$LC \to$	LA	LA
1	2	3	1	1
2	3	1	2	2
3	1	2	3	3

$L\beta$	$L\gamma$	$L\alpha$		
$LB \to$	$LC \to$	$LA \to$	LB	LB
1	2	3	1	1
2	3	1	2	2
3	1	2	3	3

$L\gamma$	$L\alpha$	$L\beta$		
$LC \to$	$LA \to$	$LB \to$	LC	LC
1	2	3	1	1
2	3	1	2	2
3	1	2	3	3

With no undefined elements and no coincidences, the process is now complete. Thus we have enumerated the arrows of the category **C** and have tables describing composition with the generators. For example, LA gives all the arrows into A. By observing the positions in which they appear in the composition tables, we may identify 1, 2, 3 of LA with $1_A, \gamma, \gamma\beta$.

Remark. Each of the algorithms described in this chapter has extensions to categories with structure; for example, categories with products. These extensions are much more powerful, and allow the computation of general algebraic structures given by operations and equations.

The extension of the Todd–Coxeter algorithm described here has been programmed by Craig Reilly and Sean Carmody and is available by anonymous ftp from `maths.su.oz.au`

Problems 7

1. Consider the graph G with one object and with n arrows $a_1, a_2, \ldots, a_n$. Consider the set E of equations $a_i a_j = a_j a_i$, $(i \neq j; i, j = 1, 2, 3, \ldots, n)$. Consider the following ordering on the arrows:

$$a_1 > a_2 > \cdots > a_n$$

Show that the set of reductions obtained from this order on the arrows is confluent. Describe the normal form of any path in G.

2. Use the algorithm for computing left Kan extensions to represent each of the following categories as a category of sets and functions:

(i) Two objects X, Y; arrows $s : X \to Y$, $p : Y \to X$ with $ps = 1_X$.

(ii) One object X; arrows 1_X, α, α^2 such that $\alpha^3 = 1_X$.

(iii) One object X; arrows 1_X, α, α^2 such that $\alpha^3 = \alpha^2$.

(iv) One object X; arrows 1_X, α, α^2 such that $\alpha^3 = \alpha$.

(v) One object X; arrows 1_X, α_1, α_2 such that $\alpha_i \alpha_j = \alpha_i$ $(i, j = 1, 2)$.

(vi) One object X; arrows 1_X, α_1, α_2 such that $\alpha_i \alpha_j = \alpha_j$ $(i, j = 1, 2)$.

3. Show that there exists a category with graph that given on page 4.

4. Apply the Knuth–Bendix procedure to the generators and relations given in Problem 10 of Chapter 1.

References

[1] Arbib M., Manes E., *Arrows, Structures and Functors: The Categorical Imperative*, Academic Press, 1975.

[2] Arbib M., Manes E., *Algebraic Approaches to Program Semantics*, Springer-Verlag, 1986.

[3] Asperti A., Longo G., *Categories, Types, and Structures*, M.I.T. Press, 1991.

[4] Barr M., Wells C., *Category Theory for Computing Science*, Prentice-Hall, 1990.

[5] Burstall D. E., Rydeheard R. M., *Computational Category Theory*, Prentice-Hall, 1988.

[6] Bird R., Wadler P., *Introduction to Functional Programming*, Prentice-Hall, 1988.

[7] Carmody S., Walters R. F. C., The Todd-Coxeter procedure and left Kan extensions, *J. Symbolic Computation* (to appear).

[8] Carmody S., Walters R. F. C., Computing quotients of actions of a free category, *CT'90, SLN in Math.* **1488** (1991) 63–78.

[9] Cockett J. R. B., On the decidability of objects in a locos, *Contemporary Mathematics*, **92**, Amer. Math. Soc. (1989) 23–46.

[10] Coxeter H. S. M., Moser W. O. J., *Generators and Relations for Discrete Groups*, Springer-Verlag, 1972.

[11] Curien P. -L., *Categorical Combinators, Sequential Algorithms and Functional Programming*, Pitman Wiley, 1986.

[12] Goguen J. A., Thatcher J. W., Wagner E. G., Wright J. B., Initial algebra semantics and continuous algebras, *J. ACM* **24** (1977), 68–95.

[13] Johnson M. S., Walters R. F. C., Algebra objects and algebra families for finite limit theories, *J. Pure & Applied Algebra*, (to appear).

[14] Joyal A., Une Theorie Combinatoire des Series Formelles, *Advances in Mathematics* **42**, (1981).

[15] Joyal A., Foncteurs Analytiques et Especes de Stuctures, Colloque de Combinatoire Enumerative , Proceedings, *SLN in Math.* **1234** (1985).

[16] Kasangian S., Walters R. F. C., The duality between flow charts and circuits, *Bull. Austral. Math. Soc.* **42** (1990) 71–79.

[17] Khalil Wafaa, Walters R. F. C., An imperative language based on distributive categories II, *Pure Mathematics Research Reports 91-29*, University of Sydney.

[18] Knuth D. E., Bendix P. B., Simple word problems in universal algebra, in (Leech J., ed.) *Computational Problems in Abstract Algebra,* Pergamon Press (1967), 263–97.

[19] Lambek J., Scott P., *Introduction to Higher Order Categorical Logic*, Cambridge Studies in Advanced Mathematics **7**, Cambridge University Press, 1986.

[20] Lawvere F. W., Display of graphics and their applications, as exemplified by 2-categories and the Hegelian 'Taco', *Proceedings of Conference on Algebraic Methodology and Software Technology*, University of Iowa, 1989.

[21] Lawvere F. W., Qualitative distinctions between some toposes of generalized graphs, *Contemporary Mathematics*, **92**, Amer. Math. Soc. (1989) 261–99.

[22] Lawvere F. W., Categories of space and of quantity, in *The Space of Mathematics*, ed. Javier Echeverria, Andoni Ibarra, Thomas Mormann; de Gruyter, Berlin/New York, 1991.

[23] Mac Lane S., *Categories for the Working Mathematician*, Springer-Verlag, 1971.

[24] Schanuel S., Negative sets have Euler characteristic and dimension, *CT'90, SLN in Math.* **1488** (1991) 379–85.

[25] Walters R. F. C., Datatypes in distributive categories, *Bull. Austral. Math. Soc.* **40** (1989), 79–82.

[26] Walters R. F. C., A note on context-free languages, *J. Pure & Applied Algebra*, **62** (1989), 199–203.

[27] Walters R. F. C., The free category with products on a multigraph, *J. Pure & Applied Algebra*, **62** (1989), 205–10.

[28] Walters R. F. C., A categorical analysis of digital circuits, *Category Conference*, Isle of Thorns, Sussex, 1988.

[29] Walters R. F. C., An imperative language based on distributive categories, *Mathematical Structures in Computer Science*, (to appear).

[30] Wehrhahn K.H., *Combinatorics. An Introduction*, Carslaw Undergraduate Lecture Notes in Mathematics 1, Carslaw Publications, Sydney, 1990.

Index

D

E

F

G

H

I

K

L

M

N

O

P

Printed in the United States
By Bookmasters